INTERVIEW HERO

INTERVIEW HERO

How to Ace Your Interviews,
Find Your Voice, and
Direct the Narrative of
Your Life

ANGELA GUIDO

communicate yourself press

Book Design by Eichner | Fukui Design

ISBN: 978-1-7323509-2-2

*I try to learn from everyone but
choose my teachers wisely.
Thank you, Kathy, Geertje, and Martina.
You helped me become more myself.
This book is dedicated to you.*

Contents

SECTION I
Interview Mindsets
5

SECTION II
Epic Storytelling
61

Acknowledgments

Sometimes I feel like a jagged rock smoothed into a polished stone by the mighty river of experience. Any wisdom I've got to share came through decades of trial and error, countless bumps and bruises.

So I want to thank all the people who've ever believed in me enough to give me the chance to fail. To all the people who let me try something with them, for them, or on their behalf: I am who I am, in part, thanks to you.

Here's an attempt at a complete list of all these special people—though I know a comprehensive list is probably impossible—in roughly chronological order:

The NJCL; Grandpa and Dad; Yale AIDS Educators and Yale bartending; Charlotte, Jock Beveridge, Haesook and Yuwon Kim from Hello Kids World; Mike from Wonderland; Anyang Technical College admin staff; all of my private students in Korea, especially Dr. Jung, Dr. Choi, and Kevin; Stephan Kim, Harry Jung, Ken Yun, Mr. Jung, and the rest of the KPMG Seoul 2000 leadership crew; Professor Mike Gibbs; an immeasurable host of amazing BCGers, most notably, Lucy Brady, Sharon Marcil, Michael Silverstein, Michelle Russell, Marin Gjaja, Jeff Gell, Doug Kush, John Budd, Julie Gish, Jill Corcoran, Christine Barton, Elizabeth Cimaroli, Rohan Sajdeh, and too many other people to name; then come Bartlett, Marjie, Mary, Joe, and Seamus; Zeke Vanderhoek, Andrew Yang, Chris Ryan, Dan Gonzalez, Noah Teitelbaum, and the rest of the early Manhattan leadership team; the awesome folks at mbaMission, especially Jeremy, Jessica, Liza, Katy, Harshad, Susan, Monica, Johnny, Dan, Kate, Helen, Lynn, Krista, Heidi, and Rachel; my travel buddy, Tanya, the chichis; and my amazing sister and brother.

My deepest thanks to all of my clients, including a few who really helped me to shape my own understanding of myself and what I'm here for. I won't name you. You know who you are.

And finally, *grazie infinite* to my amazing editor, Jalina Mhyana. No one could have asked for a better friend, compatriot, collaborator, listener, and champion.

Foreword

Founder and CEO of C-Change Media, Inc.
and Editor-in-Chief of Poets&Quants

Let me tell you the precise moment I realized that Angela Guido has magical powers.

It wasn't when I first met her.

Our first meeting occurred over a pleasant lunch on a sunny day in Northern California at a favorite restaurant. A former consultant for Boston Consulting Group, armed with an MBA from Chicago Booth, she had been working as an MBA admissions consultant and career coach for years.

Angela is instantly intriguing. She majored in philosophy at Yale, did recruiting for both KPMG and BCG, spent seven years teaching the GMAT at Manhattan Prep, and 15 years coaching MBAs. Her various wanderings in life are just as eclectic. She has lived in Korea and Italy. She has tried her hand at acting and screenwriting, and even martial arts.

We began having regular lunches whenever she would visit the Bay Area and over time I often gained useful and insightful advice, particularly when Poets&Quants ventured into the event business; first with a Pre-MBA Networking Festival in New York that brought together MBA admits with major MBA employers, and then with CentreCourt—our MBA admissions fairs.

Through those luncheons, Angela immediately earned my respect and admiration. But it wasn't until about a year ago—when I was surfing through the Poets&Quants' directory of admission consultants for a story on the most favorably reviewed counselors—that I stumbled upon an insight that reinforced just how special a person Angela is.

The writer of the review hired Angela to gain admission to a highly selective business school where the odds against every candidate are formidable. Rival consultants took one look at the applicant's stats and either ignored the candidate altogether or steered the young professional to second- and third-tier schools. It was not hard to see why: He had a 3.1 GPA from a mid-ranked public university and a 600 score on a practice GMAT test.

Yet, he wanted to apply to Harvard Business School, Wharton, Yale School of Management, MIT Sloan, and Harvard's Kennedy School. After finding a more supportive consultant in Angela, the applicant scored a 720 on the GMAT and was ultimately admitted to his dream MBA experience: Harvard Business School. MIT Sloan even offered him a Dean's fellowship worth $107,000.

But it was the person's reflection about Angela that truly captured my attention. "To work with Angela Guido is to have an MRI performed on your soul," he wrote. "After a 30-minute consultation with Angela, I was stunned by the accuracy with which she summarized my motivations, character, and potential. She roots for you. She's in your corner. She pushes you in a direction that she knows will be authentic for you. She will give you a pep talk whenever you need one, and in the end, you really want to make her proud."

Yes, that was the moment I understood her magical power, her ability to connect with others in ways so meaningful as to help them transform their lives. So when Angela finally got around to putting her valuable advice into a book, I felt privileged to give the manuscript a thorough read.

Reading *Interview Hero* is the next best thing to sitting down with Angela for an uplifting, introspective talk. It's written in a breezy, conversational style, filled with refreshingly candid advice that displays her sense of humor and even her own vulnerabilities. You instantly connect with her because she is willing to tell you things that only a good friend might divulge.

What really comes through, of course, is Angela's no-nonsense, straight-shooting counsel to "be true to yourself" rather than pander to the audience. She doesn't believe in packaging yourself as a brand. Instead, she roots for you to gain the self-confidence to be exactly who you are and who you want to be.

You can't measure yourself against others. You can't allow self-judgment to get in the way of your goals, your life. She reminds us that no matter what you do, no matter how much value you create, there will always be someone "better than you." And you will experience setbacks, disappointments, and unpleasant surprises. Angela urges us to shift our sights from goals and objectives to self-expression and connection with others.

In her view, elevating those two goals into priorities will silence the incessant voice in your head that tells you that you aren't measuring up. But it will do much more than that. By consciously working to connect with others, you'll become a happier person and a more likeable friend and colleague.

In your early days of schooling, doing well on a test defined your success. Angela reminds us that in the real world of work, healthy relationships will help to make you successful. They will allow you to land the job you want, get the assignments you need, and feel fulfilled and meaningful.

Yes, you will learn the secrets of a great interview in *Interview Hero*. But more importantly you will learn how to lead a better and more purposeful life. After reading Angela's book, I now know what her client meant when he said that working with her was like having an MRI performed on your soul: it's an exercise that yields untold benefits and insights.

Author's Note

I used to be a complete asshole, but now I'm a pretty good person.

Have you ever felt like that?

I feel that way every day. Every. Single. Day.

I mean, just yesterday I was an idiot. I did the dumbest things; I can't even believe the mistakes I made. Before that, I was a big meanie. I did unkind things to people I loved because I didn't know any better. And yesterday, I made a complete ass of myself with my words and my deeds.

But today? Today I'm better.

I'm a way better person than the idiot who did those things in the past. Hahahahahaha.

Of course, I'll say the same thing tomorrow about who I am today.

Have you ever felt like this? I imagine the answer is yes, because as far as I can tell, this experience is fundamental to the human condition. Since time seems to move in only one direction for us, if we have even a modicum of self-awareness, we're always looking back at the past with chagrin, shaking our disbelieving heads, wondering from today's enlightened vantage point how we could have possibly been so stupid.

It's one of the reasons I often feel like an impostor. I mean, with the vast expanse of past to tell me who I am, it's easy to identify with my "stupid self" and thereby undermine the person I've become. Do you do this too?

But if you think about it, this attitude is kind of silly. I mean, isn't part of the point of life to grow, to experience, and to change? To be more today than we were yesterday? In fact, the MORE more we are today, you could argue, the more successful a life we're living.

But then, jeez, yesterday sure feels foolish by comparison. It's like a snare trap: the faster you pull away from your past self and the more you evolve, the more of a loser your past self seems to be.

Well, I've got some news for ya. You'll always be more today than you were yesterday, and from a human perspective, that will always be both revelatory AND problematic. Because even if you could accept yourself by tuning out all the noise telling you that you should be smarter, faster, thinner, richer, better, and somehow different than you are today, you've still got to reckon with yourself about what a jackass you were *yesterday*.

And there are many more yesterdays than there are todays. We've only got one of those. All the gold stars, positive affirmations, power poses, diplomas, and yoga retreats in the world can't resolve that paradox, dagnabbit.

But communication can.

Ultimately, in your life, there is no one more powerful than you. And by extension, there is no voice more powerful than your own; both your inner voice and the one you share with the world. They're two sides of the same coin, in fact: when we speak with others, we're also speaking to ourselves. And when we speak to ourselves, even without words, others detect and respond to our emotions, our mood, and the subtle signals we send out. This is that 80–90% of communication we call "nonverbal."

The scary and exciting part is, we believe whatever we say—a gullibility we can put to good use. Take a look at what I wrote in the opening: "I used to be a complete asshole, but now I'm a pretty good person." You probably didn't quite believe the "good person" part, did you? Shoot, even I didn't. That sentence doesn't have any real meaning. It doesn't *communicate*.

What does it *mean* to be a good person? You have no idea of my definition from this sentence. Heck, even the word "asshole" could mean two completely different things: was I a fool, or was I a jerk?

What if, instead, I talked about myself like this?

When I was younger, I had a really hard time being objective with friends and loved ones. People would often ask me for advice, but I couldn't separate my own ambitions and desires from the questions they asked me. My advice was always unconsciously tainted by my own selfish aims, judgments, and opinions. One day, a close friend of mine pointed this out to me, and I was mortified when I realized she was right.

Over the past several years, I've worked really hard to change this about myself. I read a lot of books about consciousness; I've practiced mindfulness and meditation daily for years; I hired a coach who works with me on my perspective. Once I even took a six-month-long class on listening. Near the forests of Yosemite, for weeks on end, I just sat still and learned how to listen to someone without adding anything on my end—no thought, no judgment, not even a facial expression or "uh-huh."

And slowly, I changed.

Now, my friends often tell me that I'm the person they come to for advice because they can trust that I'll be objective and only keep their best interest at heart. I used to be kind of an asshole, really, but I'm becoming a better person.

Different, eh? Saying it like this really *means* something. To you, no doubt. But imagine how different it feels to me!

While you could say that it's honest, the opening sentence of the book deflates me: emphasis on the asshole, not so strong on the "better person." This second telling *inspires* me: emphasis on the drive to be a better person, much more forgiveness for the asshole.

I like myself better in version two, objectively, but I also like the *feeling* I get when I talk about myself in version two. I get this euphoric sensation of acceptance, inspiration, and joy through my whole body. Version one just makes me feel a bit embarrassed and like I couldn't possibly be truly understood.

What's more, I've put *myself* into this communication. I've really shared something. I've revealed what I value, and who I truly am. Now I can be seen. Now you know me.

This is the gift of communication. It allows us to show up, to be truly seen, and to connect.

Communication is a cure for self-doubt, and it's a cure for loneliness. It has the power to transform, the power to move the world, and the power to shape our experience of ourselves.

In my second real job, I was responsible for interviewing candidates for positions with my firm. So, quite early in my career, I became fascinated by the fact that two similarly extraordinary people on paper can create vastly different impressions in person. This is because interviews take place at the flashpoint of real communication: where one human being meets another and either chooses to show up as her authentic self or chooses some bankrupt strategy to win the job.

My coaching practice in the last 15 years has focused a lot on interviews for this reason. Not only is their importance paramount, but they also represent an existential choice: will I be myself, or will I instead try to be who I think they want me to be?

Option A is always right. But for people like you and me, who were such assholes yesterday, it's a tough choice. Unless we've harnessed the power of communication.

You can't fake it. Either you're being yourself or you're not. Either you're using your authentic voice or you're shamming. And you always know when people are hiding something, don't you? Don't you just kind of have a gut feeling that "something's not quite right" when others are pretending? You might not be able to say it consciously, but at an emotional level, you react with something like this: "You know, I just didn't really feel completely comfortable with her," or "He seemed impressive, but I just don't think I know him well enough to make a call." Believe me, these are not the reactions you want to evoke in your interviewer. If you want to ace an interview, being yourself is your only bet.

I know that's much easier said than done.

If you've cracked this book open and read to this point, I know you want to be more tomorrow than you are today. You want to advance, you want your career to matter, and you want to make the world a better place. If you're reading these words, this book is for **you**.

It will help you to be seen, to be known, and to connect. It will help you harness the magical power of communication in your life. Acing your interviews will be a cakewalk once you can do that. But far more profoundly than simply helping you do well in interviews, this book will help you find your voice. In other words, it will help you be your best and most authentic self when you communicate with others.

Your past assholery will be transformed into your super power. That's one definition of a hero in this day and age: it's someone who uses everything he or she's got, warts and all, to make the world a better place. As a result, this book will help you direct the narrative of your life in the inspiring direction you want it to go.

When your story shines a light on your best self, that's the self you get to be. Because what you say about yourself today is who you will become tomorrow. And how amazing you are today is only possible by virtue of the asshole you were yesterday.

There is much love here for the asshole you were yesterday. I happen to know that he, she, or they were pretty great too. So let's go forward together and shine a bright light on your whole self, your best self.

If this book provokes any questions that you want to share with me, please drop me a line. I'm always happy to hear from you. You can reach me and my team via this magical invention called email: **questions@careerprotocol.com**. Or on **Instagram: @careerprotocol**. And if I can be of service to you in any way on your quest for a career that inspires you, please just ask.

One more thing. You'll quickly find that the middle of this book is like a master class with exercises and tips and tools. I put together a workbook to help you make the most of it. If you'd like to download it free, you can get it here: **careerprotocol.com/ih**.

Heroes onward!

PS: I used up all of my swears in this chapter. The whole rest of the book is much more PG.

Introduction

Hey you. Yeah, you. I'm talkin' to you.

I know you.

You're awesome; you're ambitious; you work hard. You want your career to matter, and you want to make the world a better place for all of us.

You're what we call a leader.

I know this about you because for the last 15 years, I've been a coach to early career professionals. I've helped thousands of people define, pursue, and achieve ambitious career goals while staying true to themselves.

Part of my work involves getting very up close and personal with people and their stories. I help my clients look closely at the details of their life experiences so they can develop more self-awareness and a greater appreciation of what makes them who they are. On that rock-solid foundation, they build the life of their dreams.

My clients frequently say that I get to know them better than they know themselves, or at least better than anyone else has ever known them. So I have a pretty big and pretty detailed dataset to draw from. And in all these years, you know what?

I've never once met someone who wasn't awesome.

Each and every person I've worked with is a truly fascinating and unrepeatable collection of values, idiosyncrasies, and experiences. All of them are doing their best with what they've got, reaching for more, and trying with all their might to create a life of consequence. In all these years, I've never encountered a single loser.

That's how I know you're awesome. Because everyone is awesome in their own unique way.

But being awesome has its challenges. It can sometimes feel like you're all alone, charting your own course through the wilderness; like the world is vast, and there's no map to where you want to go. But you know opportunities when you see them—and since you know that no one is going to hand you your ideal job on a silver platter, you work hard to seize each one.

Whether you're applying to grad school or chasing that dream job, you've already put in a ton of work. You've perfected your resume, you've written essays or cover letters, and you've networked. You've solicited recommendations, made a video introduction or done a phone screen, and taken your GMAT, GRE, or LSAT. By the time the interview comes, you can almost taste it. You've come so far, and now the only thing that stands between you and your goal is the interview.

It's that last mile that makes all the difference. For people like you and me, there's almost nothing so painful as a missed opportunity— the one that got away is always the one that haunts us. If you've ever been interviewed for a job you wanted but didn't *get*, I feel your pain.

Throughout my career, I've helped thousands of people succeed in interviews, and I've discovered so many secrets to success in the process. And most of them aren't what you'd think. You've probably worked hard to find and implement advice on how to succeed in interviews. And if so, you've probably also discovered that a lot of advice out there is total crap.

People tell you to brand yourself as though you were a can of soda that needed to be explained in three or four words. They tell you to craft an elevator pitch so you can "sell yourself" in 30 seconds or less, as though you were a used car or a mattress that needs to be hustled. People tell you to get good at doing transactions to get what you want, despite the fact that solid, long-term relationships are what create opportunities and make the world go 'round. And people advise you to tell the hiring manager what he wants to hear without any regard for how you'll feel about being untrue to yourself if you actually *do* get the job.

What a load of hooey.

At some level, your only job in life is to understand, appreciate, and then share your own unique brand of awesomeness with all the rest of us. This is what we mean when we say "you need to find your voice."

If you do that, you're gonna have a career that knocks your socks off. You're gonna make wildly valuable contributions. You're gonna have a crap ton of fun. And you're gonna build bridges, relationships, and connections that enrich everyone's lives and expand what's possible.

This is what this book is about, so let me tell you a little about how it works.

Section I will help you change your mindset about interviews—shifting your perspective so that you can approach them with genuine confidence, enthusiasm, and an open mind. This section is philosophical, conceptual, and experiential, so let the ideas wash over you, and then try them out in your daily life. By the end, you'll actually look forward to your next interview instead of dreading it.

Section II is like a master class in storytelling: you'll learn how to crush answers to questions such as "Tell me about a leadership experience," or "Describe a time when you faced a challenge at work." Treat this section more like a course than a casual read. You'll want to do the exercises and track your work so you can build Epic Stories about who you are. You'll be actively preparing for any future interview as you work your way through this section. This section and the following have an accompanying workbook. If you want to go download that now, you can get it at **careerprotocol.com/ih**.

Section III is about all the other kinds of questions you'll face, such as "Walk me through your resume" and "What's your biggest weakness?" and "Why do you want this job?" Each question type requires a different approach to bring out your very best. Similar to Section II, this section is full of tips and tools to implement as you go. Once you get to the end of this section, you'll feel ready for just about any kind of question they could throw at you.

The final section will help you get ready for the interview itself. I'll teach you a process to research a job in 30 minutes. I'll cover everything you need to do to prepare for game day so you can relax and be yourself in that interview room. I'll even show you how to manage your mindset and confidence before, during, and after the interview. For instance, you'll learn how to recover from mistakes during the conversation and keep going with no loss of confidence.

By the time you get to the end of this book, you'll know more about how to succeed in interviews than all of your peers and competitors and you'll have mastered communication skills that'll enable you to get your next dream job or grad school admission. Even if you master only a small part of the material in this book, you're going to notice a dramatic improvement in your interview performance.

So use this book to ace your interviews, but more importantly, use it to find your voice and to shape your future with the stories you tell. You'll see what I'm talking about when you get in there, because this book is only about interviews on the surface. If you dig deeper, you'll find that it's about discovering who you are, connecting with your purpose, and living a life of your own design. Communication is what makes all three of those things possible.

The world is waiting for you. And the world needs you just as you are.

Let's do this.

Interview Mindsets

If you only have a hammer, you tend to see every problem as a nail.
—ABRAHAM MASLOW

We have to start with the assumption that just about everything we know and think about interviews is wrong. Not because it *is* wrong (although much of it, in fact, is), but because setting aside old perceptions is the only possible way to see things with fresh eyes. And seeing things in a new way, as though you've never encountered them before, allows you to discard old assumptions that no longer serve you. It allows you to take ownership of your perspective.

So let's start with our mindsets about interviews. In this section, I'm going to dismantle all the bad ideas we have about interviews and give you refreshing and inspiring ways to view them.

We'll start by examining the self-limiting beliefs you may not even realize are shaping your interview performance. After that, you'll be capable of applying the tactics in Section II to your interview toolkit with limitless creativity and freedom. A hammer can't debug your laptop, it can't make a strawberry smoothie, and it can't make beautiful music. So let's look at the hammer and decide if it mightn't be better to pick up a pepper grinder or a violin instead.

Let's get to it.

You've Got Interviews All Wrong

The two words "information" and "communication" are often used interchangeably, but they signify quite different things. Information is giving out; communication is getting through.
—SYDNEY HARRIS

I BOMBED A LOT OF IMPORTANT INTERVIEWS

Don't you just hate interviews? All you need to do is crush it. But how? For everything you read online, you find someone who says the opposite. Are you supposed to memorize a lot of answers to questions? Given the possible array of questions out there, that seems hard or even impossible.

OK, fine. Maybe you just need to be an amazing orator. That's not it either, though, because shy people and nonnative speakers get great jobs every day.

If you feel really good coming out of the interview, that's a sure sign that you've got the job, right? Well, I think we've all had the experience of feeling good after an interview, only to learn later that we didn't get the job.

Maybe you just need to prove that you're the best candidate. Nope again, because you can't control who else is applying.

Let's face it; it's not easy to find a systematic approach to performing well in interviews.

Then what happens if you bomb the interview?

All that time you spent, gone. Your efforts, wasted. The opportunity goes up in smoke, and there you are, no closer to your dream. For ambitious people like you and me, there is almost nothing worse than feeling like you've missed an important opportunity. I know, because that's exactly what happened to me.

In business school, I decided that I wanted to go for a job in management consulting. I applied only to Bain, BCG, and McKinsey for my summer internship. Ah, the hubris! If you know anything about consulting or MBA recruiting, you know that these are very competitive firms. They seek the very best of the best, so no matter how smart and accomplished one might be, getting an offer to join one of these firms would never be considered a sure thing.

On top of that, I was in a pretty weak position. I didn't have an impressive business background like a lot of my classmates. I had majored in philosophy. My first job was teaching English in a preschool. Then I worked in human resources at a major accounting firm. I hadn't taken math since high school. Still, I knew these firms valued intelligence and ambition over a clear track record, so I knew they would give me a chance if I could just ace that interview. I went in boldly with no backup plan.

Spoiler alert: I bombed.

These firms conduct in-depth business problem-solving sessions as part of the interview—called "case interviews." I spent months preparing for case interviews, practicing with friends and classmates. I thought I was ready for the case part, but to be honest, I kind of blew off the rest of the interview—the "fit interview"—where they ask questions about your accomplishments, life, and values. Although I hated talking about myself, I figured I couldn't be too bad at it. I mean, I wrote my resume, so I knew it by heart, right?

Oh, so wrong.

It was only during my first interview that I suddenly realized I hadn't prepared thoroughly enough. I started worrying about how I stood in relation to my peers. This was my undoing—I didn't inspire confidence in my abilities, and I didn't really shine.

What's worse, even the case didn't go as well as it could have, because I started the interview off on the wrong foot. My head was filled with chatter: when I was supposed to be analyzing the market size for consumer banking in Thailand, I was rehashing that lame answer I'd given to "Tell me about a leadership experience" 15 minutes before. It was very hard to concentrate with all that negative self-talk whirring in the background.

The outcome was just what you'd expect: no summer internship in consulting for me.

But don't worry; this story ultimately has a happy ending (as all stories do; more on that later). I didn't get any offers for the summer during my MBA, but all the firms invited me back for full-time interviews. Over the summer, I changed my approach, and I discovered some secrets to amazing interviews. In the end, I had the very high-quality problem of needing to choose between firms. Both BCG and McKinsey made me offers. I was one of only a few people in my class to get multiple consulting offers, even though I had a relatively weak professional background.

I attribute my success to the communication secrets I learned that summer. The same ones I'm going to teach you in this book.

WHY DO WE HATE INTERVIEWS?

But back to why we hate interviews. My first insight over that summer was that my performance was terrible, not because I didn't have good experiences, not because my answers were inarticulate, but because I had the wrong attitude toward the interview.

I had the wrong perspective.

My attention was focused on the wrong things: trying to seem smart and accomplished, and gauging my performance based on the nonverbal feedback I received from the interviewer. I thought the interview was a test, and I just had to be smart enough to pass it. If the interviewer smiled at me, I knew I was acing it.

Well, that didn't go super well because a lot of interviewers gave me this look.

They were nice guys (I learned later), but their strategy involved applying a little stress to see if I could still function under pressure. Their tactic was to ignore me or even give me slightly negative nonverbal cues to see what I would do. Predictably, I didn't handle it very well. The longer I talked about myself, the less confident I felt. It was a vicious downward spiral, and I couldn't escape until the interview was over and I could flee to the bathroom.

During the whole conversation, instead of focusing on my excitement about my achievements, I dwelled on how I was doing. Is he smiling enough? Is he laughing at the right point during my stories? Did I forget to include an important part of the answer? Oh shoot, was that what he was looking for when he asked about teamwork?

The self-judgment against imaginary benchmarks could have gone into infinity.

My mistake was focusing on all the aspects of the experience that made me feel judged and evaluated. And I don't know about you, but I HATE feeling judged.

Pretty much all of us humans hate that feeling, right? Because it jacks with our self-confidence. It inherently gives the opinions of others (or, worse, your *assumptions* about the opinions of others) dominion over your sense of worth. You cede control over your confidence to a stranger. And you simply can't succeed that way. Your sense of self-confidence has to reside in you—it's your domain, and you have to own it.

I know that's easier said than done, but the rest of this book is going to show you how to create that rock-solid sense of inner and outer self-confidence. So, keep reading.

But first let's take a look at why we think the interview is a test in the first place.

SCHOOL VS. THE REAL WORLD

You spend the first 21 years or so of your life in the education system. Whether you've just started your career or are 10 years in, the majority of your thinking and contributing life has been spent at school. The professional world is a bit different, so let me talk a little about the differences between those two worlds. This is information I wish I had known when I was in your shoes.

You worked in a pretty consistent way from kindergarten all the way through senior year of college and possibly even an advanced degree program. You studied hard. You learned things. You did your homework. You progressed in a fairly linear way. The halls were straight lines, and the books were square. There was almost always a right and a wrong answer, full or partial credit. Things were pretty black and white. It's very easy to figure out how to succeed in an academic environment because the rules are well-defined and you have the chance to practice them from the time you are four or five.

And throughout all those years, you're conditioned to take tests. These tests typically have right answers and are graded on a forced bell curve. So the primary kind of evaluation you know is a direct and mathematical comparison of you to all of your competitors. You know that if you study for the test, you will do well on the test. You will get a good grade, beat the curve, and succeed. It's that simple.

This kind of zero-sum competition exists in the post-school world, but it's rare. And it's definitely not what's really going on in interviews. Most of life after school is nothing like the simple linear success system of academia, as it turns out. It's a vast universe out there. If you've begun your career, you've probably already had to confront how incredibly complex and innumerable the options are, and how seemingly unfair and random the winding road to success can feel.

What's more, treating the real world like a test will lead you to do all kinds of things that could actually sabotage your performance.

Let me give you another example from my life. When I was in high school, I studied Latin and competed in Latin examinations. Yes, I was a super nerd, I know. During my first year studying Latin, I qualified for the national competition in my area of expertise: grammar. I did some investigation, and I learned that everyone at nationals would get the same grammar test. This meant that first-year, second-year, third-year, and fourth-year Latin students were all taking the exact same test, and trophies would be awarded to the highest scorers at each level.

So that summer before nationals, I decided that the only way to be sure to win my own level was to beat *everyone*. This meant I would have to learn the second half of the Latin language that I hadn't yet studied my first year. So while my friends and cousins were playing outside, I was reading Allen and Greenough's *New Latin Grammar*. I took practice tests. I drilled flash cards. Super. Nerd.

When the summer competition came around, all that effort paid off. I tied for the highest score with the champion fourth-year student.

My strategy worked because it was a test! There were right and wrong answers and a finite amount of material to learn. Admittedly it was a massive amount of material, but I was willing to put in the hard work to achieve my goal. I used this strategy to achieve a lot of goals throughout my academic life.

But things started to break down a little bit in college.

I chose to major in philosophy, where, let's just say, very little is black and white. A great paper—the basis of most of my philosophy grades—is a subjective phenomenon. There weren't many clear answers—which was the whole point! I got my worst grades in philosophy, but I didn't care because I loved ideas so much. Even though I hadn't found a way to perform well as a philosopher, I was having so much fun that I didn't care.

As a result, I never really let go of the "life and everything is a test" strategy. So, imagine my shock when I suddenly found myself in the working world, especially after business school. My strategy didn't get me very far as a consultant. I applied myself doggedly to certain concrete aspects of the job: learning how to do analysis and build great PowerPoint decks in the style of the firm. But I neglected others that didn't seem as concrete—things like building great relationships with superiors and seeking mentorship for subtle things like influence and top-down communication skills.

After a little while, I looked around at my peers who were excelling, and my mistake began to dawn on me. They were the ones who had the best relationships with managers, the strongest networks within the company, the most robust understanding of organizational politics and processes, and the clearest sense of how to get what they wanted from the job.

I ended up spending too much time on the "testable" aspects of my role, resulting in lackluster performance overall. I had focused on the things that were most similar to what I knew from school. I made the mistake of treating the working world like a test, and as a result, the contributions I could make in the first years of my post-MBA career were limited. I've had to learn the hard way that the old strategies don't work in new places, and that what got you here won't get you there.

FAILING THE TEST OF LIFE

But there was an even bigger problem with my choice to view life and work as a test: I basically felt like I was always failing, that other people were judging me a failure, and that there was something deficient in me that was prohibiting my success. At several levels I didn't really believe this, but at some level, the idea that there was something very wrong with me pervaded every thought, every setback, and even every success.

Because some of our worldview develops inside the pass/fail paradigm of academia, we naturally think that our professional lives will also be a succession of tests. If we can just ace them, we'll be successful people. But if you pause to think about how life really is, the folly of this perspective reveals itself immediately.

What does it mean to be successful in your health, for example? Does it mean you need to follow a strict diet and exercise regimen 100%? Does it mean every single blood test needs to be perfect? Does it equate to one single three-digit number on that scale? Does it mean you can never eat a donut?

And what about in relationships? How do you get a successful report card with your friends? Is someone keeping score of your good deeds and reporting that out to your network? How do you get a passing grade in listening with empathy. nurturing affinity, and supporting loved ones in pursuing their passions?

Even at work, you can bomb countless interviews and fail to get innumerable jobs and still have a remarkable career.

No, most of what ultimately matters in life has no objective measure and therefore can't be tested. You can be healthy without following a diet. You can be a loving friend, partner, and family member without keeping score. You can be a success without ever winning an award or receiving validation or acknowledgment for your efforts. But holding yourself to the standards of your schooling and approaching every little thing in life like an exam makes it hard to really appreciate and experience your own success.

Because herein lies one of the roots of impostor syndrome. No matter what you do, no matter how much value you create, there will always be someone "better than you." And there will always be setbacks, disappointed expectations, and unpleasant surprises: "failures" in life's tests, if you decide to frame them that way. You might end up—as I did—imagining that everyone else is judging you just like your sixth-grade math teacher did, and you will never be able to measure up. What's worse, you'll continue to do what I did in my early career years—focus all your effort and energy on only a small subset of things that matter, thereby sabotaging your own performance and limiting the positive impact you could otherwise have.

HERE'S A MUCH BETTER GOAL

What each must seek in their life never was on land or sea.
It is something out of their own unique potentiality for experience,
something that never has been and never could have been
experienced by anyone else.
—JOSEPH CAMPBELL

So, instead of beating the curve, why not make self-expression and connection your goal? Why not make having a great experience and creating great experiences for others your goal? I'm talking about making this your goal in interviews, but it also applies to life in general. The things that make life really worth living must be experienced; they defy measurement and quantification. Two such life-giving experiences are authentically expressing who you are in the world and connecting with others.

If self-expression and connection for their own sake aren't motivating enough, I'll give you two more reasons to prioritize them. First, if you do so, it will silence that little voice in your head that's always telling you that you don't measure up. As much as we hate feeling judged, nearly all judgment is self-inflicted.

Think about it—don't you find yourself arguing in your mind with the opinions of others? For the most part, don't you just *assume* those are the opinions of others? If you find yourself justifying your actions, behavior, and choices to other people—even in the confines of your own mind—chances are you're beating yourself up for no reason. You have no idea what people actually think about you, and most people are too busy arguing with the opinions they imagine you're having about *them* to form a genuine opinion about you.

And even if they do have a real opinion about you, who cares? You're not in sixth grade anymore, and Mrs. Forester's mean red pen can't mark you or determine the quality of your life or how success-ful you can be (I failed a lot of math tests in sixth grade. Ha!). If you're focused on expressing yourself and making a genuine connection, there's no real way to fail—every attempt is a success, and every at-tempt teaches you something new.

If you can let go of the notion that you're being tested while you're in an interview, it will free up a lot of headspace to focus on the factors that play a much larger role in determining your success than getting "the right answer" would.

Interviews mark your entry into a new world beyond grade point averages. A world where relationships, influence, and communication are the main drivers of your success. This is the second reason to shift your attention to self-expression and connection: you'll be in a much better position to influence the factors that drive interviewers' deci-sions. Let me expand upon this.

THE INTERVIEWER IS NOT A ROBOT

Because we think the interview is a test, we imagine that there's some objective scorecard in the interviewer's brain, weighing the minutiae of your performance against that of the other candidates. And, to reiter-ate, this heightens your sense of being judged, typically makes you feel a little defensive, and makes you focus on "getting the answers right."

But even the savviest and most experienced human interviewer can't run algorithms like a robot, comparing every last detail about you to everyone else in the "database." And even if he could, he wouldn't. Because humans are emotional beings. And emotions influence deci-sions more than facts.

The role of emotions in decision making has been the focus of many studies, particularly in the fields of behavioral economics and psychology. Sweet Lady Science has come to the conclusion, time and time again, that emotion "is the dominant driver of most mean-ingful decisions in life."[1] That's what a group of researchers led by Jennifer Lerner at Harvard concluded when they synthesized all the scientific research from 1970–2012 on the relationship between emo-tions and decision making. They revealed that not only has focus on this link dramatically increased in recent years (with yearly papers on the subject doubling from 2004 and 2007 and again from 2007 to 2011) but the research definitively shows that "emotion and decision making go hand in hand" and that "emotions powerfully, predictably, and pervasively influence decision making."[2]

For example, neuroscientist Antonio Damasio explains in his book *Descartes' Error: Emotion, Reason, and the Human Brain*: "We're trained to regard emotions as irrational impulses that are likely to lead us astray. When we describe someone as 'emotional,' it's usually a criticism that suggests that they lack good judgment."[3] Nonetheless, his pioneering work with somatic markers, bodily sensations, and phenomena associated with feelings reveals that without emotions, humans can't decide.[4]

His famous experiments with patient EVR[5]—a man whose frontal cortex had been surgically severed, separating the left and right sides of his brain and therefore his ability to connect emotion to information—revealed that without emotions, or at least their physical symptoms, we can't evaluate what is good, what is bad, or what we're indifferent to. All the data and analysis and pros and cons lists in the world can't help you choose something as trivial as what to eat for dinner without the evaluative charge of feelings.

Nobel laureates Daniel Kahneman and Amos Tversky further demonstrated that people often make better decisions by ignoring reason.[6] In fact, we're hardwired to be irrational, and, counterintuitively, "being irrational is a good thing. We humans don't always make decisions by carefully weighing up the facts, but we often make better decisions as a result."[7]

But you don't need science to tell you how humans function. Just look at your own experience. You make pretty big decisions on a daily basis. Stuff like choosing a job or school, deciding whether to go on a second date, creating a guest list for your birthday party, ordering your dinner, or even getting dressed in the morning. When you're choosing, don't you feel it out? Go with your gut? Listen to your heart, and see how you feel? Even if you do a pros and cons list—and think it through rationally—at some level, don't you use emotions to guide your choice?

This should be reassuring to all of you who are dreading your interviews. Even if your resume isn't the best, even if you mess up an answer or two, even if you stammer and sweat, or say something ridiculous, it doesn't necessarily count against you. What matters most are the feelings you instigate in the interviewer, plain and simple.

LET'S PUT OURSELVES IN THE INTERVIEWER'S SHOES

Say hello to Mustache Man. Let's imagine he's going to be your interviewer today. He looks like a pretty decent guy, right?

As he's asking questions and listening to your answers, what is he *personally* worried about? What is he thinking? What are his concerns? His priorities? What is his goal? He's a person just like you. So . . . what would you be thinking and worried about if YOU were responsible for making hiring decisions for your company?

If you think about it, he's probably got a lot of competing pressures. He needs to hire good people. He has to answer to his boss. He wants to make sure that his candidates are successful. He's got staffing concerns. He needs to make sure you'll be happy once you join the firm, so he has to really understand your preferences and evaluate your experiences. But perhaps most importantly, his personal reputation is on the line. If he advocates for you and you're a flop, then his reputation could very well suffer. There's really a lot going on. It's too much for the brain to manage at once.

If Mustache Man were a robot, he'd use an algorithm to weigh all those components and give you an objective score that compares you with your competitors. But since Mustache Man is human, he's going to have to leverage gut instinct to "crunch the numbers" and arrive at an informed decision about you. For this, he needs to rely on his feelings. The interviewer's goal boils down to one simple question: Will he advocate for you? In a heated discussion about recruiting decisions, will he go to bat for you?

Think about it; if you had to make a decision like that with all those competing pressures, wouldn't you rely on how the interviewee makes you feel? Wouldn't you trust that the people you liked and felt connected to were the right ones for your team? Wouldn't you advocate for the ones that "felt right" to you? It's obvious when you put yourself in Mustache Man's shoes.

WHAT DO SOME IMPORTANT INTERVIEWERS SAY?

In the next chapter we'll consider why companies conduct interviews in the first place—why they invest time and money in you before you're even hired. When you learn what companies are actually evaluating in the conversation, it's going to be very hard for you to cling to the old "the interview is a test" mentality.

Interview Hero Secrets in This Chapter:

- The interview is not a test.
- Don't use the interviewer's body language to gauge how you're doing.
- Interviews mark your entry into a world beyond school; relationships and communication become a critical predictor of success beyond "getting good grades."
- The interviewer is not a robot.
- Make human connection and self-expression your goal in the interview (and in life) and you will meet with success in the real world.

The Friendship Mindset

There are no strangers here;
Only friends you haven't yet met.
—WILLIAM BUTLER YEATS

WHY DO COMPANIES AND SCHOOLS INTERVIEW?

If you're applying for a job, think about what information the company already has on you: your resume, LinkedIn profile, cover letter, possibly a recommendation or two, a phone screen, and even a referral from a current employee. If you are applying to business school or another graduate degree program, the school has one or more essays, your resume, your grades and scores, and recommendations. Why not just hire or admit you based upon that?

I mean, your grades and scores speak for themselves—those, after all, *did* involve tests. The hiring institutions know how successful you were in an academic environment. Through your resume and LinkedIn profile, they also have information about the companies you worked for, titles you held, whether and how fast you were promoted, and the key accomplishments you achieved in those roles. So if we're talking objective measures, they have a pretty good sense of how well you've been able to perform at work, too. Your recommendations, essays, and cover letter add a bit of color commentary—they've hopefully gleaned a sense of your personality and the way you approach challenge and achievement.

So why isn't that information enough? Let me answer this question with a story.

THE AIRPORT TEST

It was my second year as a management consultant at the Boston Consulting Group, and I was working on a really challenging project in Omaha, Nebraska, in the dead of winter. I was flying to Omaha every week, spending four or five days on the ground and doing brutally challenging work. We had just been hired by the new CEO of a big company who was cleaning house so that he could run it his own way. We were charged with helping cut costs for more efficient operations. If you read between the lines there, you'll understand we were helping the company decide who it needed to lay off. Many people were laid off as a result of that project.

So, for those of us on the team, it was kind of a worst-case scenario. I worked on a lot of really cool projects at BCG, but once in a while, you get one that's no fun at all. If you imagine the stereotypical "bad consulting project," this one checked every box. We were just like those terrible consultants in the movie *Office Space*: the ones who came in, interviewed all the employees about their jobs, and then told management who they could live without.

Those were long, lonely weeks for me. The work was difficult, but it didn't challenge me in interesting ways. I was far from home, I was up to my ears in snow and barren landscape, and I wasn't contributing to outcomes I cared about. My professional mission has always been to help people have better work lives, and if anything, I was doing the opposite in Omaha. The results of my analysis were going to have a direct negative impact on people's lives. As it turns out, this was my last project as a consultant. I moved onto much more personally meaningful work after this, helping BCG recruit and empower more women: a role that fit much better with my personal values.

But that winter, I was stuck in Omaha. And thankfully, my Movie Buddy soon joined the team—a coworker of mine who shared my passion for film. We both had fantasies about going off to Hollywood to become screenwriters, fantasies we later both enacted at the same time. After long workdays we'd head out of the office and catch a 10 pm movie. Then later in the week, we'd spend hours dissecting the plot and jazzing ourselves up about how amazing it was to appreciate and tell stories. Our acquaintance eventually went beyond the office, surpassing our love of film. We became true friends.

Having a real friend in Omaha—someone whose company I enjoyed and with whom I could share experiences and emotions—changed the whole experience. Now it became more of an adventure. I had someone I could talk to in confidence about my frustrations and failings. I had someone to get out of the hotel with in the evenings and talk with over dinner. Watching a film together became our Wednesday ritual. As you can imagine, I suffered a lot less on that project once my Movie Buddy arrived.

But here's where this story concerns you and your interviews: one Thursday night we found ourselves snowbound in Omaha. All the flights were delayed, so we had to camp out in the airport for hours. Because we were together, though, this minor consulting tragedy turned into a fun evening. We enjoyed each other's company like we always did, talking about our plans and schemes for the future, and, of course, films.

At BCG, we actually had a thing called the "Airport Test" that was a big part of candidate assessment. It points to the inevitability of moments precisely like this one in Omaha: when your flight is grounded and you're forced to spend what could be hours on end with your coworker. Will you enjoy yourself? Take it from me—the question every interviewer asks himself is this: "If I'm stuck in the Omaha airport with this person, are those hours going to be pleasant?"

Just look at Mustache Man. Can you tell that's what he's thinking? He's imagining you two in Omaha. Let's hope he likes the idea of passing the hours chatting with you at gate A6.

IT'S JUST HUMAN NATURE TO WANT TO BE AROUND PEOPLE YOU LIKE

A recent Harvard study found that the quality of relationships throughout our lives determines our health, happiness, and longevity. "Close relationships, more than money or fame, are what keep people happy throughout their lives," the study revealed. "Those ties protect people from life's discontents, help to delay mental and physical decline, and are better predictors of long and happy lives than social class, IQ, or even genes."[1]

On the flip side, studies are finding that loneliness and particularly workplace loneliness are health risk factors. Research shows that "ostracism is actually a more harmful workplace experience than harassment."[2] If you have any doubt that loneliness impacts workplace culture and contentment, consider *Fortune's* 2017 article "Why Loneliness Is a Public Health Threat," which discusses findings from the 125th Annual Convention of the American Psychological Association, namely, that there is a strong "connection between loneliness and a premature death."[3] Ironic that people would feel lonely while surrounded by people, but genuine friendship and human connection are hard to come by in a work environment.

We all need to feel like we belong in our work community. In her article "The Far-Reaching Effects of Workplace Loneliness," Emily Jarrett writes, "As people spend almost of a quarter of their lives at work, job isolation can have serious, and very negative, implications."[4] So even if you don't go into an industry like consulting that often requires long days on the road, you're going to spend the majority of your waking hours with your coworkers. The quality of your relationships in the office is going to have a huge impact on your job satisfaction and overall happiness. If you've had your own Movie Buddy or another true friend at work, then you know what I'm talking about. It can mean the difference between dreading work on Monday morning or looking forward to it.

The same applies to your bosses. Have you ever had a boss you didn't like or who didn't respect you? Then you can probably remember that no matter how much you like your work, no matter how challenging and interesting your tasks are, if you kind of hate your boss, you're going to be miserable. Your prospective employers need to be sure you won't be the rotten apple, the one person who makes the workplace miserable for everyone else. There's no reliable way to gauge this on paper.

HUMANS ♥ HUMANS

But set aside the human motivations—of course we prefer to hang out with people we like, especially if we're spending long hours in a small windowless conference room in Omaha. But what about corporate objectives?

Studies, including one I contributed to,[5] have shown that companies perform better against a variety of key performance indicators when employees are happier at work. It doesn't take a genius to know that having more people you like at work will make you happier.

But even beyond the notion of employee happiness, likeability and solid relationship skills are just good for business. Robots may deliver our packages and crunch our numbers, but humans still make the decisions. And decisions—as we already established—are determined by emotions. Humans are customers. Humans buy products. Humans hire consultants. Humans manage other humans. And humans are the ultimate beneficiaries of a company's value: shareholders, customers, partners, suppliers, and service providers are all humans. There isn't a business on this planet that isn't about humans.

These facts make it clear that someone who can connect and communicate effectively with others will be a coveted candidate. As artificial intelligence takes over more and more of our analytical and manual tasks, connection and communication skills will be more and more in demand. Companies will always interview because they need to assess your human skills—emotional intelligence, communication, and relationship-building abilities. They need to know if you are likeable.

THE HIRING CALCULUS

Let's look at the hiring calculus. It's slightly different for schools and jobs.

IF THEY DON'T LIKE YOU, YOU ARE OUT

JOB APPLICANTS

The one they like most

The group of qualified applicants

MBA APPLICANTS

The most qualified

The group of applicants they like

For a job, the company is typically looking for only one person to fill a vacant position. At most, they're looking for a handful of people to create a team. So, company management will typically choose to hire their single favorite candidate—the one they like the most—from the pool of people who are equally qualified.

Think about it: as long as you clear the bar of basic skills required to get started in your new job, your long-term success at the company will be determined by how well you can function in the firm's culture—that is, how well you can rally support, win friends, influence people, and gain the respect of your peers. In other words, how likeable you are.

This same idea drives graduate school admissions decisions in a slightly different way. Schools are looking for a portfolio of candidates, so they will take the set of applicants that they like from the overall pool and then choose the subset that's most qualified from the set of applicants they like. This decision process isn't scientific, but it's why they need interviews in addition to your resume and essays and recommendations. It's not just to validate that you are who you say you are on paper. It's to ascertain if you're likeable and will fit well within their culture.

Here's an illustration of this concept, created by my friend Nicolas Constantinesco, business school faculty and former consulting Partner who's interviewed hundreds of candidates at McKinsey and KPMG:

EMOTIONS DRIVE HIRING DECISIONS

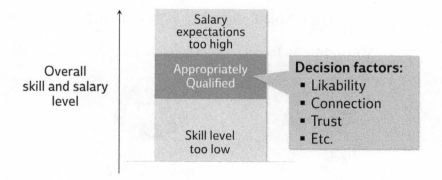

This is why it's rarely the most qualified person who gets the job, and why even my clients with terrible GMAT scores get into the likes of Harvard and Wharton. Because who you are as a complete human being and how that fits with school and company objectives and culture is more important than the parts of you that can be reduced to a score.

But Even the Airport Test Is Not Really a Test

We've already established that how the interviewer feels about you is more important than what he thinks, and his gut response will be perfectly aligned with the objectives of the company or school you're applying to.

Likeability isn't about being funny. It's not about charisma or being popular. It's not about being a sterling conversationalist. The specific hobbies or interests you have, the particular idiosyncrasies or conversational preferences you've developed, your personality type and communication style are irrelevant.

Even if you fear that you might be too shy, awkward, or introverted to be singled out as a "likable" candidate, the ability to make a genuine human connection is a gift we all share. We're born with it. Likeability is the consequence of being an authentic and decent human being who connects with other people. If that seems vague, bear with me; the rest of this book is about self-expression and connection, the two pathways to assured likeability.

Self-expression and connection are the stuff that makes you human, and the stuff that makes you likeable. But it's not the stuff that makes you perfect. That's why it's not really fair to call the Airport Test a test. It's not about right or wrong. Don't even try to come across as perfect. Think about the "perfect people" you've met. How many of them did you generally take a liking to, face to face? How many annoyed you?

Exactly.

So, one last time, don't think of the interview as a test. If anything, it's more like a test drive. The organization is evaluating the user experience of being in your company. They need to see how you handle, how you interface with other humans, how you communicate and bond. They might even decide to test you under difficult conditions to see how you perform under pressure. That's why some interviewers give you a poker face. They want to see how you respond. Can you maintain your cool? Can you still be inspiring? Can you still build a rapport? Difficult circumstances are going to arise in your career—viz the Omaha airport debacle. How will you handle it? And will they still want to be stuck sitting next to you?

GENUINE HUMAN CONNECTION: YOU ARE ALREADY FRIENDS

So, what does all of this mean for you and your mindset in the interview? We've already established that the interviewer isn't a robot, and there's no objective criteria for likeability. Affinity between two humans is a spontaneous phenomenon that's subjectively created in the moment of shared experience. Instead of focusing on getting the answers right, looking smart, seeming cool, or being the ideal candidate, focus on making a genuine **human connection**.

Back to my own story. It was the summer of 2003, and I was trying to figure out how to perform better in consulting interviews for full-time recruiting. I played back the conversations that had gone poorly in my mind; every irritated, confused, or blank facial expression I had encountered, each strand of mental monologue that derailed my confidence, and every self-doubt that had undermined me in those important moments. And I had an insight.

I realized that I couldn't control what the interviewer did or said. I would never have control over that. The truth is, I might never know if he liked me or not. Maybe he was riveted by my words and was just feigning disinterest to see if I'd crack under pressure. Maybe I bored him nearly to tears. Maybe I offended, delighted, intrigued, satisfied, angered, frustrated, concerned, or uplifted him. In the end, I would never really know. The inner life of another person is as inaccessible to us as the stars.

This inspired me to change the way I did things, which first required a change in the way I saw things. I was sick of analyzing my interviews, seeing all of my screw-ups in hindsight, drowning in conjecture, and beating myself up. So I changed my paradigm by altering my experiences from the inside out. I knew I couldn't control anyone else, so I started with me. This involved adopting a Friendship Mindset, which I consider to be the single most important secret to interview success.

The Friendship Mindset is simply this: imagine that you are *already* friends with your interviewer, and you are just going to have one of many future conversations. Your only job in this conversation is to help your friend get to know you and your experiences a little better. We all have the natural ability to be a friend, whether we're a baby or an octogenarian. Genuine human connection is our birthright. By treating the interviewer like he's already your friend, you're going to help him get to know you a little bit better in a holistic, authentic way.

You won't get every job, but if you aim to create a valuable relationship with your interviewer by being your authentic self, you'll reveal your personality, genuineness, and vulnerabilities. And this, my friend, is what makes you likeable. It has the very important added benefit of putting you totally at ease—at least this is what I've found. In my second go at management consulting interviews, after my epiphany, I actually felt like I was talking to old friends even though I had never met most of my interviewers before. And it all boiled down to my new mindset. I was so much more relaxed and clear-headed. I didn't need to wrestle with the dreaded impostor syndrome because I had no need to impress. Put simply, I was happy to be there.

ADOPT A FRIENDSHIP MINDSET

The Friendship Mindset worked wonders for me. When I viewed the interview through a friendship prism, fear of judgment disappeared. *We're already friends*, I told myself, *so why not just relax and enjoy the conversation?* If we're friends already, then he already likes me. I have nothing to prove. I can just trust him, share, open up, relax, and be myself.

How do you treat the interviewer like he's already your friend?

To make the Friendship Mindset possible, first you have to forget about your ultimate goal or objective. You have to set aside your agenda of "getting the offer" or "getting in."

I know that sounds completely counterintuitive. But here's the logic. To some extent, whether you get the job or not (or get into a graduate program or not) is out of your hands. You have no control over who else is applying, and ultimately no control over the interviewer's decision. If you focus on your goal and on the high stakes involved, you're back in testing mindset—you'll inherently feel judged—which will make you feel less inclined to strike up a friendship with the person sitting across from you and more inclined to defend yourself against imagined slights.

So just set aside the goal of getting the job, and instead, focus on building a genuine relationship with every interviewer you encounter. Forget you're in an interview in the first place. I'm not suggesting you put your feet on the desk and tell fart jokes. A professional friend is a close acquaintance you can be genuine with. Think of it this way: you'll have to see this person day in and day out if you land the job. It'll be no fun to keep up a masquerade of perfection every day if the company hires you.

In the interview, be professional, but be yourself. Act how you would act on a normal day if you already had the job and knew that everyone who worked there already accepted you just as you are. If you emerge from an interview without a job but with a new professional friend, then you can consider it a successful interview after all.

HOW TO BUILD RAPPORT: A CLIENT STORY

Here's an example of what this looks like. This is a debrief that a client of mine sent me after completing my interview training course and going into his MBA interviews with a top-five MBA program.

Spoiler alert: he was admitted.

> When I booked my interview, I was immediately matched with a member of the Admissions Committee (let's call her Rebecca). I did some quick research on her and found a couple of YouTube videos of her speaking. I could tell that her style was quite transactional and so first up I prepared myself to not worry if I felt a lack of rapport with her. I'm glad I did—she seemed very uninterested in the interview, kept looking over my shoulder and—to be perfectly honest—the way she asked questions made it seem as though she couldn't wait to move onto the next question and finish the interview!
>
> The most noteworthy aspect of this interview was that I felt I eventually built a huge level of rapport with Rebecca. After we did the standard "Any updates" and "Give me a time when" questions, I used the "Why do you want an MBA now?" question to simply have

a conversation with her about retail . . . after all, everyone has an opinion on Amazon! What went particularly well here was that she turned the conversation into a chat about Internet of Things devices, products which she clearly loved and had great interest in. She got really into it. We talked about this for about 15 minutes before moving onto other questions.

During my consulting interviews, I per~~~ ~lly decided that the best way to do this—to br~~ ~~ ~t authentic self and build ~~ ~periences honestl ~y life without with ~case scenario, the in vants to go to bat fc nd he'll want to hav

W~ Life is long. You nev ~ture career steps. B ~d yourself in a posi and helps you to bu e eager to support y

I've a~ ~ing career about t ~~ are concerned about thing ~~g the right things, impressing the interviewer, ~~ng to be the perfect candidate or at least a strong candidate, not being boring—and, my personal favorite—seeming awesome without reeking of arrogance.

Adopting the Friendship Mindset resolves many of these concerns. But even if you treat the interviewer like a friend, if you're not careful, you run the very real risk of seeming arrogant. Arrogance ranks high among undesirable qualities in an airport layover companion, so coming off as self-satisfied or conceited will tank your chances of being admired or liked.

Unfortunately, the burden to prove non-arrogance is doubly high for women. For a host of interesting reasons, our culture punishes women far more severely than men for appearing full of themselves. The next chapter is going to give you a new window into what arrogance is all about and how to avoid it with confidence.

Interview Hero Secrets in This Chapter:

- People like to work with people they like; if you aren't likeable, your chances of getting an offer are slim. "Likeable" doesn't mean you have to be popular or outgoing—relatable is what you're going for.

- Make genuine human connection your goal and set aside the objective of "getting the offer." Try to forget you are in an interview.

- Adopt a Friendship Mindset: you're already friends with your interviewer, so help him get to know you better by being open and authentic.

- In the interview, be who you are in your normal life; be professional but be you.

- No fart jokes allowed. (My editor thought I should cut this one, but I decided to keep it 'cuz . . . just in case. Ha!)

Confident Humility
and Enthusiasm

There is a real magic in enthusiasm.
It spells the difference between
mediocrity and accomplishment.
—NORMAN VINCENT PEALE

THE A-WORD

A year after I moved to Florence, I made a new friend. She was a brilliant author who had fallen on hard times—she and her 17-year-old daughter had recently been deported for no apparent reason from the country where she was a resident. She had landed in Italy and was trying to rebuild her life to its former glory and reunite with her husband, who was a citizen of the country she'd been kicked out of. It probably adds a little intrigue to the story if I tell you she's an American citizen and her husband is English. She's also the editor of this book and she encouraged me to add this story.

One night shortly after we became friends, we were walking home from an event, talking about our pasts. I'd been explaining my work and some of the things I had achieved before coming to Italy. After I was done, I turned and asked her what she had done before coming to Italy. Relaxed and totally at ease listening before, she immediately bristled. She then navigated a familiar and painful machination that I've watched so many people go through, and which I myself know only too well.

"Well I don't want to brag," she began. "But just months ago I curated a poetry series at the Ashmolean Museum at Oxford University, where I was a student in the History of Art department. I actually won a writing award that paid for me to study talismans at Viennese museums. And before Oxford I earned a master's in creative writing." But not wanting to brag, as she had promised, she then added: "Don't get me wrong, I also know my weaknesses and faults—I've got a list as long as my arm. I'm just saying that's what I was doing before I ended up here, though you'd never guess it, seeing me now."

It pained me to listen to this incredibly talented and accomplished woman suffer so greatly through the simple act of telling someone who she was and what her passions were. But it was a pain of recognition. Because we all struggle from time to time—or even all the time—asserting who we are in the world in a way that does us justice without demeaning or belittling anyone else. We don't want to be arrogant, but it's only fair to be proud.

If you haven't guessed, the A-word is "arrogant."

Where's the line and how do we strike a balance, especially in interviews when we're expected to talk ourselves up? We need to project an air of confidence, but we don't want to err on the side of self-aggrandizement.

TALKING ABOUT OURSELVES IS WEIRD

Let's face it. Talking about ourselves is weird, especially since we're taught that humility is a virtue. Talk about inner conflict! In the interview we're wrestling with various syndromes: we've got tall poppy syndrome—which is when we don't want to stand out too much for fear that our heads will be chopped off. This leads us to act meek and unassuming. On the other hand, we're beset with impostor syndrome—the secret belief that we're frauds—so we try to stand head and shoulders above the rest to convince ourselves that we're good enough. This arrogance/modesty duality is like having an angel on one shoulder and a devil on the other. Which one do you listen to?

You have no choice. You've GOT to talk about yourself in interviews, and you've got to project confidence while doing it. Really, there's almost no other time in life when you're expected to behave this way.

Therapy, counseling, coaching, mentorship conversations, venting, getting advice about a problem, and countless other times in life when we're permitted to talk about ourselves are nothing like this. Typically, in those conversations, we're dwelling on some problem or weakness we're trying to resolve—a subject that's very comfortable for many of us. But turn the discussion toward success, and most of us just get weird. Isn't that strange? Aren't you more comfortable talking about your problems and weaknesses to others than you are talking about your strengths and what makes you great? I know I am!!

Adopting the Friendship Mindset goes a long way to resolving some of this conundrum. If you set aside the notion that the interview is a test, you'll avoid the temptation to *prove* you're awesome, which usually tends to make you seem arrogant. You've seen it a hundred times before.

When someone is acting like, "Eh, I'm awesome!" How do you feel about that person? Major Airport Test fail, right?

But we still have to deal with the fact that there are all these other competing concerns running in the background. Even if you treat the interviewer like an old friend, you've probably had friends that you thought were just a touch arrogant at times. And remember the hiring calculus—when the company is only hiring one person, they take *the person they like most* from the pool of qualified talent. Likability is so important. If you come off as arrogant, you're screwed. How do you make sure you're not that guy?

CONFIDENT HUMILITY

The Friendship Mindset is just one of three essential paradigms that will help transform the experience of talking about yourself to strangers. The second is Confident Humility. Confident Humility makes you relatable, trustable, and likable. You can't fake it: humble brags are transparent, and false humility makes us all cringe. Human beings have really sophisticated radar systems that detect when someone is *pretending* to be humble, but the good news is that you don't have to fake it.

Let me go back to my story to show you what this quality means and how you can instantly create it for yourself.

When I was interviewing for summer internships during my MBA, I struggled a lot to present a confident façade when inside the alarm bells were screaming: Impostor! Impostor!! Fraud!! Who do you think you're fooling!!!?

I knew that confidence was indispensable. Without confidence in your professional life, you won't speak up in meetings, ask for what you want, push back on unreasonable demands, or generally remain true to yourself. When you lack sufficient confidence in a given situation, it's nearly impossible to perform your best. And companies want strong performers, so lacking confidence is not an option. You need to project strength or you will fail to engender trust in your abilities as a professional. But . . .

INTERVIEWS ARE CONFIDENCE-KILLERS

Interviews create the perfect circumstances for confidence implosion that's rarely replicated in adult life. I certainly had never felt anything quite like it before running the gauntlet of MBA internship interviews myself. It was just a stranger and I staring at each other in a room— a stranger whose job it was to judge me! I was being judged, and if I was judged insufficient, rejection would ensue. And let me tell you, I *hate* rejection more than anything! My self-confidence was in the guillotine and my fate was in the hands of the interviewer. Or so it seemed.

I said it before: most humans hate feeling judged. Especially if that judgment results in rejection—one of the most crushing types of failure because it rarely allows for recourse and typically bars us from gaining something we really want: a job, admission, a relationship, a new future. But even without the possibility of rejection, feeling judged means feeling vulnerable and exposed. That goes double if you've danced with the devil of failure once or twice.

See, I fail at pretty much everything I do. At least once or twice. Sometimes many, many, many times before I succeed. As a perfectionist and someone who wasn't brought up with a growth mindset, I find failure to be about as inspiring and enjoyable as oral surgery without anesthesia. I mean, it just sucks not to measure up to my own expectations. But it's an experience I'm doomed to repeat pretty much every day and even every hour of my life.

And there is no time when my internal "you suck" monologue rages so loudly as during interviews. I would imagine the other person judging even my most cherished accomplishments—never mind the failures—and finding them lacking. Maybe that huge project I completed that meant so much to me seems like a cakewalk to Mustache Man.

And then there's all those failures he doesn't know about. Hard to feel like anything but a fraud.

This was my repeated experience in interviews until I discovered that I didn't have to keep any of that stuff a secret.

That's how I discovered Confident Humility.

Know this: confidence happens in communication. I'm making this blanket statement without evidence, but my hope is that the rest of this book will help you experience this truth in your bones. We have exactly as much confidence as we give ourselves through our self-talk, and exactly as much confidence as we allow ourselves to experience when we speak to others (even when we suspect they might be judging us).

What we tend not to realize is that confidence without humility is fraud. It's tempting to sugarcoat life, put the spotlight only on the high moments, and sweep failures and struggles under the rug. But when you do that, not only do you seem arrogant, but you are truly vulnerable. Not only because you're hiding part of the truth, but also because the real secret to confidence and connection lies in embracing and communicating your full humanity, eff-ups and all. That means you have to appreciate and celebrate conflict and failure and then tell Epic Stories about them.

UNDERSTANDING THE NATURE OF CONFLICT

Let's make this really practical. When answering questions such as "Tell me about a time you made a difference," "Tell me about your greatest accomplishment," "When did you lead a team?" I realized that I couldn't just focus my response on the successful outcome. I also had to reveal the challenges I faced along the way.

Take the example of a big project I managed that was a huge success in the end. As I prepared for interviews, I took time to understand the ultimate impact of my work: how much money and time were saved by virtue of my ingenuity, the positive outcomes that would not have happened without my ideas, and the other verifiable measures of my success such as praise from managers and clients and awards that resulted from my work. I knew, of course, that a "happy ending" is an important part of every story.

But then I turned my attention to the challenges I faced along the way. Wasn't there an interpersonal conflict on the team? Didn't I need to convince someone who didn't believe in my ideas? Weren't there severe time or budget constraints that required extra creativity? And didn't that learning curve I had to climb seem insurmountably steep when I started out?

I started being honest with myself about the ways I was challenged by the experience, where I struggled, and at what points things seemed daunting and hopeless. I realized that as I talked about my career success stories in interviews, I needed to include the obstacles I had to overcome in order to achieve my objective, how I strategized about those obstacles, how I thought and felt about them, and how they shaped my course of action.

I learned a very simple and liberating truth: if you are honest about the struggles you faced en route to success, then you will be able to showcase even the most exceptional accomplishments with your humility intact. You'll also avoid feeling like a fraud. And that will in turn allow you to relax, enjoy the conversation, and shine.

ARROGANCE IS SKIN-DEEP

To go back to my friend's struggle to talk about herself, I was struck by the fact that far from presenting an air of Confident Humility, she actually did the opposite—she presented a picture of self-flagellating arrogance. I already knew her well enough at that point to know that she wasn't a braggart, but imagine if she had introduced herself this way to someone who didn't know her, as you could conceivably do in an interview.

This is why communication can be so treacherous—who are you on the inside? No one will ever *really* know. People have to make decisions about who you are based on what they can see.

I learned the Korean language in my twenties, and it changed my brain in interesting ways, as language immersion always does. It gave me new ways to look at the world. One interesting grammatical fact is that in Korean, it's impossible to construct a sentence like this: "She is sad." In Korean, adjectives that describe internal states can only be used in one of three ways:

1. In the first person to express your own inner state: "I am sad."

2. When quoting someone who has spoken in the first person: "She said she was sad."

3. And lastly, when paired with the verb "to make or do": "She does sad," or "Stop doing sad."

In other words, it's baked into the grammar that you can't make assertions about someone else's inner states. You can only comment that she's showing external signs of sadness. When you speak about others, you are speaking about what you are seeing on the surface, not necessarily what is underneath. I think this is a brilliant and insightful tribute to the nature of reality.

And this is why communication is everything in life. Well, just about everything. And certainly, it's everything in an interview. No one can really know who you are on the inside—it's who you are *in communication* that determines how people see you. It's what you do and say and how you make people *feel* that will determine how they view you.

And how *you* feel when you're speaking is often a very good indicator of how you are making others feel. We humans are pack animals, after all. Feeling peaceful and self-assured? Then others probably feel pretty good too. Feeling combative or defensive? The person listening is probably having a tense or equally combative response. Feeling bad about yourself? It's getting all over others too.

FOUR COMMUNICATION MISTAKES YOU MAKE WHILE TRYING TO AVOID SEEMING ARROGANT

I had to laugh a little at my friend's Airport Test fail, but again, it was a painful laugh of recognition. I had been there so many times myself. I understood that she felt really lousy about herself—that inside she wondered if her life was ever going to be OK again. She was in a dark place and couldn't yet identify a silver lining.

She had wanted to make herself known to me and was justifiably proud of the life she had before. We were becoming friends, and she wanted me to relate to her as the person she knew she was. But as the words were coming out of her mouth, she was also struck by the fact that they tasted arrogant. Impostor syndrome kicked in, and unsure how to recover from that bad feeling, she had to bring herself down a notch to recover from it. So she tried to pile on some vague cliché about her weaknesses to make her words match more how she felt. But of course, that made no one feel better, least of all her.

For most of us, it just feels bad to brag, so we go to great lengths to avoid that feeling. Typically, when we're "avoiding bragging," we're making one of four mistakes. My friend made three of them. Let me show you.

Here's what she said again: "Well I don't want to brag, but [Mistake 1] just months ago I curated a poetry series at the Ashmolean Museum at Oxford University, where I was a student in the History of Art department. I actually won a writing award that paid for me to study talismans at Viennese museums. And before Oxford I earned a master's in Creative Writing [Mistake 2]. Don't get me wrong, I also know my weaknesses and faults—I've got a list as long as my arm. I'm just saying that's what I was doing before I ended up here, though you'd never guess it, seeing me now [Mistake 3]."

Can you guess what the mistakes were?

Let me explain so you can understand how the next key mindset functions.

Mistake 1: Never preface a conversation with a disclaimer; it only steers the listener's attention to what you're trying to avoid. And since the listener is now hyper-aware of what you're avoiding, he can't help but wonder why. It can be perceived as inauthentic, manipulative, and suspicious.

The worst case of this is, "No offense, but . . ." The listener automatically armors herself against what you're about to say, because if it were something positive, there would be no need to preface it that way. When you say, "I don't mean to be _____" (fill in the blank with offensive, too blunt, arrogant, braggy, daft, whatever), you're trying to get yourself off the hook for being precisely _____.

Move toward something you *do* want to convey in the conversation instead—focus on something genuinely positive that makes you feel good to talk about, and then you don't have to apologize in advance.

Mistake 2: My friend cited accomplishments like facts with no vivid detail, no emotion, and no Confident Humility. This may SEEM like it's less arrogant because you are "letting the facts speak for themselves," but it actually comes off as completely arrogant when the facts are about you. No dice quoting someone else either. My mom is very fond of saying things like, "My students just think I'm so great." And when I point out that she's bragging, she replies, "No, I'm just telling you what they said about me." Sorry, mom. It's still bragging if you're the one quoting it. Ironically, adding some emotion instead of flat facts could have allowed my friend and my mom to show Confident Humility. More on that below.

Mistake 3: My friend threw vague dirty laundry out there without putting it in the context of the accomplishments she was expounding. Self-deprecation is not charismatic. Being self-effacing and genuinely humble is, but tearing yourself down isn't humble; it's pitiable. If she had cited a specific challenge or weakness she was grappling with, she might have endeared the listener, but throwing shade on yourself just evokes pity—in you first and foremost. She got no credit for her accomplishments, nor credit for humility.

Mistake 4 (my friend didn't make this one): This one involves deflecting attention from you onto someone else or the nebulous "team." This is the notorious "we" in conversations that should be almost exclusively about *you*. For instance, if given the question, "Tell me about a time you led a team," many people might answer, "I was coordinating a group of engineers on a project. We did this and we did that, and in the end, we achieved amazing things."

Can you spot the problem here?

Giving credit where credit is due is one thing. But beware of using "we" too often when you should be focusing on "I" and "me." Hiding your role in a successful operation makes you look disingenuous and ineffectual and—ironically—even more arrogant because you appear to be taking personal credit for a group's work. The interviewer asked you to tell her about a time that *you* led a team, after all, and here you are talking about what everyone else did. She'll be tempted to draw the conclusion that you didn't do much and therefore need to take credit for the whole team's outcomes.

THE FEELS ARE YOUR FRIENDS

The remedy for all four of these mistakes—a foolproof way to shine when you talk about yourself—is the third key mindset I suggest you adopt. Well, more than a mindset, it's an emotion—a feeling you want to share with your interviewer. And that's enthusiasm.

Enthusiasm is contagious, and it's inalienable. In every moment there is something to be excited about if you just look for it. In all of your experiences, there is something fascinating, beautiful, poignant, and exciting. Instead of talking about what you've done, talk about *what you love* about what you've done: all the positive emotions it made you *feel*.

It works every time.

Later my friend asked my advice about how to introduce herself because she knew this was my area of expertise. And here's what I told her: instead of trotting out what you've done and hanging it out there for judgment, focus on what you're passionate about instead. It defies judgment. We all love to love things, and therefore we can all relate to that feeling of enthusiasm.

Here was her improved answer to "Tell me about yourself":

"So far in life I've loved bringing people together through the arts. For instance, I used to curate poetry at Oxford. I revamped the existing program and linked it to social media and created booklets for each event. Even though the community frowned upon my innovations at first, it was an amazing journey. In fact, hilariously, the museum had to rope off the exhibits and hire guards when we held readings because my efforts helped each event reach capacity. Talent scouts attended the readings, and as a result, many of the poets were asked to speak at literary festivals. It brought me so much joy to see my 'crazy idea' turn into a platform that not only enriched and challenged me, but also brought the arts community together in meaningful and surprising ways. For now, I'm trying to figure out my next steps, but I know poetry is going to play a huge role."

In this version, the listener is pulled into the drama and the surprise of the story. A guard at a poetry reading? The local community didn't support her at first? It doesn't occur to me that she's bragging at all because she's honest about the challenges she faced and her feelings about them. Her accomplishments took the form of a narrative that sucked me in. Instead of thinking, "Wow, this lady has low self-esteem!" I would be wondering how she managed to achieve such success in the face of such obstacles. What secrets can she teach me about social media and community building? How did she organize such a huge project? And can I hire her to work in my company?

WE ALL WANT TO FEEL MORE ALIVE

See the difference between these two ways of presenting yourself? In my friend's initial attempt, she came across as arrogant and awkward because she listed her experiences like bullet points on a resume instead of telling a vivid story with challenges and suspense. In the revised version, her story offered vulnerability and intrigue. She came alive while telling it, and that pulled me into her experience. Because one thing we all want as humans is to feel more alive. This is the gift of enthusiasm.

Framing accomplishments as challenges and passions turns dull bullet points into engaging stories. If my friend had told her story this way in the first place, she would have achieved her goal: I would have seen her the way she wanted me to see her. In my mind's eye, I would have visualized the whole scenario. I wouldn't be walking across the piazza with my friend as she is now, but in the museum audience seeing her as she was *then*. I would have felt like I really knew her, liked her, and wanted her on my team because I could relate to feeling so passionate about something.

We'll talk about storytelling in the next section of the book. Combined with the Friendship Mindset, Confident Humility, and enthusiasm, good old-fashioned storytelling is your key to Interview Heroism. If you tell vivid stories, the interviewer won't be staring you down across a desk, but rather she'll be imagining herself in your story, in your shoes, fleshing out your narrative in her mind and feeling what you felt right alongside you: the death-defying lows and—most importantly—the enlivening highs.

When we encounter stories, we visualize, imagine, and *feel*. Stories have an ineffable power: they allow us to temporarily escape our own realities and thoughts and to live through the adventures of another for a while. They allow us to empathize and connect not only with the speaker, author, or character, but with all of humanity. Engaged with a story, we're not alone, and the world is a vast and magical place.

Don't worry if you're not a gifted raconteur. In the next section, you'll gain a variety of tools that will help you craft awesome stories—stories that communicate who you were, who you are now, and who you want to become.

And if you're a woman, the storytelling chapters will be extra specially valuable to you. For better or worse, the band of communication that registers as arrogant is far broader for women than it is for men. Society holds women and men to different standards of expression where success and accomplishment are concerned. And even if the perception on the outside were not different, in my vast experience coaching women, the experience on the inside is. Women *feel* arrogant talking about their successes more readily than men do. Look to your own experience: as you read what my friend said, you might have recalled a number of times you've heard other women make some of those mistakes. It's probably harder to recall examples of when your male friends did so.

Interview Hero Secrets in This Chapter:

- Everyone thinks they're a fraud, everyone gets nervous and insecure, and everyone struggles. You don't have to hide that from the interviewer.
- Channel Confident Humility by being honest about where you've faced challenges and how they made you feel.
- Avoid the four critical communication mistakes you make in the name of avoiding arrogance: beginning with negative

preambles, sticking to "the facts," tearing yourself down, and overusing "we."

- Enthusiasm is contagious, and it defies judgment: if you share what you love and how you feel about it, your enthusiasm will infect the listener as well.

- Stories make your experience come to life—they create a feeling of empathy and aliveness that connects you and the listener through your shared humanity. We all want to feel more alive and more connected.

The Seven Stages of the Interview

*There's nowhere you can be that isn't
where you're meant to be.*
—JOHN LENNON

KNOWLEDGE VS. WISDOM

As you read the previous chapters, you hopefully had a few "aha" moments and gained new insight into your own experiences, struggles, and feelings about interviews. I hope that the three key mindsets: Friendship, Confident Humility, and enthusiasm will work magic for you in all of your professional communication.

But I also know that—as humans—we don't learn our most valuable lessons through reading and thinking. We learn by doing. It's your experience that teaches you—not printed words on a page or the interesting ideas of other people. Even my ideas, no matter how brilliant I might think they are (ha!), won't change your life until you embed them in your own experience. That's why this book is just getting started and didn't end with Chapter 3.

Implementing these communication strategies in your professional life is going to require practice. And practice requires tools and techniques so that you can operationalize these conceptual ideals. And boy, have I got some tools and techniques for you!!!

The rest of this book is going to break down each part of the interview in finite detail so you can understand what is happening in the conversation. You'll learn how to approach different question types with answers that engender affinity, respect, and trust. How people perceive you is everything in an interview, even if they're mistaken. It's not enough to *think* someone is your friend and to *feel* enthusiastic—those values need to be reflected in the content of your communication.

So let's work on the content of your communication. It's my hope that the tools, frameworks, and processes I'll present in the rest of this book will serve you far beyond interviews and transform you into a dazzling communicator in every area of your life. Because humans are always humans, the same principles will serve you equally well in interviews, sales conversations, first dates, networking events, online chats, and just about any other situation in which you are talking to one or more humans.

You're about to become a brilliant communicator. And this is how you will become the director of your own life narrative and—therefore—complete life experience.

But if and *only* if you actually practice.

Ideas are worthless without implementation. Knowledge has little value without experience. I encourage you to use the rest of this book like a training manual. I'm going to talk at you less and invite you to act more. I've got homework and downloads to help you, and I hope you'll use all of them.

Now I'm going to get into the tools. Ready? Let's do this.

STEP BY STEP, OH BABY

Does anyone remember NKOTB? No?

OK never mind. Let's start by breaking down the interview into seven stages. Most interviews proceed through most of the stages in the order outlined below—starting at the top and working toward the bottom. But there are no rules, and the questions—whether they're all included, some are skipped, the focus is entirely on one or two questions, or you're asked 20—are entirely at the whim of the interviewer. Even when firms have general guidelines or specific policies for interviews, a conversation between two people will always follow the will, interests, and mutual chemistry of those people.

So apart from Stage 1 and Stage 7—which will always happen in the first and last spot, respectively, in the sequence—the rest could theoretically come in any order. We'll deal with each one in turn in subsequent chapters, but let me talk through them in order now, so you can understand the pattern of affinity and human connection and how it proceeds from casual and general to intimate and specific.

Stage 1: Breaking the Ice

Stage 2: The 30,000-Foot View

Stage 3: Your Past and Behavior

Stage 4: Your Values and Vulnerabilities

Stage 5: Your Future

Stage 6: The Interviewer's Experience and Advice

Stage 7: Appreciation

HOW THESE STAGES MAP TO THE MAJOR QUESTION TYPES:

1. Chitchat While You Are Sitting Down	⇒	Breaking the Ice
2. Walk Me Through Your Resume	⇒	The 30,000-Foot View
3. Behavioral Questions	⇒	Your Past and Behavior
4. Point-Blank Questions	⇒	Your Values and Vulnerabilities
5. Why Questions	⇒	Your Future
6. What Questions Do You Have for Me?	⇒	The Interviewer's Experience and Advice
7. Your Thank You Note	⇒	Appreciation

Let's look at them one at a time.

Stage 1: Breaking the Ice

This funny expression reveals a truth about human connection: it starts cold. Between you and any stranger there is a vast glacier—an expansive and frigid wasteland separating your identities and experiences. To traverse that landscape is no small gesture—to break that ice and warm to another person is an act of kindness, generosity, and courage. It's also the hardest step in friendship, and as a result, it is incredibly empowering and uplifting to both parties. So when you wake up the day of your interview, turn on your inner heat lamp and be warm. Here are some tactical ways to do that.

The interview in some ways begins the moment you enter the building. You would be wise to assume you are being evaluated from the time you walk through the door—and nothing will make a better impression than genuine warmth. So, chat with people in reception. Smile at other interview candidates. Be a good person.

> *Actions speak louder than words, and a smile says,*
> *"I like you. You make me happy. I am glad to see you."*
> —DALE CARNEGIE,
> *How to Win Friends and Influence People*

Then think about that moment when the interviewer comes to you and sticks out his or her hand and says, "I'm going to be interviewing you today." Even if you're meeting at a crowded Starbucks, this is the moment when the official conversation begins. You've probably read that people take almost no time to form a first impression. In later chapters I'll talk about how to make a killer first impression in terms of what to wear, how confident you feel, and how to shake hands. All that stuff's important.

But far more important is how you two break the ice. Meeting someone for the first time can be awkward—not only for you but also for your interviewer, believe it or not. It's a state change to go from complete and utter strangers to acquaintances: akin to how warmth turns physical ice to vapor.

What topic of conversation will facilitate that chemical reaction? How will you gracefully strike up your new friendship and put the interviewer at ease? You probably didn't think that was your responsibility. It doesn't have to be, but you're going to be much better off if you take responsibility for it yourself. Because you'll feel secure that you can start the relationship off on a positive foot. That in turn will make you feel more powerful and confident.

Communication is messy and multidimensional, and happening all the time without end. Even by not communicating, you're communicating. You're expressing a desire to be left alone, for example, a diffidence and lack of willingness to be the first one to put yourself out there. You can't control most of this mysterious dance between two strangers, but there are a few small things you *can* control, and doing so will serve you well.

In Stage 1 of the interview conversation, you can take control of the small talk. Having a few relevant topics at the ready for light discussion in those first moments will make a big difference in your self-confidence and avoid awkward pauses. In my experience, roughly 90% of the time, interviewers come into the room without having prepared anything to discuss to break the ice. They'll be relieved if you cross that divide and melt the ice first.

Stage 2: The 30,000-Foot View

The first question out of the gate is typically something like, "Tell me about yourself," or "Walk me through your resume." Not a question in fact, but an invitation. In this second stage, you're going to give the interviewer the lay of the land of your life. It's the 30,000-foot view, the one you would see from an airplane.

The point of this from the interviewer's perspective is threefold:

- It lets you both settle into the conversation. It's a more general and less intimate question than some that are coming soon, so this is a gentle way to help you ease in and help him release the distractions he brought into the room so he can focus on you for the rest of the conversation.

- It gives him a sense of the big picture of your career and life so that he can place the rest of what you say in context. It also helps him make some choices about where he would like to probe deeper and get to know you better.

- It gives you a chance to own the moment—to present yourself from the starting gun in the way YOU want to present yourself. You're given this chance to show the interviewer what you really want him to know about you. This question is a very generous act on the part of the interviewer because it allows you the opportunity to take a stand for who you are. Whatever you say will determine how he will relate to you for the rest of the conversation.

It's this last aspect of the "Tell me about yourself" that almost no one thinks about even though it's your key to a stellar first impression. Nearly everyone squanders this opportunity to take ownership of his or her own narrative by painting the precise picture you want the interviewer to see. By some accounts, since this question comes first, and since it sets the stage for the conversation and determines how much the interviewer likes you in those formative first moments, it is the most important. This is why I have dedicated an entire chapter to this important question. You will never answer this question the same way twice if you are doing it right.

Stage 3: Your Past and Behavior

Now come the behavioral questions. If you've looked into interview styles including Behavioral Interviews, Personal Experience Interviews, or Competency-Based Interviews, you will have encountered these questions. Stuff like, "Tell me about a time you led a team," or "Discuss an example of solving a problem creatively." We'll begin with these questions in the next section because they evoke a full-blown narrative response. To answer these questions well, you need to become a great storyteller, a skill I cannot wait for you to develop or improve because it will enrich your career and your life on so many levels above and beyond your interview performance. Much more on this in the ensuing chapters.

Stage 4: Your Values and Vulnerabilities

Typically after, but sometimes before or instead of, behavioral questions, come what I call "point-blank" questions. In this broad category, you find questions that don't evoke a story or a summary of something, but rather elicit a direct and clear answer to a question fired at point-blank range.

- What's your greatest weakness?
- How do you define your leadership style?
- What are you learning these days?
- Why did you change jobs?
- What's your favorite book and why?
- Do you think the internet should be regulated?
- Why should I hire you?

As well as questions from the new paradigm of Strengths-Based Interviews, such as:

- What are you good at?
- What things give you energy?
- Describe a successful day you have had.
- How do you measure success?

Point-blank questions require a different strategy from behavioral questions. You don't have the luxury of two to four minutes to expand upon your experiences and tell a robust story. You've got to cut to the chase and give 'em an answer. But that doesn't mean you should just give 'em any old answer. If you examine the above carefully, you'll notice that these questions get at deeper concepts in your life—they dig below the surface of what you did and what you thought and how you felt, and invite insights about your values, your vulnerabilities, your concerns, and your preferences.

With these questions, we're now getting closer to the very core of your being.

Another name I use for these questions is "values and vulnerabilities questions." In a later chapter, I'll provide frameworks that will help you exploit the incredible opportunity these questions offer: a chance to reveal your character and engender trust and affinity.

Stage 5: Your Future

If questions about values and vulnerabilities cut closer to the quick of your personality and being, then questions about the future get right to the core. We're at our most vulnerable when we contemplate the future because the future is a secret place where we store our wishes, dreams, and fears. It's impossible to look into the future without touching these very tender emotions. For many of us, our deepest insecurities, fears, and anxieties come out when we look forward.

So when they ask questions such as . . .

- Why do you want to work for our company?
- What are your career goals?
- Where do you see yourself in ten years?

- What do you expect to struggle with in this role?

- What do you hope to gain from attending this school?

- How will you contribute to our culture? How will you raise the bar?

- What weaknesses of yours will affect your performance in this role?

. . . they are now getting to the very bottom of who you see yourself to be and the place you see for yourself in this world. The best answers to these questions will bravely reveal these aspects of your individuality. If you answer these questions honestly, they should make you feel a bit vulnerable, and they should inspire both you and the listener.

Most people don't achieve an exciting emotional pitch when they answer these questions because they view them as a transaction between employee and employer—or between student and school. They construct answers that will placate or impress the interviewer or aim to project certainty where there is doubt, determination where there is questioning. Questioning and doubt are authentic and real. Expressing them requires Confident Humility. This is the better strategy.

I like to think that this is why these questions come last—to allow you to build up trust and understanding with your conversation partner and feel safe enough to let yourself be authentic. It's your chance to inspire the interviewer with your vision and bravery rather than just conciliate with an essentially manipulative response. Success in these questions hinges on your level of internal self-awareness. I've dedicated two chapters to these.

Stage 6: The Interviewer's Experience and Advice

Once you've weathered the gauntlet of questions about you, you've now earned the right to ask some more intimate questions of your interviewer. It's a critical moment when he turns to you and says: "OK, that's all I have. Do you have any questions for me?" There are five categories of questions you could ask here.

The 1st: Questions related to your interview performance

- How did I do?

- Will you be giving me the offer?

- How did I compare with other candidates?

- What concerns do you have about my candidacy?

- What else can I do to win the job?

I don't recommend this line of inquiry. It's almost never a good idea, except, perhaps, in the case of interviews for sales positions in firms with competitive sales environments, where "closing the sale" is one of the skills they want you to demonstrate. But in every other circumstance—and often even in that one—the interviewer likely only has partial control over the outcome. It isn't his job to decide, to extend the offer, or to give you feedback if the answer is yes or no. So these questions will make him uncomfortable and destroy all the goodwill you created by engaging the Friendship Mindset up till this point. They put you back in pass/fail test mode. That will feel bad to the interviewer too, because it changes your budding friendship into a transaction—you're trying to get something from her instead of connecting.

In a later chapter, I'll lay out a framework for research and show you how to figure out if your interview is one of those where you need to be closing at the end. But for 95% of you reading this book, these questions are a bad idea.

The 2nd: Logistical questions about next steps

- When can I expect to hear?

- Will you be contacting me in the next week about the rest of the process?

- What are the next steps I should be planning?

These questions are fine to ask. But I recommend you ask them in the hallway as you are shaking hands rather than as the first response to "What questions do you have for me?" for reasons that will become clear below.

The 3rd: General questions about the firm, the team, and the job

- Could you tell me what challenges the firm is facing in the next couple of years?
- How many people are on this team?
- How would you describe the responsibilities of the position?
- What is the company's management style?
- How much travel is expected?
- Is relocation a possibility?
- What is the culture like at this company?

And many, many more. These are question you will *definitely* want to have answers to before you accept a position at the firm. But I recommend you get them answered *before* the interview. Informational interviews—the topic of a later chapter—are one of your best interview prep tools. One-on-one conversations with people who work at the firm not only give you important insider information about corporate fit, but also help you understand how the firm interviews and what exactly you should be expecting. They're also your best chance to build real relationships with people at the firm who might be able to advocate for you *after* your interview when hiring decisions are being made.

Asking these questions at the end of the interview could actually backfire—especially if you're recruiting at a fairly high level—for a managerial position or post-graduate school rotational role, for example. The interviewer will think you haven't done your research and that you don't even know what you're getting yourself into. You could very well destroy all the goodwill you just created during the conversation.

The 4th: Logistical questions about the job itself

- How will I be trained?
- Is this a new role, or did someone hold it before?
- What types of skills is the team missing that you're looking to fill with a new hire?
- Can you show me examples of projects I'd be working on?
- Whom will I report to directly?

THE SEVEN STAGES OF THE INTERVIEW 57

- What opportunities will there be for advancement or professional development?
- Would I be able to represent the company at industry conferences?
- What are the most immediate projects that need to be addressed?
- Can you tell me about the team I'll be working with?

These are questions you *could* ask at this point with minimal downside risk. They reveal that you have a nuanced understanding of what matters at work and that you're taking steps to prepare yourself for the role. They will work best if you are interviewing directly with the person who will be managing you or at least with someone on the specific team you would join.

Still, these aren't your best bet for the sixth stage of the interview. And for higher-level positions, these might best be answered post-offer, as you are weighing your options and negotiating the terms of your contract.

The 5th: Questions that allow the interviewer to share his or her experiences or give you advice

These are your best bet, bar none. Dale Carnegie famously said, "Talk to someone about themselves and they'll listen for hours." But it's also true that if you lend people an open ear and show genuine curiosity about who they are, they'll talk for hours. My clients who go in for 30-minute interviews and emerge two hours later do so because they brought the interviewer into a dynamic discourse and engaging dialogue about the *interviewer and his or her interests and experiences*, not just themselves.

We all want to be known and acknowledged. Asking great questions and listening attentively is a great gift. In a way, you're returning the favor of 30–60 minutes focused entirely on you. So consider asking questions about the interviewer's experience and advice. Here are some examples.

- How did you get up to speed when you first joined the firm?
- What have been the key levers you relied on to achieve great performance?

- What has helped you be really successful here as opposed to just getting your job done?

- What changes have been implemented since you joined, and how have these changes affected your work?

- What do you wish you had known before you started?

- What has been your favorite project so far, and what are some of the valuable lessons it taught you?

- What would you say is your favorite aspect of firm culture?

- Who has been most instrumental in helping you succeed here, and how did you cultivate that relationship?

- How do you measure your own success in this role?

- What makes someone a top performer here? What advice do you give someone who wants to be a top performer in this firm?

- Are there things you would change about this company?

- What advice do you have for me to hit the ground running if I'm offered the position?

- What three pieces of guidance do you find yourself most frequently offering to your team members to help them thrive?

The possibilities are virtually endless. These questions align perfectly with the Friendship Mindset and enthusiasm because you are reciprocating the interviewer's kind attention to you and your experiences. You give him the chance to manifest enthusiasm for his own work and life.

The questions you choose should be tailored to the knowledge and experience base of your interviewer and how that aligns with your objectives and interests. For example, if you're speaking with an HR manager who has never done your job and isn't a part of the team you'll join, asking him about how he measures his own success in his role will probably not be all that relevant to you. On the other hand, a question like: "In your opinion, how do successful people in roles like this quickly establish their reputations?" would be a great one. He has probably interacted with several people in jobs like the one you are being interviewed for, so he probably has some interesting insight and advice to share that could help you succeed.

Stage 7: Appreciation

The thank you note is what you're working toward all throughout the discussion. It's the fuel that propels your relationship out of the realm of transaction and into the realm of true friendship. When you take the time to genuinely thank someone, and in the process acknowledge what you appreciated most about your time together, you solidify the connection from one of necessity to one of choice.

Here's a sample thank you note:

> Hi Mustache Man,
>
> I can't thank you enough for your time yesterday. I loved sharing the story about creating my former company's strategic plan with you, and your questions really forced me to reflect on what I valued so much about that project. Thanks for the incisive and insightful dialogue. I know your advice about staffing dynamics will prove invaluable should I be given the chance to join your team. Looking forward to hearing good news soon, but in any event, I hope it's all right if I keep in touch. It was a pleasure to meet you.
>
> Best,
>
> Angela

That's 100 words including the greeting and closing: It's brief and tight. But it's also personal and heartfelt. It establishes a friendship by paying back just a little of the energy that Mustache Man invested in getting to know me.

You can be sure that Mustache Man will be looking forward to hearing from me and will likely leave the door open for any future contact—be that advocacy for me to get hired, mentoring me if I get in, feedback should things not work out, or even referral to other jobs should the opportunity arise.

All right. Now it's time to dig deep into each of these stages and help you get ready for your interview at every level, including topics of chitchat, questions for the interviewers, and amazing answers to each of the four main questions types.

Just to recap what those are, here you go.

The four main question types:

1. "Walk me through your resume"
2. Behavioral questions
3. Point-blank questions
4. Future questions

We're going to start with behavioral questions, which demand Epic Storytelling skills. In the following chapters you'll learn how to tell engaging stories about yourself. In order to project Confident Humility and create an affinity with your interviewer—or anyone else in life—just sit back, relax, and entertain them with stories.

Interview Hero Secrets in This Chapter:

- The conversation will go through seven stages which mirror the pattern of increasing intimacy.

- Each stage is an opportunity to connect and build a relationship in a deeper way, so you'll want to be ready with tools and tactics to do so.

- There are four main question types in an interview: "Walk me through your resume," behavioral questions, point-blank questions, and future questions.

- That thank you note is what moves you from interview transaction to the possibility of real friendship—don't skip it—ever!!

SECTION II

Epic Storytelling

People never learn anything by being told,
they have to find out for themselves.

—PAULO COELHO

In this section you're going to learn how to tell an inspiring story about any life experience. Think of this less like the section of a book and more like a master class in personal storytelling. It contains theory, examples, exercises, and loads of stories. I encourage you to treat it like a class and go download the workbook at this link here: **careerprotocol.com/ih**.

Here's how it will go.

First, we'll dig into story theory and some science that explains why stories are so important to us. Then I'll give you an incredibly powerful framework to help you construct your own success stories. In Chapter 7, we'll examine failure and learn how to tell the most inspiring stories about times you fell on your face. Chapter 8 will outline some advance storytelling techniques to juice up the impact of your stories. And finally, in Chapter 9, I will give you a highly detailed process and multiple tips to prepare stories and practice them before you go live in interviews.

Why Stories Matter

Stories render our shared humanity.
—I SAID THIS.
I know it's lame to quote myself, but you know what?

OK fine, here's another one:

One of the ways to reincarnate is to tell your story.
—SPALDING GRAY

MY FIRST JOB

When I graduated with a degree in philosophy, I had two job offers: one working with a reputable market research firm that consulted big companies on consumer insights, and one teaching English to three-year-olds in South Korea.

I chose the latter.

It made no sense to friends and family—or to me, for that matter. I didn't speak a word of Korean. I'd never been a teacher in an official capacity before, nor did I think it was a job well-suited to me. I didn't even like kids all that much. But despite my discomfort with the unknown, deep down inside, I knew it was the right thing to do.

So, with only $40 in my pocket, I boarded the first international flight of my life with nothing else but a whole lot of hopes and fears and the promise that my employer would meet me at the arrivals gate.

Filled with anxiety and self-doubt (what had I done?), I scanned the crowd at Kimpo Airport, as they spelled it in those days, for someone with a sign bearing my name. An hour passed. Then two. At the three-hour mark, I was trying to negotiate with taxi drivers who barely spoke English to take me to an address that I couldn't read (because it was written in Korean) and to accept all the remaining U.S. dollars I had for a ride that should have cost twice that in Korean *won*. Then, finally, four hours late, my employer arrived, and my new life began.

I flourished in Korea. Against a one-year expectation, I stayed five years. I became fluent in the language and made many new friends and connections, and through a series of introductions, I eventually landed a job managing training and human resources at KPMG, a major global accounting firm. It was a job I was by no means qualified for, but I loved it and found a way to make a big impact on the company's 700+ employees. It showed me some of the things I value and inspired the decision to get my MBA. And it planted the seed for the work I do now—teaching emergent leaders the skills they need to achieve their dreams.

Turns out teaching suited me after all. I never would have known it before.

It took me a long time to understand the decision to move to Korea and teach little kids, but what I've come to realize is that I'm much more interested in working with actual humans than with data about humans. I care more about helping people grow than about helping companies sell them more stuff. And I am willing—quite literally—to go to the other end of the earth to help people improve themselves. The decision to work in Korea ultimately led me to my destiny even though it made absolutely no logical sense when I boarded that plane.

OK, what I just did there was tell you a story.

Let's call that Introduction A. Imagine if instead of writing that, I had begun the chapter this way:

I really care about helping people. I think helping companies sell more stuff is a waste of time. I don't consider myself to be very brave, but everyone tells me I am. I've had a great career, and I'm very fortunate to have been able to pursue my purpose in life.

Let's call that Introduction B.

You probably notice a lot of differences between Introduction A and Introduction B. But what I want you to pay attention to is how each one makes you *feel*: how you feel about me, the person you're reading about, and how you feel about yourself.

BEHIND THE SCENES OF A GOOD STORY

Now set aside the fact that both of those texts were about me, and let's analyze how you felt about the person in them, whom I'll refer to in the third person for the sake of not distracting you by appearing now to be arrogant.

When you read Introduction A, you probably felt inspired by the story. You may have been touched by the courage and willingness to take a scary leap the character exhibited. If you were hiring someone, you could imagine wanting to hire this person in the story—someone who took risks, bootstrapped herself from a lowly position to a higher one, sought to have impact, and exhibited strong self-awareness.

But take a look and see if that story also made you feel a little inspired by your *own* successes. That story might have reminded you of a time you made a similarly difficult decision that seemed illogical but ended up being right for you. You might have felt uplifted, with an expanded sense of possibility, or a greater connection with your own sense of purpose. In fact, you might right now be grappling with a career choice, and hearing what that person chose to do at her own crossroads might give you permission to trust yourself and chart your own course.

For these reasons, the character in Introduction A was immediately likeable: she made you feel good about her and good about yourself.

But even more importantly, you probably also felt more connected to her. You probably feel like you know her, like you understand her character. You came to your own conclusion about the kind of person she is. If the character were facing a difficult decision, you could probably predict what she would do.

These are the feelings of friendship, by the way. Friendship is defined by shared experience. The emotion is connection and camaraderie: mutual upliftment and inspiration.

Consider now Introduction B. Reading that one, you probably felt at best uninterested, bored, and disconnected. At worst, you may have felt put off, insulted, or repelled by the character's self-satisfied air. Let me play back for you the line-by-line reactions I would have had, were I reading Introduction B written by someone else:

I really care about helping people.

Reaction: Oh yeah? Prove it! and . . . What a suck-up!

I think helping companies sell more stuff is a waste of time.

Reaction: That's so judgmental! What about all the people who love marketing? What about everyone who works at Apple? Nobody cares what you think anyway!!!

I don't consider myself to be very brave, but everyone tells me I am.

Reaction: Nobody cares what anyone else thinks either. If you're so brave, quit bragging about it and prove it with a story that shows instead of tells.

I've had a great career, and I'm very fortunate to have been able to pursue my purpose in life.

Reaction: I'm just supposed to take your word for that? If you could tell me what your career was all about, then maybe I could judge if it's great or not. But I don't really trust your own evaluation of yourself. Conflict of interest. And by the way, saying that you're fortunate doesn't make this any less of a brag. Completely smug and Airport Test FAIL!

I'm exaggerating a bit for effect, but if you think about it, you probably had some of these same reactions as you read Introduction B. That character certainly didn't come off as likeable; you don't feel like you have any real insight into her character or even her life. And you probably even felt a little personally invalidated by what she said. She insulted everyone in marketing, and touted her "great career" without evidence, so that might have left you questioning how adequate your own career has been and whether or not you too are aligned with your purpose.

This version accomplishes precisely the opposite of Introduction A. Rather than giving you insight into my character, inspiring you, and connecting us through shared experience, it distances us, puts you off, and even possibly deflates you a little bit.

This happens because of an important feature of human nature: free will. Because we're all free to choose our perspective, no one likes to be told what to think. If you tell people what they should think, their immediate response will be to think the opposite until you prove the thought one way or the other.

By that same token, no one really cares what anyone else thinks. I don't mean people don't care about your experiences or your feelings. They may also be interested in your thinking—your reason and logic. But opinions are the farts of the mental realm: just as meaningful as passing wind.

Furthermore, if you assert a strength like it's a fact, you leave the door open for people to take it as an affront to themselves. The seemingly competitive nature of reality means that any points in your court are points taken away from mine. This is an illusion, but it's one many of us unconsciously use to keep score. We don't know how successful we are, or how happy to feel, without some kind of relativity.

YOU ARE TELEPATHIC

To immediately disarm this win-lose mindset, choose the power of story instead. Stories are what connect us. They're what we all share. They're what we have to offer each other. Stories are, in short, the threads with which the tapestry of human relationship is woven. When you want to motivate, persuade, or be remembered, start with a story of human struggle and eventual triumph. It will capture people's hearts—by first attracting their brains.[1]

The word "telepathy" is derived from two ancient Greek words: τῆλε, tele, meaning "distant," and πάθος, pathos or -patheia, meaning "feeling, perception, passion, suffering, experience." I like to think that storytelling is actually a kind of telepathy—making another person feel and perceive something at a distance. You create in the mind of your listener a concrete picture of an experience, and she then has all the same feelings you had while living it.

As an interesting sidebar, I find it meaningful that feeling was synonymous with suffering to the Greeks: pathos stood for both meanings. They clearly understood the human condition. To live is to feel and to feel is to feel pain. This is a tautology. If you cut off the pain, you also cut off the joy. The fact that telepathy requires attention to pain will become very relevant in the next chapter.

Recent studies have shown how and why this works. Paul J. Zak, at the Center for Neuroeconomics Studies at Claremont Graduate University, did some fascinating research on the chemical effects of stories on the brain. He took blood samples and brain scan images of two groups of people: one group watched a short film about a father and his struggle to grapple with the impending death of his son due to cancer. The second group watched video footage of the same father and son walking around a zoo.

The first group of subjects had measurably increased levels of cortisol and oxytocin in their blood, chemicals associated, respectively, with our ability to focus and our ability to experience empathy and connection. Likewise, their brain scans revealed increased activity in the areas of the brain that are rich in oxytocin centers that help us feel empathy. The group watching random zoo footage had none of these indicators.

It likely won't surprise you to learn that after the videos, when asked to donate money, the subjects who had watched the cancer story were far more likely to do so. They gave more money to a cause that worked with sick children, but they also gave more money to a random stranger in the lab whose identity they would never know.

Zak's research reveals a rare peek under the hood of human connection and shows how stories affect us at a chemical level: this is telepathy in action. You are manipulating the listener's brain chemistry with your words. Please use this power only for good—namely, to create connection and the aliveness of shared experience in your interviews and relationships.

YOU ARE ALSO A MIRROR

Doctor Giacomo Rizzolatti and his team at the University of Parma discovered mirror neurons. While measuring the brain activity of macaques in the lab, they discovered something amazing by accident. When the monkeys picked up peanuts, a certain neuron fired in their brains. Rizzolatti's team was astonished to find that when a lab technician picked up a peanut, the same neuron fired in the monkeys' brains as if they had picked up the peanuts themselves. The team realized it had stumbled upon something significant and wondered if there were parallels in human behavior.[2]

Rizzolatti and others have extended this research to humans, and it has yielded startling conclusions. For instance, a basketball player's brain comes alive in exactly the same way when he watches game tapes of other players making free shots as it does when he's shooting them himself, according to research conducted by Salvatore M Aglioti, Paola Cesari, Michela Romani, and Cosimo Urgesi.[3] When we watch people do things, our brain behaves as if we're doing them ourselves.

Though I'm not aware of research that has extended mirror neurons to storytelling, I anticipate such insights aren't far behind. Whether Lady Science proves this or not, just look at your own experience and you will understand that stories work in a similar way to basketball game tape. We're all united in the human experience, so any story you have lived is a mirror for mine. I can't help but see myself in your story.

When I talked about being stranded at an airport in Korea, you felt an echo of a time when you too were lost and felt in way over your head. Your brain too was panicking and feeling a little sorry for itself. You felt empathy for me, and this connected you with me on the deepest level possible—mirroring that core underbelly soft spot where we're all afraid that we're not enough and that the world is too big and scary for us to survive.

Mirroring is often talked about in terms of body language—as a tactic to manufacture connection. If the interviewer runs a hand through his hair, he will feel connected to you if you do it too. If you cross your legs, the interviewer might, as well. But these are a clumsy instrument to create connection—and they're easily seen through. Storytelling is a far more elegant and honest way to relate: the interviewer won't be able to override the chemicals that have been released into his synapses any more than he can ignore the feelings those chemicals encourage: connection, trust, empathy.

You're placing your own experience directly into the experience (or, you could say, brain) of another person. You're creating a shared experience of humanity. How marvelous!! Is there anything more delightful that to feel human connection at this level? It's the remedy to loneliness in our "social media–afflicted" world.

When you tell a genuine story, people listen and relax. They connect with you as a human or as a character that they really like. You bring the listener into your world by building mental bridges. When you adopt the Friendship Mindset and share your stories, the interviewer will mirror you, and relax into an attitude of interest, enjoyment, and inspiration. He'll be making a new friend too.

THESE ARE YOUR FEELINGS ON STORIES

But for your purposes, stories are important for an entirely different reason—and that's the effect they have on *you*. I started this book with a reminder of how stressful interviews can be; how the very act of being in a small room with someone who is evaluating you can destroy your self-confidence before you utter word one. Thankfully, telling an inspiring story builds up your sense of self before the interview dynamic has a chance to tear you down.

This is something I discovered the summer of 2003 when I was trying to improve my own interview performance. And it happened by accident. I never would have figured it out if it weren't for the fact that I was a movie buff. I don't think there was ever a better summer for blockbuster movies than the summer of 2003. We had the third *Lord of the Rings* film, *X-Men 2*, the first installment of the *Pirates of the Caribbean* franchise, and, most importantly to me, *Finding Nemo*. This movie really touched me. In some ways I could see myself in the main character, Marlin—a kind of paranoid, cowardly guy who learned to overcome fear in his heroic quest to find Nemo. I burst into tears when Nemo and Marlin were reunited. Didn't you?

Think about how you feel after you watch a great film. Didn't you just feel like a million bucks when the good X-Men conquered the bad guys? How about after watching *The Lord of the Rings* gang beat Sauron? Didn't you leave the theater feeling like anything was possible, that the world is a wonderous, exciting, and safe place, and that you could do absolutely anything you put your mind to?

If you think about what's going on here, it's pretty strange. These are all completely implausible fictional characters. And these emotions and experiences were produced in your brain by colorful moving pixels on a giant screen. There were (seemingly) no actual humans involved—no facts, no truths, no real experiences. And yet, you left the theater uplifted. The experience changed you on a chemical level, and you *felt* it.

The illusion became real in you.

We already looked at the science of brain chemistry, above, and why those feelings happen. But that summer I wasn't interested in how it worked. I just wanted to harness the power of stories to do better in interviews. I figured if a cartoon fish could make me feel so much emotion, then if I told a great story about myself, I could make the interviewer feel those great emotions too.

I had grown up in the theater, and although I didn't like to have attention on me personally, I found it was pretty easy to be on a stage pretending to be someone else. If I could just think of myself as a character in a movie, I reasoned, it would be easier to tell my story.

So I sat down with my resume and started exploring my own experiences in each and every bullet. And I started to practice telling them with real feeling—just like I did in high school plays—in the shower mostly. I noticed that when I was telling a story, I could just relax and be myself. I got so into the story as I was telling it, that I wasn't self-conscious. I couldn't have cared less what my shampoo thought of me. In fact, I'd get so excited and into the experience of storytelling that I'd forget I was lathering until the suds started dripping down my face and burning my eyes.

When I wove stories organically into interviews, I found I could connect with the interviewer as another human being. It brought me more concretely into my own world and created all kinds of positive emotions. It *worked*. I left interviews feeling like I was on cloud nine, like anything was possible—just like I feel when I leave a theater after watching a great movie. I inspired myself. And that part I didn't expect. Nor did I realize how important it was until the real interview.

On interview day, my stories made me more confident even in those moments when I felt like I was rambling or the interviewer seemed bored. I could just bring myself back to the story and there was the inspiration just waiting for me. My stories were my Kryptonite against whatever was thrown at me: difficult questions, a bad mood, an interviewer's poker face, impostor syndrome. Once I started telling a story—a story I had told others in the past, one that was tried and true—I knew I would be just fine.

Now, like I said, this was an accident. I didn't know I was supposed to inspire myself, but that's what happens when you tell great stories. It happens almost like magic. Now, the truth is, I didn't fully understand what I was doing. I was just following my intuition. Many years would pass before I figured out the best way to tell a story and how to teach it. By that time, I was working on BCG recruiting, and I had to help hundreds of people prepare for the firm's competitive interviews. That's when I finally learned the building blocks of great stories.

That's what you'll learn in the following chapters.

GOOD NEWS: YOU ALREADY KNOW
HOW TO TELL A STORY

Now, the good news is, you already know how to tell a story. As a human being, this is something you do every day. Our brains are made for it and our languages are built around it.

If you ever said something like this . . .

- "And then she said . . ."
- "Yesterday I was in a meeting when . . ."
- "You will never believe what my boss did today . . ."

. . . you were telling a story. Humans are social creatures, and stories are a big part of how we build relationships in the first place. Think about it. When you're catching up with an old friend, getting to know new ones, or just hanging around on a Friday night with the ones you've got, what are you doing? At least some of the time, you're telling stories—you're recounting experiences from your day, your week, your life.

NOT ALL STORIES ARE CREATED EQUAL

Let me tell you the story of how I was forced out of Chicago.

I had been living in this apartment for a year, and during that year there had been four major water disasters. The basement flooded twice due to rains and poor city drainage. Then the air conditioner on the floor above me broke and drained into my closet, ruining all my linens. By the time raw sewage backed up from the city pipes, through my kitchen sink, flooding my living room, the floor had already been replaced twice. This was the third time. My landlords were really uncool about it all. They'd take forever to fix things and send workers at all hours of the day despite the fact that I told them I worked from home and needed some notice.

Just after all the flooding was over, and I renewed my lease so I could take a trip to Italy for two months, the heater in my apartment broke. I was already in week one of my eight weeks in Italy by the time it happened, so the pipes froze before anyone knew what was going on. And when the heat was turned back on, my entire apartment was flooded and destroyed for a fifth time: the floors, the walls, the ceilings, everything.

When I came home two months later, I had to get a lawyer involved because the landlords hadn't fixed anything. There was no running water, no drywall in four rooms, and there were holes in the floor big enough for a person to fit through that went into a different basement that was publicly accessible from the street. On top of leaving the apartment in this horrible illegal state, they were trying to blame me for the heater breaking. I didn't even know where the furnace was located in my building.

As I was packing all my things, I was desperately trying to find another apartment in that neighborhood because I really loved it. Most of the apartments I looked at were terrible, but I finally found the perfect place. It was the whole first floor of a three-floor walk-up building, the price was right, and it was only half a block away from my favorite coffee shop. I couldn't have been more excited about my new home. On the day of the open house, the only other possible tenants were two groups of 20-something young men. And the landlady was a writer just like me! I figured that, as a pretty boring 30-something woman who had a decent income and worked from home, I would be shoo-in.

So I put in my application for the apartment, and she told me she would let me know by Friday. When the landlady hadn't called me by Friday evening, I called her. "Oh yeah, I meant to call you. I decided to give the apartment to those other guys who were looking at it because they were there first."

I felt so betrayed.

At that point I decided that the whole city of Chicago really had it in for me and that it was time to leave. I had been so happy in Florence, so I looked online to see if there were any apartments available near the neighborhood I liked, booked one for summer, and headed out to see if I could make my life work in Italy. It was the most stressful time of my life, but I managed to survive it.

OK. That's a dramatic and fairly interesting story, but imagine how it feels to *me* to tell it. I have to relive that drama with my landlords. I have to experience the painful rejection of having three hard-partying young men chosen as tenants over me. And I have to conjure the incredible anxiety of worrying about a lawsuit while being uprooted from the building I had called home for so long. And even for you—maybe you liked the juicy gory details of the saga, but did it make you feel better once it was over? Now you're probably worrying if your landlord will do the same thing to you if your pipes ever freeze.

HERE IS A DIFFERENT STORY ABOUT THE EXACT SAME LIFE EXPERIENCE

I took my first trip to Italy with my sister when I was 25. We visited Milan, Rome, Florence, and Venice. I loved all of it, but there was a particular moment in Rome, standing in front of the Fontana di Trevi, that I consider part of my destiny. I looked up from the fountain at the surrounding buildings, and I realized that they were all apartments.

"People live here????? I want to live in Italy some day!" I thought to myself with a pang of joy and whimsy. And then for some reason I added, "While I'm still single." I then promptly forgot about that moment until 12 years later when I returned to Italy again with my sister. On this later trip, I remembered my wish with a sense of wonder. Here I was, 12 years older, and single again, and with the means to actually move to Italy if I wanted to.

But it was too big a leap to take all at once, and I wasn't brave enough. I just didn't have the wherewithal to leave everything I knew behind and start my life over at the age of almost 40. So instead, I started taking extended vacations to Florence. I fell in love with the city—like every time I left, it felt like I was leaving a loved one. I was just so happy there.

I consider fate the force that steps in and intervenes when we're ignoring destiny. And she was standing by. As it happened, one week into my second extended stay, my apartment in Chicago suffered severe water damage due to a heater breaking. When I got home, I had to pack quickly and put my stuff in storage while I looked for a new apartment. It was a big dramatic mess.

Sometime during my packing, it had occurred to me that this might be my moment. It seemed like it might be time to see if I could build a life in Florence. But then I found the perfect apartment in Chicago. The landlady's daughter had severe allergies, and the only other applicants for the unit were two groups of 20-something guys. In other words—people with a high likelihood of having raging parties at which there might be smokers. The landlady had told me about emergency room visits for that reason in the past. So I packed my boxes, assuming I would take them out of storage again six weeks later in Lakeview, and I was happy with that potential outcome. It was a nice apartment.

But as fate would have it, those boxes still haven't been opened. I didn't get the apartment. I had decided before taping up the last box that if I didn't get that one, it meant it was time for me to move to Italy. Within a week of arriving in Florence, I knew I wouldn't be leaving anytime soon. The love affair continues to deepen with each passing week, and I still haven't had the chance to thank that landlady who didn't let me live in her building for helping me fulfill an ancient wish and a nearly lifelong dream.

Both of those stories are completely true, and they're both interesting and engaging. But one is edited to highlight my hardships, the ways I was victimized, and what sucked about the experience. And one was edited to show the inspiring version of events, that the world is a magical place and that I'm on a journey that's still unfolding before my astonished eyes.

TELL INSPIRING STORIES

In case it wasn't completely obvious, the second version is better. Especially for an interview. Life can be rough sometimes, and in the middle of my apartment crisis, you can bet I had the need to vent once or twice (or 25 times). There were days I really thought my life as I knew it was ending, and it would never be the same. I wanted to gripe and complain at times, yes. But the interview—or really almost any professional interaction—is not the time to do that.

You want to tell inspiring stories in interviews. You want to build your relationship on a foundation of positive emotion, inspiration, and enthusiasm. If you connect on the basis of complaining, negativity, or victimhood, you might earn your interviewer's sympathy, but you will never earn your interviewer's respect.

But perhaps even more important than the effect the second story has on you, the reader or listener, is the effect it has on *me*. I know, it seems weird. "Why does the story I tell matter? I lived it!!" you might think. "And why would it have any effect on me, when I already know the ending? Heck, if I've practiced my stories a dozen times in the shower, they'll lose all significance and, in the interview, I'll bore myself to death, right?"

I understand the logic of these questions. I do.

But consider the negative voice in your head that tells you you're a phony, a fraud, that you're no good, that you shouldn't even try. If you're anything like me, you've heard that voice a million times, and each time, it's like a blow to the gut. In fact, if you home in on your experience, you can probably find the place in your body where that voice hits you—mine is actually on the back of my neck; I start to feel like my head is on fire. My heart races, my palms sweat, and my mind reels. Its effect is multiplied if I'm talking when it happens. I derail and start rambling incoherently. So, seen from the wisdom of your own experience, you'll probably agree that the stories we tell ourselves are pretty potent.

Why not maintain your emotional equilibrium by drowning out the negative inner stories with positive ones? Imagine the exact opposite of the physical symptoms I outlined above. A warm glow, muscles relaxed, body language open and unthreatened, and a big smile on your face. And psychologically? No rambling train wrecks. You're in control; you're having fun. You've *got* this.

When I tell the second story, I feel like I'm a fascinating character in an epic drama that's unfolding around me where enchanted forces that I can't see are shaping my life into something beautiful. I feel empowered, uplifted, touched, and inspired.

I come alive.

And coming alive is kind of the whole point of life, isn't it?

> *People say that what we're all seeking is a meaning for life.*
> *I don't think that's what we're really seeking.*
> *I think that what we're seeking is an experience of being alive,*
> *so that our life experiences on the purely physical plane*
> *will have resonances with our own innermost being and reality,*
> *so that we actually feel the rapture of being alive.*
> —JOSEPH CAMPBELL, *The Power of Myth*

INTRODUCING A NEW DEFINITION OF STORYTELLING

The storytelling craft may very well be as old as time. Certainly, the entire concept of time makes little sense without a story. We're just drifting in an infinite sea of indistinguishable moments that each bleed indifferently into the next unless we have a way to mark the beginning of something, the middle of something, and then the end of that thing. And so arises narrative to shape our perception of time itself, and—consequently, whether we recognize it or not—our experience of everything in it, including ourselves.

Some anthropologists believe that the art of storytelling gave rise to language itself—beginning with cave paintings.

"I was hungry. I slaughtered a bison with arrows. I ate it. The end."

Whenever it started in the history of time, it's with us now. And you have an innate ability to tell stories. But knowing how to tell *brilliant* stories is, well, another story. The fact that the word "story" is thrown around so willy-nilly these days makes doing so even harder.

So what is a story? If we go to the dictionary, we find this:

story

noun sto·ry \ ‹stȯr-ē \

1   a : an account of incidents or events
    b : a statement regarding the facts pertinent to a
        situation in question
    c : ANECDOTE; *especially*: an amusing one[4]

If a story is an account of incidents or events (or even facts), then it must be about the past. Events and incidents and facts can only take place in the past leading up to the present. So, going forward, whenever someone uses the word "story" to refer to something that hasn't happened yet, you will know that's not the correct usage of the word. A story can only be told about something that has already happened. Even if it's fiction or fantasy—it's from a fictitious past or from the past of some imagined future.

I'm not entirely satisfied with the definition of "story" I found in the dictionary for our purposes, though. And—as I said—the word has been terribly abused in modern business culture. We need something more enlightening and evocative; the kind of story that uplifts and inspires.

So let's coin a new term that we'll use for our Interview Hero purposes: an Epic Story.

The word "epic," as you know, means "heroic or grand in scale or character." And let's go with my personal screenwriter's definition of story over *Webster's*: "A story is what happens when a character wants something and has to overcome obstacles to get it." This conception of narrative goes all the way back to ancient Greece and Aristotle's essays about drama.

An Epic Story, therefore, is a grand telling of events that unfolded when a character wanted something and had to overcome obstacles to get it.

Remember the caveman? Case in point.

An Epic Story is what we're going for when we talk about building storytelling skills. An Epic Story is a narrative that conforms to specific rules and features, follows a specific linear format, and has a powerful effect on the reader or listener. It captures her attention and touches her emotions. It also has a salutary effect on the speaker—it inspires and uplifts her.

Of course, stories can also be horrific, depressing, or cautionary; but for the purpose of interviewing and building connections, in this book we're going to focus on feel-good stories. Stories about you and your life.

You're about to learn how to tell an Epic Story. After teaching my clients this skill, they've told me that they use it every day of their lives thereafter: in sales meetings, in consulting presentations, at networking events, in interviews, and even on dates. Aren't dates just romantic interviews, after all?

Storytelling is essential to the fiber of human relationships, so you're not just building a skill for interviews here; you're building a life skill.

In the interview, you won't tell Epic Stories in response to absolutely every type of question. An Epic Story is best used to respond to questions like "Tell me about a time you led a team" or "Describe a challenging project at work." When you're in the behavioral question zone, Epic Stories are your magic wand.

These of course usually aren't the first type of question posed in an interview. Typically, the first question is, "Walk me through your resume," or "Tell me about yourself." We're going to talk about that soon, but before you can learn how to use the techniques of storytelling for non-story answers, you need to be able to differentiate between an Epic Story and every other way to talk about yourself. Once you know how to construct a real narrative—an Epic Story—you'll use the same narrative elements for all the other question types; the same skills and ideas, just not in the exact same format.

HOW NOT TO TELL AN EPIC STORY

Because people have been preparing for job interviews for at least a century, there are already a lot of tools out there to help you boost your self-confidence, talk about your accomplishments, and perform well under stressful conditions. Behavioral interview preparation advice generally encourages you to answer questions like "Tell me about a leadership experience" in three or four discrete steps. Here are a few of the most well-known frameworks:

The oldest and most well-known is the STAR framework: situation, tasks, actions, results. The idea is to answer interview questions by describing the situation you were in, then outlining the tasks that were required of you or the target you were aiming for, what actions you took, and then finally the results you produced.

You may have also heard of the SOAR framework: situation, obstacles, actions, results. It's basically the same idea as the STAR framework, but it introduces the notion of obstacles into the second step.

Then along came the CAR framework: challenge, action, result. It's the same idea, just omitting the situation and rolling it into challenge, which is basically the same thing as obstacle.

I've never found these frameworks to be terribly helpful for teaching the art of storytelling, which is the bedrock of successful interviewing. These systems can help you understand the chronology of a story and construct a nice clinical answer to behavioral questions, but they don't enable you to tell an Epic Story because they leave out several of the defining elements of a great narrative. They also make it very easy to construct stories that aren't based on your desires, don't reveal your true character, and don't touch the emotions of your audience. That's why STAR answers can be boring.

Epic Stories are never boring. No matter how boring your life may seem to you, tell an Epic Story about it, and you become instantly fascinating.

THE HERO WITH A THOUSAND FACES

Myths are public dreams, dreams are private myths.
—JOSEPH CAMPBELL

Let me officially introduce you to my first storytelling guru, Joseph Campbell, the author of the storytelling bible *The Hero with a Thousand Faces*. During the Great Depression he spent nine hours a day, for five years, reading.

True story.

He read everything from religious texts to ancient mythology, newspapers, novels, history, and biographies. He read everything he could get his hands on, and he discovered that there's a hidden pattern in almost every great story. He called this "The Hero's Journey." You've probably heard of this before, and you may have even seen an image like this:

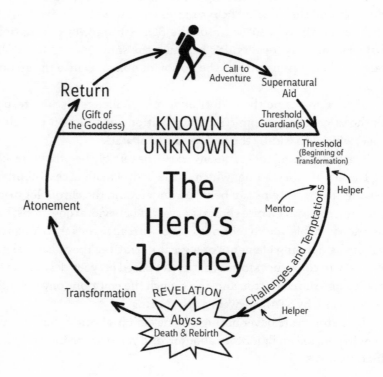

Intuitively, you know what the Hero's Journey is: you've been living this every day of your life, and you've seen this familiar structure play out a million times since childhood: in cartoons, fairy tales, novels, sitcoms, and movies. It's everywhere. The Hero's Journey framework is incredibly rich and nuanced with multiple steps. If you're interested in the ideas of story theory and its implications for life experience, I encourage you to read Campbell's groundbreaking work. This framework resonates with the entire human experience at the very deepest level.

But you don't need to read Campbell to understand it. If you've seen a mainstream Hollywood movie or modern American TV show, and I'm guessing you've seen hundreds if not thousands, you know exactly what the Hero's Journey looks like. Film is the flagbearer of the storytelling artform in the modern era. In fact, it was my study of screenwriting that led me to understand what constitutes an Epic Story and how to tell one myself.

Even though I'd been toying with these ideas for a while, I had a major epiphany after switching from consulting at BCG to managing the women's initiative. It was a part-time role, so when I wasn't helping women prepare for interviews or planning conferences, I was writing screenplays. I devoured every book I could find on the subject, I took college classes about script development at a local university, and I joined a writer's group with a bunch of accomplished writers for the stage and screen.

And when that wasn't enough, I traveled to the coasts to study with the leading story masters of our day. Meet my second story guru, Robert McKee.

Stories are the creative conversion of life itself into
a more powerful, clearer, more meaningful experience.
They are the currency of human contact.
—ROBERT MCKEE

While McKee's book, *Story: Substance, Structure, Style, and the Principles of Screenwriting*, is about becoming a great writer for the screen, it's also about the incredible hologram that is our shared human experience. It's essential reading for anyone who wants to look under the hood of a story or human psychology. If you want to really geek out on narrative structure, his book is a must-read.

But for interviews—for live human interaction that unfolds in 30 minutes or so—we don't need to do such a deep dive. We only need to understand a few key components to get started. By this point, you understand the myriad benefits of telling Epic Stories in interviews and in absolutely every facet of your life. You know the science and mythology behind it. We just need to put these concepts into action. I've developed a really easy-to-follow framework that allows you to leverage Campbell's Hero's Journey and Robert McKee's essential teachings so you can tell your own Epic Stories.

Interview Hero Secrets in This Chapter:

- Talking about yourself is hard—it's very easy to come off as arrogant if you just give your opinion or self-description.

- Stories affect the listener at the level of brain chemistry to engage his attention and evoke his empathy, while stories connect us through shared humanity.

- Telling a great story about yourself will inspire you, first and foremost, engaging you in the story and overriding your negative self-talk and self-consciousness.

- You already know how to tell stories, and you always have a choice about how you tell them: I recommend you tell inspiring stories instead of disempowering ones.

- Epic Stories are what you want to tell in interviews. Epic Story: a grand telling of events that unfolded when a character wanted something and had to overcome obstacles to get it.

- Forget about STAR, SOAR, and CAR; they won't get you to Epic Story. The Hero's Journey is a more powerful approach.

How to Tell an Epic Story

*Do not allow people to dim your shine
because they are blinded.
Tell them to put on some sunglasses.*
—LADY GAGA

In this chapter, I'm going to show you how to create your own Epic Story about one of your accomplishments. I'm going to take you on a little learning journey here. Instead of explaining everything, I'm going to lead you through it step by step, so that by the end of this chapter, you'll have developed a new skill that you can use in just about any conversational situation to make a connection, entertain, and inspire others. This is what's going to make you an Interview Hero.

And speaking of heroes, guess what? The hero in your story is you!

THE HERO

All Stories are journeys of character.
—MY THIRD STORY GURU, JULE SELBO, *Screenplay*

hero

noun he·ro \ 'hir-(,)ō \

1 a : a mythological or legendary figure often of divine
       descent endowed with great strength or ability
   b : an illustrious warrior
   c : *a person admired for achievements and
       noble* qualities
   d : *one who shows great courage*
2 a : *the principal character in a literary or
       dramatic work*[1]

In an Epic Story about your experiences, you are the hero in the last three senses bolded above. Epic Stories center on one single main character: the protagonist. The word "hero" in narrative theory (definition 2a) generically describes the main character of a story. Now that doesn't mean that that character is necessarily heroic: it means that he or she is the center of the story. For example, Macbeth is the "hero" of the play *Macbeth*, because he's the main character, but we'd probably all agree he's not a very heroic figure. So at the most basic level in the Epic Story framework, the "character," or "hero," is the person the story is about: you!

But in an Epic Story, you're also the hero in the heroic sense: "a person admired for achievements and noble qualities" and "one who shows great courage." This is the beauty of an Epic Story: it naturally reveals the heroic nature—the most noble qualities, the achievements, and always the courage—of the main character.

To make this really concrete, I'll go back to *Finding Nemo*. If you haven't seen that movie, I recommend you go and watch it right now. Not just because it makes this chapter easier to follow, but also because that film—and just about any film by Disney or Pixar—brilliantly demonstrates the Hero's Journey in action and the framework I'm about to outline. These are two production companies that have built billion-dollar businesses on the Hero's Journey alone.

For the rest of this chapter, I will reference *Finding Nemo*, but if you haven't seen the film, just substitute any other film you know and love that has a strong main character and use that whenever I talk about *Finding Nemo*. Again, Disney and Pixar films all work: *Toy Story*,

Frozen, *Up*, *Wall-E*, you name it. Hold your favorite one in mind as I go through this chapter if you don't know *Finding Nemo*.

Though Nemo is the title character of the film, if you think about it for a moment, you'll realize that it's Nemo's father, Marlin, who is the hero of the story. The hero is always the character whose desires and actions drive the narrative: Marlin is the one who's doing the finding; he's the character that goes on the Hero's Journey.

NOBODY LIKES TO BE TOLD WHAT TO THINK

Stories recount actions, not opinions. Think about this: how do we get to know a character in a story? How did you come to know what kind of a character Marlin was in *Finding Nemo*? Recall that at no point did the narrator come on screen and say anything like . . . "Marlin was a little bit of a control freak. He was a nervous fish and an overprotective father. But he meant well. He just cared about his son and wanted to protect him. He was afraid to go very far from home because of things that had happened to him in the past . . ."

Of course not!

All of that would have been the narrator's opinion. Most films don't have a narrator, and even the ones that do, if the narrator is talking, it's rarely to give his opinion. This is for the reasons I discussed in the last chapter. If you tell people what to think, their knee-jerk response will be to believe the opposite until you prove you are right. And ultimately, no one really cares what anyone else thinks.

On top of all of that, opinions are boring. In a film (and a story) the audience's attention needs to be captured and held. Action does this way more effectively than opinion. Likewise, the story needs to connect with the audience's emotions. Opinion can't do that. The narrator's opinion about Marlin doesn't help you make a personal emotional connection with him (or the narrator, for that matter). As humans, we all want to be able to form our own opinions. I learned in my screenwriting classes that for the most part (with a few exceptions) using a narrator is lazy writing.

Given how useless and problematic opinion is, it might go without saying that in interviews, you should almost never answer a question with an opinion. But just for good measure, let me say it. Steer clear of answering questions with adjectives and descriptions.

Imagine I ask you: "What kind of leader are you?" Here's a bad answer:

> "Well, I'd say I am a compassionate leader. I know how to connect with my team and empower them to perform well."

Humans are very sensitive to being manipulated, and you aren't a credible source of information about yourself. There's a conflict of interest there: it's impossible to be objective about yourself! Not only am I *not* going to believe you ("Oh yeah? Prove it!"); I'm going to think you're arrogant. All of that creates emotional distance, not connection, which is what you want. Eschew these problems by doing what the writers of *Finding Nemo* did—use actions to reveal your character. Omit your opinion, and instead *show* me your actions. Here is a much better answer:

> "As a leader, I always try to sit down with each member of my team to understand each one's personal objectives on the project before we get started so that everyone can benefit from the experience. This helps me be a more constructive leader and mentor."

This is a much richer and more meaningful response. You've *shown* me that you are compassionate and that you know how to empower your teams. I can form my own opinion about you: and opinions we form ourselves are the ones we most agree with. Ha!

This answer is still not a story, but it illustrates Storytelling Rule #1: actions, not opinions.

STORYTELLING RULE #1:
Stories are made of actions, not opinions.

And this is something you already know. It's the A in all the other frameworks: STAR, SOAR, CAR. The A stands for "action," and it's the primary content of any great story. I've assembled Eight Rules of Storytelling, by the way, that I will reveal to you one by one as you go through this chapter and the next. But first, let me break stories up into their four most fundamental parts.

THE FOUR C'S

For our purposes, there are four pieces in an Epic Story. This framework is called the Four C's, because, well, there are four steps and each step conveniently starts with the letter C. But instead of giving it to you all up front—as I said—I'd like to walk you through it one step at a time while you build up your own Epic Story in the process. Just knowing about this framework will be interesting, but it will make no difference until you use it.

So let's just jump in and use it!!

I'll recap everything at the end, so don't worry if you lose sight of the big picture as we're going. Just follow the experience. This will be a lot easier for you to do if you have the accompanying workbook. You can download that for free right here: **careerprotocol.com/ih**.

Ok! Let's construct an Epic Story!

START AT THE BEGINNING

Step 1: Choose an Accomplishment

Your Epic Story is going to focus on a single discrete accomplishment. So imagine you are in an interview, and the interviewer says, "Tell me about an accomplishment."

Pick one from your life to work with for the rest of this chapter. The first one that comes to mind is good. It can be from your professional life, personal life, community life, family life, extracurricular activities—whatever. Choose an achievement that was meaningful to you and one that happened in a confined period of time: say, over the course of a week or a month or a year at most. You may ultimately want to apply this framework to every major life and work experience, so you just need an easy one to start with. Don't overthink it at this point.

Now here's Storytelling Rule #2:

STORYTELLING RULE #2:
All stories have a beginning, middle, and end.

You knew that, right? Stories are about past events, so they must have ended already! And for it to be a story, it has to start somewhere!

Step 2: Brainstorm What Happened at the Beginning of Your Story

Now that you have your accomplishment, think about the beginning of the story. You want to recall some of the concrete details that set up the story so the listener can follow it and make sense of it.

I'm going to call this part of the story *context*. It's just the setup: the basic information the audience needs in order to make sense of it. In *Finding Nemo*, this was the first 15 minutes of the film, where we learned about Marlin and Nemo's life and a little bit about their past. We got to know where they live, what their life generally looks like, and the fact that they're fish: just the essential information. From your other frameworks, this is the "situation" and—to some extent— the "task."

Here's an example from my life:

> It was my first consulting project at BCG Chicago, right after my MBA, and I had to make the contract that would dictate the post- merger integration of two consumer goods companies.

This is far more concise than you need to be, but notice how in just one sentence I've conveyed the most important background information you need: the situation, the place, the time, and the task.

Stories happen in space and time.

Something magical happens when you start talking about past events in space and time. Imagine if I turned to you and said one of these things:

- I was at the office yesterday when . . .
- Last week, when I was going to the grocery store . . .
- I was sitting in my senior-year chemistry class when . . .
- Two weeks ago, while my mom was driving, she . . .

These are blank imaginary teasers, but as you read them, didn't you find yourself really wanting to know what comes next?

Now contrast that with how you feel reading these:

- I have always thought . . .
- Tomorrow, I'm going to . . .
- One day, I will . . .
- In general, I . . .

The difference may be subtle, but you should be able to feel it. These sentences are nowhere near as provocative as the previous ones. That's because they're not grounded in our shared time-space reality.

The thing about opinions and the future is that they aren't "real." Your opinion can't be experienced by others in the external world. Likewise with plans, conjectures, dreams, and ideas about the future—those are the fodder of your interior world, which is a landscape I can never, by definition, traverse.

But out here, in space and time, we're both together. So if you start talking about something you did yesterday or last week and you place it in space so that I can connect it to my own physical reality, now you have my undivided attention. As you think about the context of your story, be sure to include language about when and where you were.

The story trigger in my example was: "It was my first consulting project at BCG, right after my MBA . . ." When you read this, your brain knows to pay attention because it's about to encounter a story.

Here are some more good examples of beginnings that are located in space and time:

- I was working late one Friday night . . .
- It was my second week at work . . .
- It started before I had any idea about company culture . . .
- On my last project at my company . . .
- When I was still a junior analyst at the firm . . .

These are just examples. Find your own. But notice how each one of these—even though it contains almost no information—is alerting your brain to the fact that you're reading a story. You're naturally going to pay attention to whatever comes next. And so is your beloved interviewer, Mustache Man.

That Mustache Man says, "You have my attention!!" This is how stories work. So be sure to figure out the space and time of the accomplishment that you're going to tell an Epic Story about.

Before we move on to the next part of the story, take just 30 seconds to jot down in your workbook the circumstances and the background information of your accomplishment story. Be sure to focus on concrete time-space reality details that will bring the listener into your world. Just brainstorm and write down anything that comes to mind.

Written Exercise 6.2:
Write down the details of the beginning of the story.

- What were the circumstances?
- What was the task in front of you?
- Who else was there?
- When was it?
- Where were you?

THE END OF THE STORY

We'll come to the middle later. It's the hardest part of the story to understand and the major failing of all those other frameworks. It's even the hardest part of a screenplay to write—many an author has lamented over the "sagging middle," a lackluster second act in the traditional three-act structure.

But before we come to the middle, let's fast-forward for a moment and build the end of the story. It's easier to navigate your way through the middle of your story if you have a clear idea of where you're headed. So let's see where your happy endings have taken you, and then we'll go back to the middle of your story to bridge the beginning and ending.

Step 3: Brainstorm What Happened at the End of Your Story

This is the "R" in all those other frameworks (STAR, SOAR, CAR): the result. On the surface, it's the happy ending, the success, the result you produced, the impact you had. But it's also the *internal change* you experienced: what you learned and how you grew as a result. Go ahead and take a few moments to write down all of the positive outcomes that resulted from this accomplishment.

Of course, we know the ending of *Finding Nemo*. Marlin finds Nemo. But it's much bigger than that: Marlin has changed by the end of the story—he's a different fish altogether. He's become more adventurous, more trusting, and in a challenging situation, he lets Nemo take a big risk to save others instead of insisting, "You just can't do these things, Nemo," like he did at the beginning of the story.

This is why I call this last piece of the framework "change." All heroes must change in the course of an Epic Story. Name any work of literature, film, or playwriting with a strong central character, and you will see that the character changes. If he changes for the better, we have a comedy (in the classical Greek sense). If he changes for the worse, it's a tragedy. The central idea of many dramatic films and books is a protagonist failing to change. This too is change—for the worse: where once there was harmony, the hero is now at odds with his environment.

THE HERO'S JOURNEY IS JUST A TEMPLATE FOR THE GROWTH OF A HUMAN BEING

The destination of the Hero's Journey is always change within the hero. What transpires in the middle of the story changes him. In the crucible of the journey, the hero is shaped. The person who emerges isn't the same person who went in.

Here's the ending in my story:

> The contract was a success, the merger went off without a hitch, garnering praise from the CEO, and I learned a lot about client management.

As you write a brief summary of the end of your story, include any concrete and measurable results: dollars earned or saved, hours removed from a process, promotions, accolades, awards or honors. **But don't neglect how you grew, what you learned, and how you changed as a result of this experience.** Be sure to include any insights you had, lessons you learned, how your confidence changed, how your career changed, and any other personal growth outcome you can think of. Take a second and write them down now.

> **Written Exercise 6.3:**
> ## Write down the details of the end of the story.
>
> Include specifics about the results you produced and how you grew and changed through the experience. Include:
>
> - External outcomes and results, including ones that are concrete and measurable
> - Internal results and changes, including insights, lessons learned, personal growth, and changes inside you

THE MIDDLE OF THE STORY

Now, back to the middle of the story. The middle is the most important part of the story. This is where all the action happens. It's Act 2 within a three-act structure, and it's the hardest to write because it's the longest and the most important. This is where all the other frameworks you have used tend to fail: they don't give you a road map to navigate this all-important second act. In STAR, SOAR, or CAR, this section is just called "action."

But . . . which actions? That project of mine with the post-merger integration took three months. How do I condense that efficiently and powerfully into a minute and a half to three minutes?

It's easy to get lost telling your own story here because it's not that easy to know which actions are most important. If you've ever found yourself talking too long or losing your listener's interest in the middle of the story, the problem was Act 2. Let's solve that problem now.

There are two steps in the middle of your story. The first is "conflict."

CONTEXT > CONFLICT > CHANGE

Think again about a film—in the first 25% of it, you're still meeting the characters and getting to know their world. The action really begins when the protagonist is challenged in some major way. We call this the "Inciting Incident" in film, but for the purposes of your Epic Story, it's just the obstacle that stood in the way of getting what you wanted.

Let's go back to our hero, Marlin. In the beginning of *Finding Nemo* we find out where he lives. We learn a little bit about his backstory and what has happened to him before. And we discover his relationship with his son, Nemo.

Then, all of a sudden, disaster strikes. Nemo is fish-napped by an Australian diver. Now, let's imagine there's a hole in the net and Nemo swims to safety and Marlin and Nemo are reunited and happy again. If the "story" ended here, we can probably all agree that this wouldn't really *be* a story. Not by any definition. It's just something that happened—and it's not even something very interesting. Nemo got caught in a net and then he escaped ten seconds later. The end. There's no story here because the defining feature of a story is conflict.

STORYTELLING RULE #4:
Conflict defines the story.

Marlin's Hero's Journey was launched by the loss of his son. This is the Inciting Incident that forced him out of the safety of the reef and across the ocean to find Nemo.

It's worth noting here that all great characters are human (even fish). They're flawed, and they face challenges. Especially heroes. When you learn to write action movies, you learn that the most important character in a film isn't the hero; it's the villain. The stronger and more invincible the villain is, the more heroic the protagonist will have to be in order to defeat him. *The Dark Knight* is such a potent and moving film not because Batman is so cool, but because of Heath Ledger's extraordinarily dark and maniacal Joker.

And this just mirrors reality. Think about it: don't you value your accomplishments in direct proportion to the level of difficulty you faced in achieving them? The more intimidating the obstacle, the more valuable the victory. It's why a marathon and a 5K aren't the same thing at all. The greater the conflict, the more meaningful the success. The more the hero has to change to achieve his aim, the more rewarding the trophy is. This is because in life, the trophy is never actually the point—it's just the McGuffin that spurs you on to grow, change, and transform into the person you are meant to be.

Though great villains are important in film, and in real life, the obstacle doesn't have to be a person, though it certainly *can* be. Take Marlin's conflict, for example. What made *Finding Nemo* so inspiring is that Marlin had to face so many different, seemingly insurmountable challenges on the journey. At first, he didn't even know where his son had gone. Then once he figured that out, he had to brave sharks, an angler fish, deadly stinging jellyfish, the East Australian Current, and a hungry pelican to save him. At the beginning of the film, you could never imagine a scaredy-fish such as Marlin facing such terrifying predators.

UNDERSTANDING THE
NATURE OF CONFLICT, PART II

When I first started screenwriting, I struggled to understand the nature of narrative conflict. Because it can take so many forms—as in Marlin's case—it was hard to pin it down to one simple idea. But after years of trying and failing to write great stories, I finally figured it out. What is conflict? Here is years and years of screenwriting study boiled down to one single sentence:

Conflict happens when the protagonist wants something and has to overcome *obstacles* to get it.

The concepts of both desire and resistance are essential: the hero has to want something, and it can't be easy for her to get. If you want an ice cream cone, and you just go get one and eat it, you'll have a nice day. But there will be no story to tell about it. If you get swept up into a tornado, fall through a wormhole, lose your wallet, or run into an angry ex-lover on your way to the ice cream shop, now we're talking. This definition of conflict is so important, that you'll notice I slipped it into the very definition of an Epic Story.

Step 4: Define Your Conflict Sentence

So, think about this as it relates to the story you're building about that accomplishment. Go back to the beginning of the story and consider what you wanted and what your objective was. Be as honest as possible.

Written Exercise 6.4:
Identify your objectives.

- What did you want?
- What was your objective?

Here's my example:

I wanted to impress my teammates and do a great job for the client.

The more honest you can be about what you wanted, the more powerful the act of telling the story will be. Notice how I had two objectives. The second was a noble one; the first was a bit shallower and more selfish. We're all human, ya'll. We all want to look good. That's the whole reason we occasionally experience embarrassment: we fail to look good. And that is a painful experience. Risking looking bad is a great motivator, so I'm being honest with myself here about the fact that I wanted to impress others.

The best stories rest on a foundation of solid self-awareness and self-honesty. So dig around and find your motives: both the public ones and the private ones—the ones that maybe you wouldn't necessarily admit to in the interview. Your conflict sentence is the bedrock of the story, the skeleton. So you will probably never say it during the story, but you'll know it, and that's what will give your story depth and power.

Once you've looked at what you wanted, consider the obstacles you overcame to accomplish the outcome. What was challenging about the situation? What did you have to overcome to achieve your goal? List out every single obstacle, hindrance, setback, and limitation you can remember, even if the only thing standing in your way was you.

Written Exercise 6.5:
Identify the obstacles.

- What was standing in the way of what you wanted?
- What was challenging about the situation?
- What obstacles did you have to overcome to achieve your goal?

Here's my list:

> I had to overcome a compressed timeline, an unmotivated client, and my own complete inexperience.

When you've figured out both of those things, the core of your story will boil down to one single sentence. This is the conflict sentence.

I wanted _____, but I had to overcome _____.

Pause and reflect on this sentence and then write the conflict sentence of your story down. Be as specific and clear as you can.

Written Exercise 6.6:
Define the conflict sentence for your story.

Fill in the blanks:

> I wanted _____, but I had to overcome _____.

Here's my example conflict sentence:

> I wanted to impress my teammates and do a great job for the client, but I had to overcome a compressed timeline, an unmotivated client, and my own complete inexperience.

You may never utter this sentence in the course of telling your story, but nonetheless, it defines your narrative. Again, you can think of this as the skeleton of the story, while the part that you relate out loud will be the flesh. The better you can define this conflict sentence, the easier the story will be to tell. Indeed, once you start reminiscing and digging back into the details of the story, you'll remember new things—new challenges that stood in your way and new ways you grew in the process.

THE HERO'S RESPONSE

Now that you understand the conflict in your story, it's time to choose the actions that make up the middle. You've probably struggled once or twice to understand the right level of detail to go into when recounting the story of an experience, but in the end, the right details are easy to identify when you've nailed the conflict sentence.

The story is composed of the hero's response to conflict.

Because the conflict defines the story, the actions that will drive the hero toward change are the ones he takes expressly to overcome those challenges and get what he wants. It took Marlin weeks to find Nemo, but we saw the whole thing happen in two hours. We never saw Marlin eating; we didn't see him sleep or wash. Even parts where he was just swimming long distances, we didn't see. Because those actions just happened. They weren't part of his response to the hurdles he encountered along the way.

It's very important to notice that before he lost Nemo, the last thing you would have expected Marlin to do was venture out into the open ocean: it terrified him. But when faced with a choice—lose your son forever or do something you can't imagine doing—that's exactly what he did. He chose to brave numerous dangers to get his son back, and those choices changed him as a person (er, fish).

STORYTELLING RULE #5:
Choices define the character.

"It is our choices that show what we truly are, far more than our abilities." This truism from J. K. Rowling in *Harry Potter and the Chamber of Secrets* reveals the entire point of many interview questions in the first place. The interviewer wants to understand the choices you make when times get rough. Will you keep going or will you fold? Will you take a shortcut or do it the hard way? And just as importantly, when a road is blocked, *how* will you find your way? What is your way through? What is the precise mark of your courage?

This is the final piece of our framework: **choice**. The interviewer will come to trust you by "watching" what you choose to do in the face of challenges. This is also how you will reveal your individuality: given a challenge, no two people react in exactly the same way. It's the unique choices you make in the process of overcoming the conflict that show us what you're made of, how you think, and what you do when the chips are down.

Step 5: Distinguish and Articulate Your Choices in Response to the Conflict

You now want to think about the choices you made. Once you've distinguished the obstacles you encountered and what was challenging about the situation, it's time to think through what came next. How did you think and feel about the obstacles in your way? How did you strategize to overcome them? What was your "plan"? And then what actions did you take to surmount the obstacles?

This part of the story is almost certainly going to require some reminiscing. More on that in a moment. This is what we're working toward: adding one final piece to your conflict sentence: your plan, your strategy, your choices.

> **I wanted _____, but I had to overcome _____, so I decided to _____.**

Back to my example:

> I wanted <u>to impress my teammates and do a great job for the client</u>, but I had to overcome a <u>compressed timeline, an unmotivated client, and my own complete inexperience</u>, so I decided to <u>coach my client counterpart to take ownership of the process</u>.

This sentence reveals my unique strategy and the primary choice I made to achieve my goal. You might have an inkling of what your complete conflict sentence is, but before you commit to it, let's explore choice a little more.

To help you further explore your own choices, let me tell you the complete story of my consulting project, so you have a vivid illustration of what matters in the "choice" part of the story and how all Four C's come together to create an Epic Story. As you read this, pay attention to how you feel about me—the hero of the story—by the time you reach the end.

HOW LENNY AND I WON THE DAY

Context: It was my first consulting project, and I had to make the contract that would dictate the post-merger integration of two consumer goods companies. This required me to collaborate with every function of the client organization (a multibillion-dollar consumer goods company) and create an exhaustive list of business processes that needed to be taken over after the merger. We'd then decide who would own each individual process, how the target company would hand it off, and when the hand-off would be executed. If we forgot anything, we'd risk not realizing synergies and making the whole deal worthless.

Conflict: The timeline was tight, and I had no idea what I was doing. But much more detrimental to the project was the fact that my client counterpart, Lenny, failed to keep order at meetings. The process started to fall apart when other team members challenged his leadership, and we really didn't have time for delays.

Choice: At first, I was frustrated because my hard work wasn't producing the results I wanted and the outcome seemed out of my control. Because I was just a young consultant, fresh out of business school, I knew these 20-year career professionals weren't going to listen to me. I realized that if I could bolster Lenny's ability to own the process, the rest of the team would fall in line, making my job and the whole process a lot easier.

So, my strategy was to schedule meetings with Lenny before every plenary session: I became his guide, his coach, and his cheerleader. I would give him pep talks. I would walk through the presentation deck with him. Then I would challenge him with questions that I knew people would raise in each meeting. I would boost his confidence, saying: "You've got this, Lenny. You can answer these questions. You know what you're doing."

Eventually, these meetings paid off. There was a turning point in one session where Lenny was delivering some information about our process, and Mike, a longtime antagonist of Lenny, stood up and asked a snarky question, attempting to undermine Lenny's authority. And Lenny, for the first time, had a great response. Mike sat down. He was quiet. The whole mood in the room changed, and the project went much more smoothly from then on. Lenny was in charge.

After that, there was a lot more work to do: I had to build a giant spreadsheet with over 300 lines with all those business processes; then I had to work with lawyers to translate it into a legal document.

Change: But once Lenny took ownership of the process and the rest of the team viewed him as the leader, they gave the input for their respective functions more readily and helped contribute to meeting the deadline. In the end, the contract was a success and the merger went off without a hitch, garnering praise from the CEO. I learned a lot about client management, but what I'm most proud of is that Lenny got his first promotion in 10 years as a result of that project.

I'm going to further dissect this story in Chapter 8 so that you can learn some even more advanced storytelling techniques, but for now, just notice how you feel reading it. You very likely feel that you know me. You can relate to the challenges I faced whether you've ever been in a situation exactly like that or not. You probably also trust me: you know you can count on me to navigate difficult human and political challenges. You understand how I think and act, and how I treat other people. You can see what I value: I'm clearly a person who cares about helping and empowering others. And hopefully, you can imagine that if you were hiring, you'd want me on your team.

You reached all these conclusions by yourself after "seeing" the choices I made in response to conflict. I showed you who I am without telling you. I didn't use any opinions or adjectives. Notice how an Epic

Story passes the Airport Test and shows Confident Humility without arrogance.

THE ART OF STORY IS IN DETAILS AND SPECIFICS

Now it might interest you to know that in the process of crafting and then telling this story about Lenny for the first time many years ago, I actually felt my sense of self-awareness expand, and I inspired myself in a new way. This is what will happen when you tell authentic Epic Stories—and it will happen because they force you to reflect on the choices you made and the specific actions you took when faced with conflict. This is because . . .

> *True character is revealed in the choices a human being makes under pressure—the greater the pressure, the deeper the revelation, the truer the choice to the character's essential nature."*
> —ROBERT MCKEE

Our choices show what we truly are—not just to others, but also to ourselves. Through examining and appreciating the choices you've made in the face of challenges, you'll inspire yourself with who you are.

There are two more rules of storytelling that will help you work through this part of your story.

STORYTELLING RULE #6:
Stories are made of concrete details.

This rule is an extension of Storytelling Rule #3: Stories happen in space and time. Look back at the story about Lenny and observe all the very specific and concrete details I included. I'm going to talk about vivid moments in Chapter 8. The vivid moment in the Lenny story happened when Mike challenged him at the meeting and you could actually picture it like you were there. But consider these details from the story:

> So my strategy was to schedule meetings with Lenny before every plenary session: I became his guide, his coach, and his cheerleader. I would give him pep talks. I would walk through the presentation

deck with him. Then I would challenge him with questions that I knew people would raise in each meeting. I would boost his confidence, saying: "You've got this, Lenny. You can answer these questions. You know what you're doing."

If I had just said this instead: "I decided to coach Lenny before each meeting," and left it at that, the story would have been much less powerful and much less real for you, as the listener/reader/audience. Because a story happens in time and space, we need some concrete details to be able to connect with it. It's really about bringing the listener into your world in a tangible way so she can step into your shoes and experience your story firsthand. This is how you'll make her feel like she knows you, trusts you, and wants you on her team. This is how you'll do voodoo on her brain chemistry.

As you construct your Epic Story, the rich details won't be on the surface. Your short-term memory has a small cache, so you need to activate the long-term neurons when you brainstorm and construct stories. In putting together my own story about Lenny, I had to really think for a while before I remembered what had happened in that meeting. I couldn't immediately recall when I realized that trying to lead the process on my own wasn't going to work. I had to really dig around in my long-term memory before I remembered that I had decided to help Lenny take charge. I had to unearth those details. As you prepare for interviews, give yourself due time for this reflection.

Below you'll find a set of questions to guide you.

THE POWER OF EMOTION

It's easy to forget how we felt before, during, and after intense moments of our lives. That's why reflection is so important. For instance, the negative emotions I felt at the beginning of my story had been snuffed out in memory when things started going my way again. And not being able to remember those negative emotions, I had also lost touch with how proud and inspired I felt when I learned Lenny got promoted. The feelings we feel while living an experience are like flames—they go out once the experience is over and we move onto the next thing. But—like a flame—they can be instantly rekindled and relived through storytelling.

Both the negative and the positive emotions matter in a story because of Storytelling Rule #7.

STORYTELLING RULE #7:
All heroes feel.

Your feelings at your darkest hour are an essential element of the story: revealing how you felt in the face of challenges draws the listener further into your world and connects him with you. It causes him to empathize. On the positive side, you will also reveal how you felt about the change: what made you feel proud, inspired, relieved, joyful, excited, and happy at the end of the Hero's Journey. When you reveal these positive emotions, the listener will share your victory and see himself in it too.

If you include how you felt when faced with conflict and include how you felt when you achieved change, you guarantee your interviewer will be able to connect with you as a human being. He will see himself in you, and that feeling of connection will uplift and inspire him. This is why great actors make millions of dollars—because they manifest emotions on the screen and evoke them in us. Those shared emotions make us aware that we're never alone in this world. There is always someone else going through exactly what we're going through.

You're not in a film, so in the interview, you will have to *tell* us how you felt. The story you tell will show your actions and tell your feelings at the time. The key emotion you will actually *express* in the interview (show as opposed to tell) is—as you already know—enthusiasm. Because you are going to get inspired and excited in the telling.

You read my story above about Lenny, but imagine you had heard me tell it out loud. You would have felt my enthusiasm because this story makes me come alive when I tell it. I'm so proud that I was able to get that project done in the first place. But I'm even prouder that it left a lasting positive impact on someone's career. I love the way I approached the problem—from the standpoint of human development. That's my personal take on what matters most in a business environment. And I stayed true to those values even at a very difficult time. That inspires me because it shows me that my outward manifestation aligns with the person I think I am on the inside. There is almost nothing that will bolster your self-confidence more than knowing you've stayed true to your values in difficult circumstances.

EXPLORE YOUR STORY AND
REMINISCE ABOUT CHOICES

Now that you see how the complete Epic Story works, it's time to pin down the choices, specifics, and emotions in your own story. Answer these questions in your workbook.

Written Exercise 6.7:
Remember your feelings.

Use feeling words that are as precise and vivid as possible.

- How did you think and feel about the challenges you faced?
- Was there a particular moment when all hope seemed lost? What was that like?
- How did you feel when you achieved your goal?

Take a moment and reminisce about your feelings. Use vivid words that really capture what it felt like to you. Instead of "worried," try "terrified," "crestfallen," "panicked," "downcast," "deflated," "anxious," "alarmed," "vexed," "agitated," "agonized," or "troubled." Instead of "happy," try "proud," "overjoyed," "elated," "giddy," "delighted," "ecstatic," "lucky," "blessed," "thrilled," or "rapturous."

Get out that thesaurus and find the precise language that re-evokes the feelings you felt. You do not have to say these words in your story if they aren't part of your natural vocabulary, but you do want to feel them as you tell the story, so take the time now to name them with laser-like precision.

Written Exercise 6.8:
Review your choices.

Answer these questions about your strategy and key actions:

- Did you have a strategy to overcome the challenges? What was your plan to get what you wanted? (Even if you didn't have a clear strategy in mind when you started taking action, looking back, what can you now see was your inherent strategy?)

- What was the rationale for that strategy? Why did you think that strategy would work? Why do you think it did work in the end?

- Did you try a strategy that didn't work at first? Did you flounder? How did that make you feel?

- What two or three core actions were most important in helping you achieve your goal? Why were those the most important?

WANT TO GET MORE INTIMATE WITH EPIC STORIES?

Here's an easy exercise to do for more homework:

Pick a movie with a strong main character. Watch the movie and take notes on the Four C's: context, conflict, choice, and change. See if you can observe the Seven Rules of Storytelling in Action. Take note of how the movie makes you feel, and see if you can pinpoint the specific source of your emotions as they come up: are you inspired by the character's choice? Do you feel empathy for his or her situation? Is it something else?

Use these insights to shape and enhance your own Epic Stories.

LET'S RECAP

OK, there you go—that's the Epic Story framework served up with a healthy dose of narrative theory and philosophy. Once you've explored an experience in this way—in depth and detail—you'll be ready to tell an Epic Story about it. Feel free to start practicing now!! I'll give you more techniques and tactics to hone your telling techniques and prepare for multiple stories in Chapters 8 and 9.

I'll recap the whole thing for you now, but first, one last bit of philosophizing because I can't help myself:

If you're one of the umpteen percent of humans who suffer from impostor syndrome, if you doubt yourself, if you worry that people won't understand how great you are, or even worry that you aren't that great in the first place, then you need to start telling Epic Stories about your life.

From his extensive study of all the heroes humanity has ever known, Joseph Campbell concluded very simply that "The privilege of a lifetime is being who you are."[2] Because we're all heroes on the journey of life. You have lived. You have tried. You have faced your personal dragons, and at least some of the time you have won. When you tell stories about those victories, you connect with the finest qualities inside you and allow your light to shine. That's a great gift—both to you and to the person listening.

Now the recap!

Interview Hero Secrets in This Chapter:

The Four C's of Epic Stories

CONTEXT   CONFLICT   CHOICE   CHANGE

- **The five steps to creating your own Epic Story:**

  Step 1: Choose an accomplishment.

  Step 2: Brainstorm what happened at the beginning of your story.

  Step 3: Brainstorm what happened at the end of your story.

  Step 4: Define your conflict sentence.

  Step 5: Distinguish and articulate your choices in response to the conflict.

- **Use these questions to explore and outline your story:**

Context

- What were the circumstances?
- What was the task in front of you?
- Who else was there?
- When was it?
- Where were you?

Conflict

- What was challenging about the situation?
- What obstacles did you have to overcome to achieve your goal?
- What did you want, and what was standing in your way?

Choice

- How did you think and feel about the challenges you faced at that time?
- Was there a particular moment when all hope seemed lost? What was that like?
- Did you have a strategy to overcome the obstacles?
- What was your plan to get what you wanted?
- What was the rationale for that strategy?
- Why did you think that strategy would work?
- Why do you think it did work in the end?
- What two or three core actions were most important in helping you achieve your goal? Why were those the most important?
- What was the rationale for your choices?

Change

- What was the happy ending?
- What measurable results were produced (by you directly or any others involved: dollars earned or saved, hours removed from a process, promotions, accolades, awards or honors)?

- How did you grow, and what did you learn?
- How did you change (Confidence? Career trajectory? Other personal growth?)
- How did you feel then, and how do you feel about these changes now?

Seven of the Eight Rules of Storytelling

Storytelling Rule #1: Stories are made of actions, not opinions.

Storytelling Rule #2: All stories have a beginning, middle, and end.

Storytelling Rule #3: Stories happen in space and time.

Storytelling Rule #4: Conflict defines the story.

Storytelling Rule #5: Choices define the character.

Storytelling Rule #6: Stories are made of concrete details.

Storytelling Rule #7: All heroes feel.

You'll learn Storytelling Rule #8 in the next chapter! Let's get to it!

When the Hero Falls on Her Face

*The fishermen know that the sea is dangerous and
the storm terrible, but they have never found these dangers
sufficient reason for remaining ashore.*
—Vincent VanGogh

FAILURE IS A GOOD THING

The Florence airport has a notoriously difficult runway. Situated on the only open plain amid the idyllic Tuscan hills, it's frequently overpowered by dangerous crosswinds, causing flights to be canceled and landings rerouted to Florence's kinder and gentler neighboring runways in Pisa or Bologna. Pee-your-pants turbulence is virtually guaranteed on one of every eight or so take-offs (in my anecdotal experience). And even when the crosswinds aren't terrorizing pilots and passengers, the runway is scandalously short. In fact, it's so problematic that pilots require special training to be allowed to land here. They need to hit the ground at the very front of the runway and break extra hard to avoid careening off into those beautiful hills.

I didn't know this when I first moved here. So imagine my terror when the pilot—mid-landing attempt—rapidly pulled us back up into the clouds. *What's going on?* fellow passengers and I asked each other. No one had an answer.

Fifteen minutes later, after circling the city again, the pilot went back for a second attempt. And he pulled up again. At this point, anxiety in the cabin had escalated to a fever pitch, and everyone was murmuring, praying, breathing deeply—all the things we do to manage abject fear. Bizarrely, neither the pilot nor the crew made any announcements as to why this was happening. So when he finally landed on the third attempt, everyone cheered, clapped, and hugged each other.

I soon learned that this was a regular occurrence in Florence. On later flights, pilots explained the reason for the occasional pull-up, and others even asked passengers to brace themselves before landing for the hard braking that inevitably ensued. Communication helped a lot. But failure on attempted landings in Florence is par for the course. One in about six flights I have taken in the last several years has required multiple landing attempts. And let me tell you: *this* kind of failure is a very good thing. In fact, it's part of the pilots' training: if anything doesn't feel right about the approach, pull up and try again. Pilots have to fail to land multiple times in Florence to avoid a far more catastrophic failure that would cost lives.

FAILURE IS ESSENTIAL TO SUCCESS

This is why at some point in your interview career, you're going to be asked about failure. Companies need to ask about failure because they know what all airlines with operations in Florence know: if you aren't willing to fail small once in a while, you're bound to fail huge.

They also know that appetite for failure is one predictor of success. I like to say that if you want to understand people's potential for success, you only need to look at their capacity to fail. History is teeming with examples of people who succeeded only by virtue of their willingness to tolerate repeated failure. Thomas Edison, Stephen King, and Michael Jordan are just a few people who've talked about their repeated dances with setback and rejection. They could have easily curled up under the covers, felt sorry for themselves, and given up. Instead, they kept getting right back on the Hero's path. Your graduate school or future employers are looking for their next Michael Jordans: resilient people who know how to grow and aim for excellence in the face of setbacks.

But failure is essential to success for many more reasons. Let's start with this one: success may be what makes you competent, but failure is what makes you lovable. It makes you human and more relatable to others because *everyone has experienced failure*.

STILL, TALKING ABOUT FAILURE SUCKS

Almost nobody likes to talk about failure. Why is that? In fact, it almost seems counterintuitive to prepare failure stories for interviews. I mean, isn't that the kind of stuff you're trying to hide from interviewers? Let's take a moment and think about why failure sucks and why we don't like to talk about it. What is it about failure, and admitting to it, that's so shameful?

Never mind the fact that failure bars you from getting what you want, failure can shatter your self-confidence. It just feels crappy to fall short of expectations, whether they're our own expectations or someone else's. Far more devastating than the fact that failure makes you look weak, incompetent, or foolish, it makes you *feel* weak, incompetent, or foolish. Those aren't feelings we enjoy. And the last place we want to feel them is in that interview room. All of these conditions and presuppositions cause most of us to dread the inevitable failure question, to pull punches when we answer them, or to avoid preparing for them altogether.

But don't forget the Friendship Mindset! The interview isn't a test! And what's more, knowing how to fail, pick yourself up again, and move on is an essential skill that employers screen for. So you're going to have to embrace failure stories if you want to get that job. See? Here's Mustache Man with a little reassurance that you're OK and failure is OK and talking about it is absolutely A-OK!!

Failure evokes so many different kinds of negative emotion. You don't want any present-tense source of shame, embarrassment, or self-disappointment to creep into the conversation. But sharing your past encounters with those emotions will endear you to the interviewer like almost nothing else you will do during the conversation. That's because failure is pretty much inevitable. We've all been there, and you'll have failure in common with absolutely everyone who ever interviews you.

Like George Bernard Shaw said, "If you can't get rid of the skeleton in your closet, you'd best teach it to dance." So that's what we're going to do. We're going to tell great Epic *Failure* Stories, inspiring stories about failure.

Let's dig in. In interviews, failure questions can take many forms. Some examples:

- Tell me about your biggest failure.
- When did you make a mistake?
- What's your biggest regret?
- How have you grown through failure?
- How did you fail in your last job?
- How did you overcome a major setback? How did you recover?

The list goes on . . .

Step 1: Pick a Failure, Any Failure

All right, we're going to make this really tangible just like we did for success. And this is going to be fun!!

I know that sounds odd. We hate failure so much that even going near it can feel painful, but this process of exploring and then telling stories about your failures is so awesome and empowering because it allows you to gain objectivity about the experience, release negative emotions, and then turn the setback into something you're proud of. For serious. So let's go through this together. I'll be your guide.

Pick a failure to work with. Write it down with no frills—just tell it like it is. The example can be culled from any aspect of your life: professional, community, school, extracurriculars. Even personal failures will work. To make it as easy as possible, let's define failure. And to do this, we begin by defining the word "fail":

fail

verb [feyl]

1   to fall short of success or achievement in something
    expected, attempted, desired, or approved:
    The experiment failed because of poor planning.[1]

The first thing you want to notice is that although the very sound of
the word "fail" might evoke all kinds of prickly feels, it actually has a
fairly benign meaning. Failure happens pretty much anytime you fall
short of the success you expected, attempted, or desired. By this definition, I fail at least a few times every single day. To-do list anyone? I
pretty much always want things that I don't get right away, try things
I don't achieve up to my standards, and expect things that don't happen. No biggie.

So just pick any old failure that fits this definition for this exercise. And be sure to pick a failure that's in the past—something you
can now see in perspective and analyze somewhat objectively. In other
words, if you think you might get fired tomorrow because of something you did yesterday, that's not a good one to pick. You can deal
with that one later when you have some distance.

> ### Written Exercise 7.1:
> ## Pick a failure and write it down.
>
> Choose a time in the past when you fell short of the success or achieve-
> ment you expected, attempted, desired, or approved.

Now. When I get to this point in my live workshops, there is always at least one person who can't think of a failure to work with.
"But I've never really failed," she says. Or "I don't really view anything
I've done as a failure." This is a nice, seemingly enlightened view, but
it's not honest. Acting like there's no such thing as failure is typically
a subterfuge to mask emotions that have been swept under the rug.

When you hit "send" on that email and realized it was a big mistake, when you didn't meet that deadline, when that meeting didn't go

as well as you thought it would—those are all failures. Failure doesn't have to be dramatic; it just has to be a time when you fell short of success or achievement in something expected, attempted, or desired. If you can't think of a single time that happened to you, then you must be a professional couch potato. At the end of this chapter, I'm going to recommend that you use the Epic Failure Story framework not just to talk about failures in interviews, but to proactively debrief on your disappointments and use them to maximize your personal growth. That will be a much more confident, resilient, and truly enlightened approach than pretending failure doesn't happen. It will set you free from the fear of failure and make you invulnerable to shame.

But for now, all we're going to do is work with the mechanics of failure so we can tell stories about it. You can go back later and apply this to all of your failures. For now, just pick one and write it down in your workbook.

THREE TYPES OF CONFLICT

As you learned in the last chapter, an Epic Story happens when a character needs to overcome conflict to achieve change. Remember that conflict is what happens when the protagonist (you) wants something and has to overcome obstacles to get it. Well, at a certain level we could make the case that all of life is about conflict. I mean, think of everything you've been through just today. You probably had to deal with traffic jams, a line at the coffee shop, or maybe somebody who was in a bad mood. Perhaps you didn't get an email or a text that you had been eagerly waiting for, your favorite shirt had a stain on it, the cat scratched up the sofa, your roommate didn't put out the garbage, you missed your train, the Uber had 3X surge pricing, or it was raining and you forgot your umbrella. The list of conflicts we face daily goes on and on and on. We're really used to encountering conflict. There always seem to be obstacles standing in the way of what we want.

Step 2: Come Up with a Conflict Sentence for Your Failure

Let's look a little closer at the failure. This is the same exercise we did in the last chapter. What did you want, and what was the obstacle? This is the DNA of any story, whether it's a success story or a failure story.

What was the thing that you wanted, and what was the thing that was in the way?

Written Exercise 7.2:
Come up with a conflict sentence.

Fill in the blanks:

I wanted _____, and I was struggling to overcome _____.

For the purposes of your Epic Story, there are really only three kinds of conflict. We boil all the obstacles we face down into only three categories. You probably already know what these are: man vs. nature, man vs. man, and man vs. himself, with man, of course, meaning "human" and including women. The last is my personal favorite, and the one I most commonly find myself dealing with. But let's take a moment and locate the nature of the conflict in your failure story.

THE THREE TYPES OF CONFLICT

Conflict	The Obstacle
Man vs. Nature	External forces or circumstances
Man vs. Man	Another person
Man vs. Himself	You or your view of yourself

If it's a man vs. nature conflict, the thing you're struggling against is an external force or circumstance. In traditional literature and mythology, the minions of mother nature are baffling in their array: Scylla and Charybdis; the Labyrinth of King Minos; Medusa; the Sirens, the Fates, and the Harpies; lions, tigers, and bears; the weather or climate change; and even time itself. The list is virtually infinite. If we extrapolate these beasties into their modern expressions, we could also include technology and large, complex organizations that seem to have a nature all their own. For our purposes, though, any external circumstance fits into man vs. nature. If you were racing against the clock or wrangling your iPhone, that would classify as nature. If you're battling a big organization, the government, an established process, or a whole culture resistant to change, that would be man vs. nature, too.

Man vs.man is pretty self-explanatory. You're having a problem with another person. Sometimes when you examine your experiences, you might think that the conflict—the obstacle in your way—was the entrenched processes or culture of a team, a group, or a committee of people (this would be man vs. nature). But when you really drill down and look closer at the details, you'll often find that even though on the surface you struggled against a whole team, in reality it was just *one* other person that was standing in your way; one person, or perhaps two.

If you're talking about team dynamics or organizational dynamics in your failure story, be sure to look closely and pinpoint whether it was truly the complexity of the whole organization that you were battling, or if it was really just one or two people who stood in your way: a boss that didn't believe in you, that one reticent team member who wouldn't toe the line, the client who refused to buy into the plan no matter how many people tried to sway him.

The final type of conflict is man vs. himself. I think we can all summon recent examples of this one, where you were your own worst enemy. For example: you didn't know how to do something; you didn't believe in yourself; you were ignorant about the topic at hand; your negative self-talk led to a freak-out; you didn't have adequate training. That's man vs. himself.

Tragedy happens when the hero fails to change in the face of changing circumstances. If you examine some of the experiences that you still regret or that you would label failures, see if you can find this particular mistake. See if you can identify places where you just didn't realize you needed to change until it was too late. That would be a man vs. himself conflict.

THE FAILURE CONFLICT SENTENCE

Now we're going to go a little bit deeper with your conflict sentence. First, what is success? Well, remember, this was our sentence for success stories:

I wanted _____, but I *had* to overcome _____.

It turns out that the difference between success and failure is just one little word. In the case of failure, you wanted something but you *failed to* overcome the obstacle. That's the only difference.

I wanted _____, but I failed to overcome _____.

Step 3: Identify the Nature of Conflict in Your Story

Depending on what obstacle you failed to overcome—external circumstances, another person, or yourself—the failure will have a particular flavor to it.

You Failed to Achieve Your Objective and . . .

Conflict	The Failure
Man vs. Nature	External forces or circumstances bested you.
Man vs. Man	You damaged a relationship.
Man vs. Himself	You let yourself down.

Take a moment and decide which kind of failure you experienced in your example. Was it man vs. nature, man vs. man, or man vs. himself? In many cases, the failure might encompass more than one of these dynamics. It could in fact be all three kinds of conflict that got the better of you. Be sure to home in on the specifics: define very clearly the one to three obstacles that blocked your success.

Written Exercise 7.3:
Categorize the conflict.

Define the nature of the conflict that barred your success. Clarify specifically what it was and which of the three categories of conflict it falls into.

As you do this, you might already start to feel a little more relaxed about that failure. The conflict is one you've likely encountered many, many times before. Sometimes you beat it. This time you didn't. No big deal. It's bound to happen again!! Let's see, though, if we can turn this little turd of an experience into a nugget of gold.

LET'S EXAMINE WHY FAILURE IS ACTUALLY AWESOME

I already talked about how the ability to fail is essential to success, but let's look closer at what's good about failure. How is failure constructive for you personally? Take just a second and contemplate this. Is there a reason why failure is useful to you? Is it valuable?

The benefits of failure, when you look closely, are actually pretty awesome.

One huge upside to failure is that it forces you to learn about yourself and your limits, boundaries, and abilities—and then take concrete and efficient action to expand. It helps you reassess your strategy, which makes you more self-aware and determined to do better in the future. It gives you a thicker skin, so you'll be shatter-resistant the next time around. Failure also forces you to revisit your values and priorities. How many times have you failed to get something you wanted, only to readjust your expectations and attain something that was even more valuable?

Have you ever noticed that success isn't a very good teacher? Success feels really good, yes. We all like to win. But when we're successful, we're not learning and growing as much as we are when we're stumbling and messing up.

Knowledge is cheap, but wisdom is earned. And the difference between knowledge and wisdom is experience. As a beloved client of mine used to say, I could tell you how to bake a cake. I could even bake a perfect cake for you. But until you eat it, you won't know what "cake" really is.

You won't have the wisdom of experience. As it turns out, we gain the most wisdom through failure. You have to get your hands dirty and lick your fingers. Life is messy, and perfection just isn't an option. If you want to live up to your potential, you will need to fail again and again.

In interviews, failure is your secret sauce. Failure stories are ultimately growth stories, and growth is what makes you interesting. Think about it. Would you rather hear a story about someone who easily gets everything he wants, or one about someone who embarrasses the heck out of himself trying to get what he wants, then manages to put the pieces back together against all odds? If there was never any stumbling, learning, or growth in your life, your personal story would put people and—let's be honest—*you* to sleep. There would be no character arc, no development of your personality or character.

So far, we've discussed how failure can change the way people see you, and how you see yourself. But did you know that your failure can actually change the way you see others? It gives you humility and empathy for others who might be struggling, because you know firsthand what it feels like to be in their shoes. You know embarrassment. You know shame. You know disappointment. And by the way, so does your interviewer. We all like stories about hard-won victories because we get to experience the grit, tenacity, and ingenuity of a character in the process of growth. Nobody roots for the guy who's always winning—that honor goes to the underdog.

Your failure story will get you closer to winning the acceptance letter or the job offer than the most stellar success story. Think about it—everyone interviewing will come prepared with success stories. They'll all be brilliant, accomplished, and poised—just like you. But you'll have an edge. While the others stammer, avert their gaze, and sugarcoat their failures (and bore the interviewer half to death with predictable answers), you'll intrigue him with accounts of your Epic Failure Story—the bloody knees and laurel wreaths that are the badges of true character.

No doubt about it: viewed from a certain angle, failure is awesome. So let's complete your Epic Failure Story, though a better name for it would be "Epic Growth Story."

TAKING RESPONSIBILITY

The next piece of your Epic Failure Story is taking responsibility for the failure. So let's add two simple pieces to our failure conflict sentence:

> **I wanted (<u>goal</u>), but I *failed* to overcome (<u>conflict</u>), because I (<u>mistake</u>), causing (<u>impact</u>).**

The "because" reveals the reason for the failure. The result is the negative impact on you and others. Taking responsibility for the part of the failure that is yours in a self-aware and authentic way is what will make your story (and your life) powerful. Being honest about its impact on you will endear you to the listener. These are also what will transform your confidence and turn the failure from a source of shame to a source of pride and joy.

Step 4: Identify Your Mistake

Start by finding your personal mistake. While the failure might be big and dramatic and while many people may have played a role, if you look closely, you should be able to find your personal error. It's often something quite small and seemingly insignificant. Here's the definition of mistake:

mistake

noun [mi-steyk]

1   an error in action, calculation, opinion, or judgment caused by poor reasoning, carelessness, insufficient knowledge, etc.
2   a misunderstanding or misconception.[2]

I think we can all name a handful of mistakes we've made even just today. To err is human. No big deal. Take the Florence landing example. The pilot's mistake was something small, like starting the descent 10 seconds too late or miscalculating the approach by 20 feet. See if you can pinpoint the mistake you made that resulted in your failure to beat the conflict

Here are some ideas to get you thinking:

Mistakes of ignorance

- I didn't understand how important something was.
- I didn't have enough information.
- I didn't know how to do something.

Mistakes of timing

- I did something too late or too soon.
- I realized something important too late.
- I didn't know how long it would take to do something.

Mistakes in judgment and reasoning

- I didn't know how something really worked.
- I didn't take something important into account.
- I thought an action would produce a certain result, and I was wrong.

Mistakes of diligence

- I left out something important.
- I made a careless mistake.
- I wasn't detail-oriented enough.

Mistakes in influence or communication

- I was too detail-oriented: I lost sight of the bigger picture.
- I didn't communicate something the right way.
- I didn't take someone's viewpoint, perspective, or feelings into account.

Mistakes of missed opportunity

- I didn't seek help when I needed it.
- I didn't take someone else's feedback on board.
- I didn't use all the resources available to me.

These are just a few ideas, so dig deep into your own experience and find the perfect phrasing of your own mistake. Be as specific and detailed as possible.

A WORD ABOUT OVERREACHING

If you work with the ideas above, you should be able to pinpoint the aspect of the failure that truly belonged to you. When you're honest about your own mistakes while not overreaching and blaming yourself for circumstances out of your control or the choices of others, then you truly have power over your own failures. You can take 100% responsibility for the failure—no matter how many people contributed to the negative outcome—by accurately identifying your personal mistake.

As they say, hindsight is 20/20. Our mistakes often become clear only after the fact. That's part of why failure is so valuable: because it forces us to go back and replay the tape and decide how we can make better choices next time. But oftentimes the thing we did wrong couldn't have gone any other way at the time. We just didn't know any better. When you tell stories about failure, they will resonate powerfully with your listener if you've taken responsibility for what was yours without pummeling yourself for things out of your control.

It's important to rigorously distinguish between your personal error and the bad choices of others or unavoidable circumstances. Sometimes failure is a group effort. Ha! But if you overreach or blame yourself for things that weren't in your control, you're stuck in self-flagellation land—you could go on and on beating yourself up for things you ultimately had no power over. The world is big, and a lot of it isn't under our control (frustrating, I know!), so be gentle with yourself. Acknowledge that most of the time, you are doing the very best you can. Take full credit for the thing you realistically could have been expected to do differently and—if appropriate—acknowledge that there were other aspects of the experience that weren't in your direct control.

Written Exercise 7.4:
Locate and describe your mistake.

Take full responsibility for your personal error or failing in the experience and write down exactly what your mistake was. But do not overreach and take the blame for things that were out of your control or that you could not reasonably have been expected to do or to know.

Step 5: Be Honest about the Impact

Next, you want to outline the impact that your mistake and the failure had. You want to be honest with yourself but be gentle. Don't overreach and don't beat yourself up. Sometimes the greatest innovations and achievements are born of prior failures. The world keeps turning and we go on living. So try to be clinical about this and just delineate what resulted from the mistake or the failure. Include all three kinds of impact:

External Consequences: Missed deadlines, lost dollars, increased costs, and other externally verifiable impact

Relational Consequences: Lost trust, hurt feelings, negative emotions, and problems caused for others

Personal Consequences: Impact on you in terms of negative emotion; loss of opportunity, confidence, or desired outcomes; and any other impact on you, your career, or your personal effectiveness

Here is a complete Epic Failure conflict sentence from one of my own biggest failures:

> *I wanted to* build an airtight model and get a good review on an important project, *but I failed to overcome* my own inexperience and our tight timeline, *because I* focused too much on the details of the model and didn't collaborate or communicate well with the rest of the team, *causing* significant reworking of the model, a frustrated manager, a bad review on the project, and a lot of personal embarrassment.

Pretty crappy, right? Yeah, that project was a learning experience, to say the least!! And speaking of learning experience, let's get to the growth part of the story—the awesome positive results of failure.

Written Exercise 7.5:
Identify the impact.

Be honest with yourself about the impact that the failure and your mistake had in the external world, on other people, and on yourself. Include the negative emotions you felt at the time.

ALL STORIES HAVE A HAPPY ENDING

Despite the fact that you didn't achieve your initial objective, your failure story still has a happy ending: it's just not the one you initially attempted, desired, or expected. Yes, you fell short and met with defeat. But here's the eighth rule of storytelling:

All stories have a happy ending.

Defeat is temporary. Setbacks are impermanent. Mistakes are recoverable. Failure happens in a discrete moment in time. If your story doesn't appear to have a happy ending, that's because *it's not over yet*.

I'll be the first to admit that sometimes you need a little bit of distance from failure to be able to see the happy ending. That's why I asked you to pick an episode that happened a little while in the past for this exercise.

The thing about human life is that we're repeating this cycle all the time. Anyone who is capable of vision—of seeing possibilities that do not yet exist—is on intimate terms with failure. But that's part of what makes life fun—that it's possible to dream and create beyond what already exists. If your dreams manifested instantly, that would cause a whole other set of problems. To have everything we want and be all that we want to be, we have to tolerate not getting it immediately at least some of the time. Hence the critical importance of learning to fail well.

You're probably in the midst of failing right now in some capacity. I know I certainly am. We're failing day in and day out and overcoming our failures day in and day out. So when you want to tell an Epic Failure Story in interviews, be sure to choose one where the story is over—where you can point to exactly what it is that you've learned and how you've grown as a direct result.

GROWTH, THREE WAYS

Step 6: Identify and Celebrate How You've Grown

No question you've grown through failure, so let's look at the three types of growth that correlate with the three types of conflict.

THREE TYPES OF GROWTH

Conflict	How You Grew
Man vs. Nature	You changed externally.
Man vs. Man	You deepened your capacity for relationship.
Man vs. Himself	Your view of yourself expanded.

In the case of man vs. nature, typically you changed externally. For example, if your failure involved missing a meeting because your taxi got stuck in traffic, you probably decided that next time, you'd change your routine. You'd leave your house a little earlier, move closer to work, get a bike, or rent a parking spot by the office. When nature bests you, you make some external change. This might involve taking a class, improving your skills, and changing your habits. These are things you do in the external world to become a better person and to achieve more success the next time you're up at bat.

When the conflict is man vs. man, you're typically growing in your capacity to sustain meaningful relationships. You're becoming humbler, more empathetic; you're learning how to listen and communicate better, and how to trust. In the future you'll find yourself more open to intimacy, more confident in relationships and communication, and maybe more forgiving of others' mistakes.

If the conflict is man vs. himself, then your view of yourself expands. I think we can all relate to the experience of failing, picking ourselves up and trying again, and ultimately being really impressed by what we achieve. You learn to appreciate the extraordinary person that you are when you find the inner fortitude to move on from failures with no loss of enthusiasm. Your self-confidence, awareness, and appreciation grow, and you become bigger in the process.

Written Exercise 7.6:
How did you grow?

Take at least three minutes and brainstorm all the ways you grew as a result of this setback, mistake, or failure. How did you change? How did you become a better person and professional? What new experiences have resulted and what new achievements have you attained as a result of growing from this failure? Be sure to include any subsequent successes that you achieved thanks to the learnings from this failure.

Once you have an idea of all the ways you've grown, the first thing you want to do is stop and pat yourself on the back. Look at how amazing you are. One of the things no one else can do for you in life is learn. Only *you* can take life's lemons and make them into lemonade.

Only you can confront your failings and mistakes with self-honesty and commit to doing better next time. And only you can grow from failure instead of curling up into a fetal position and calling it quits. So take a moment to acknowledge that you did that. You expanded. You grew. You became more of who you were meant to be. All because of a little mistake, setback, or failure. How cool!

The next step is to construct your complete growth sentence so you can begin to share all this awesomeness powerfully with others:

> **I wanted (goal), but I failed to overcome (conflict),**
> **because I (mistake), causing (impact),**
> **and as a result, I gained (growth).**

You didn't get the outcome you were aiming for, but instead you got something even better—something much more valuable, something in the form of growth.

Take a moment and customize this growth sentence as it relates to the failure you're working on. How did you fail? What mistake did you make, and what was the impact? And then how did you grow as a person afterward? Be sure to include everything you can think of. Most failures bear multiple fruits.

Step 7: Put it all together in your Epic Growth sentence.

Here's my completed growth sentence:

> *I wanted to* build an airtight model and get a good review on an important project, *but I failed to overcome* my own inexperience and our tight timeline, *because I* focused too much on the details of the

model and didn't collaborate or communicate well with the rest of the team, *causing* significant reworking of the model, a frustrated manager, and a bad review on the project, *and as a result I gained* **an appreciation for the value of mentorship and more productive teamworking habits**.

Once you've completed this sentence, you've taken complete ownership of your personal growth, exerted your power over that failure, and begun to direct the narrative of your life. Remember, not all stories are created equal and you always have a choice about how to communicate something, both to yourself and to others. When you frame failure as a growth sentence, you're taking a giant step to becoming the master of your own destiny.

You'll never be able to control circumstances or other people, but when you own your experience and who you are—warts, mistakes, and all—you expand your power to create the life you want. Taking ownership of your failures expands your capacity for success.

You're human. And you're magnificent. Isn't life grand?

THE COMPLETE EPIC FAILURE STORY

All right, now let's integrate this growth sentence into our Four C's story-telling framework of context, conflict, choice, and change so you can turn your failure into an Epic Story. Here's the outline of an Epic Failure Story:

Context

- The background information needed for the story to make sense

Conflict

- What you failed at and the impact of that failure, including your emotions

Choice

- What specifically you took responsibility for
- The strategy and actions you chose to recover from the failure and grow

Change

• The results of your choices: how you grew and improved as a result

Here is the whole story from my own Epic Failure.

Context: I was working on a really cool analytical project for a pharma company when I worked in consulting. I wanted to execute my part of the analysis perfectly and get a good review, so I worked extra hard. I built a really intricate and detailed model in Excel.

Conflict: But I failed to get my manager's input. I toiled away in silence for a couple of weeks, and by the time I shared the model, a lot of time had been wasted and my manager didn't really know what to do with my analysis. He had to reverse-engineer my model before he could share the results with the client.

In the end, I got a negative review on that project, even though my model was correct and the conclusions it enabled were part of our final presentation to the client. I was really disappointed in myself, and I felt so foolish and naïve for not having recognized how to collaborate effectively with my team.

Choice: I realized that my perfectionist approach was making it really hard for other people to work with me, so I changed my strategy. I decided to communicate with my manager at regular intervals on all future projects—seeking input and providing clear rationale for my work so that it could be as useful and easy to understand as possible.

Change: On successive project reviews, I got much stronger marks. On top of that, I actually learned much faster with my manager's support and input, so it was a win-win situation. I might not have figured that out had I not done it so horribly wrong the first time around.

What kind of emotions did you experience while you were reading that story? What did you think of me? You probably didn't think that I was a loser or a victim or that I was being dishonest. Notice how I'm being genuine and up-front about how I messed up. I'm taking full responsibility for my part in the failure. No excuses, no beating around the bush. I'm not being a victim or blaming other people. I'm also showing how I leveraged that negative experience to grow and become a better person and a better professional. All of these things engender confidence, affinity, and trust. This is what you want to do with your own failure stories.

But in this story, I also want you to notice the nature of taking responsibility for a failure. The truth is that, in my story, my model was almost perfect. I actually predicted exactly the right numbers that I was trying to achieve, they were well backed up by research, and my assumptions were smart. In terms of *my* objective, which was to make a perfect model, *I actually succeeded*. I could have used that fact to be defensive or to deflect the comments of my manager, but my model itself wasn't the failure. The failure was my lack of communication and how my insular working method slowed down my team, so that's what I took full responsibility for.

LEARN, GROW, CHANGE

Most people don't know how to talk about failure in an inspiring way. This is odd, seeing as failure is a cornerstone of the human condition. From cradle to grave, either we're succeeding in achieving our objectives, or we're failing. Either you want something and you succeed in overcoming the obstacles, or you want something and you fail to overcome the obstacles. We repeat this pattern our whole lives.

But eventually we learn, we grow, and we change. We learned how to create fire, how to farm, how to make a wheel, how to create metal and glass, and so on. Now we have space shuttles and artificial intelligence. If you look at the history of humanity as the story arc of one character, you see how many times it fell on its face, how it persevered, learned, and grew. And continues to do so endlessly into infinity.

Because failure is inevitable, it's happening to you right now. It happens every day, but hiding it and feeling bad about it are entirely optional. If you're aiming high, you're bound to fall down from time to time. You can use this framework to view your own failures with clarity and gratitude and move on with your self-confidence intact. That's what I encourage you to do.

COMMUNICATION SHAPES
YOUR EXPERIENCE OF LIFE

The way you tell your story ultimately informs and shapes your experience. Remember the two stories about my eviction from Chicago—and my inspiring escape to Florence? Absolutely every aspect of your personal communication is in your power. Only you have the ability to transform a cringe-worthy experience into a soul-affirming story. No one will do it for you. So don't let those embarrassing episodes go to waste! Use this framework to proactively dissect your failures after they happen (not just before an interview) and then use them to build bridges, to entertain, and to inspire—yourself first and foremost.

Telling your personal story with compassion and insight is crucial whether you're speaking to another person or just mulling the story over **in your own thoughts**. It's so easy to let your inner voice tear you to shreds and rewrite your story in the most unflattering way. If you tell your story often enough, though, your positive spin on it will become ingrained in your neural pathways, and your inner voice won't be able to overpower it.

But perhaps the most important reason to get good at talking about failure is this: when you see how you've grown as a result of setbacks, mistakes, and failures, then *you* will really know what you're made of. If your self-confidence stands on a rug under which you've swept all memory of failure—all the negative emotional charge of all your screw-ups—you're standing on shaky ground. The very next failure you face might rip that rug right out from under you and plunge you into the abyss of self-doubt and self-flagellation. That happens from time to time no matter what you do: we're all human this way. But if you confront your failures, take responsibility for them, and then celebrate them for the growth they caused or inspired, then it's harder to deny how powerful you truly are.

So appreciate your wisdom, appreciate the lessons you've learned by getting your hands dirty, by trying and occasionally failing. This is what will make you a hero in your own experience. That's the most important lesson in this entire book.

Interview Hero Secrets in This Chapter:

- Failure is essential: if you aren't willing to fail small once in a while, you're bound to fail huge.

- We need failure to grow, because success isn't a very good teacher. When we're successful, we're not learning and growing as much as we do when we're stumbling and messing up.

- Failure makes you lovable, humble, relatable, compassionate, resilient, and brave.

- Knowing how to fail, pick yourself up again, and move on is an essential skill that employers screen for. So you're going to have to embrace failure stories if you want to get that job.

- What did you want, and what was the obstacle? This is the DNA of any story, whether it's a success story or a failure story. In the case of failure, you wanted something but you *failed to* overcome the obstacle. That's the only difference. I wanted _____, but I *failed* to overcome _____.

- Taking responsibility for the part of the failure that is yours in a self-aware and authentic way is what will make your story (and your life) more powerful.

- Defeat is temporary. Setbacks are impermanent. Mistakes are recoverable. Failure happens in a discrete moment in time. If your story doesn't appear to have a happy ending, that's because ***it's not over yet***.

Stakes, Payoffs, Vividness, and Villains

Believe in your flyness, conquer your shyness.
—KANYE WEST

ow that you've got the basic framework of an Epic Story down, let's look at some more nuanced components of a truly great narrative. They are:

- High stakes
- Brilliant payoffs
- Strategic "we"
- Vivid moments
- Great villains

HIGH STAKES

In the context part of the story, it's essential that the listener understand **what is at stake**. This is what creates dramatic tension. It's related to what you want, but it might go way beyond that. Let's go back to the Lenny story I shared in Chapter 6. In my story, the stakes are in bold:

It was my first consulting project, and I had to make the contract that would dictate the post-merger integration of two consumer goods companies. This required me to collaborate with every function of the client organization (a multibillion-dollar consumer goods company) and create an exhaustive list of business processes that needed to be taken over after the merger. We'd then decide who would own each individual process, how the target company would hand it off, and when the hand-off would be executed. **If we forgot anything, we'd risk not realizing synergies and making the whole deal worthless.**

For a story to satisfy the audience, there needs to be a big payoff at the end—a reward for their attention. This is the happy ending, and it's why so many people were angry about the *The Sopranos* series finale: there was no payoff. I'll get to payoffs next, but what holds their attention until the payoff is what's at stake. The thing at stake could just be the loss of the payoff or the outcome you desired. But usually, when you fail to reach a goal, there are other consequences.

Think in terms of the three kinds of negative impact I outlined in the last chapter:

External Consequences: Missed deadlines, lost dollars, increased costs, and other externally verifiable impact

Relational Consequences: Impact on other people and relationships, lost trust, hurt feelings, negative emotions, and problems caused for others

Personal Consequences: Impact on you in terms of negative emotion; loss of opportunity, confidence, or desired outcomes; and any other impact on you, your career, or your personal effectiveness

Any one or all of these could be part of the high stakes in your story. Here are some specific examples of high stakes to get you thinking:

- I wanted to get the promotion, and if I didn't hit it in January, I'd have to wait another year.
- I needed to win this client or it would set the firm back by a few million dollars.

- If I failed to finish the report on time, my boss would not be kind in my annual review.
- If I didn't finish the marathon, then half the money my friends and associates had pledged wouldn't go to the charity I was supporting.
- If I hadn't passed the test, I would have been deeply disappointed in myself at a time when I really needed the confidence booster.

So when you're building your own Epic Story, be sure to think about what was at stake and include that somewhere in the first half of your story. It can fit either in the context or in the conflict part of the narrative.

Written Exercise 8.1:
Identify the stakes.

For this exercise, go back to your success story. Take note of what was at stake. What would have been the negative impact if you had failed?

BRILLIANT PAYOFFS

Let's talk a little more about happy endings. One of the commandments of screenwriting is "Thou shalt save the best for last." Indeed, if you'll recall all of your favorite films, you'll remember that stuff goes crazy toward the end of the story. New villains emerge from the shadows, dragons multiply, and the hero gets put in increasingly impossible situations. The conflict reaches a fever pitch before the hero can have his way. In Freytag's Pyramid (another important framework in narrative theory), this is called the *climax*.

This "commandment" signals not only that the action has to be most intense close to the end of the story, but also that there needs to be an amazing payoff at the end of it. The audience/listener/reader needs to feel a sense of satisfaction and reward for having given focus for however long he or she was watching or listening or reading.

And—importantly—if you've used the Four C's to construct an honest story that emotionally connects, the interviewer will actually share in the good feelings of victory when you achieve your goal. Just like you did when Frodo beat Sauron and Marlin found Nemo and the X-Men beat the bad guys of the year: their victory was also yours.

So, you need a powerful ending to your story, and it's absolutely critical you don't pull any punches at the end. Here was the payoff from my story:

> In the end, the contract was a success and the merger went off without a hitch, garnering praise from the CEO. I learned a lot about client management, but what I'm most proud of is that Lenny got his first promotion in 10 years as a result of that project.

In my story, you might have noticed, there were three kinds of happy endings:

External Payoffs: Concrete, measurable results—things that verifiably changed in the outside world

Relational Payoffs: Qualitative results that show people were positively affected by the changes

Personal Payoffs: Personal growth and other personally beneficial outcomes

Let me expand upon each of these.

Three Kinds of Happy Endings

External payoffs—concrete and measurable results—are important and need to include numbers when possible, so at least some of your stories will end with numbers and measurements. These have to be real. Don't make them up. Don't fictionalize them, but really look for times where the impact of your work could be measured—preferably in terms of dollars and time.

Here are some examples:

- . . . this saved the company $10,000 per month.
- As a result, the process took three minutes instead of the usual six weeks.
- This created five new revenue opportunities worth a total of $2 million.

- The project won an internal award for innovation.
- I got promoted six months ahead of schedule as a result.
- The company realized its synergy plan.
- The management team could make decisions in real time for the first time in company history.

Notice how all of these examples are concrete and could be objectively verified. The revenue I helped generate is on the P&L. You can call my boss and hear about how I saved the company all that time with my innovative macro. Anyone can go into my office and see that award hanging on my wall. It's real and it's tangible.

Wherever possible, include concrete and measurable results. Qualitative results are also good, though, and they're especially important if you can't think of any quantitative results. Here are some examples:

- The CEO praised the plan as the most comprehensive in the firm.
- The team dynamics changed for the better.
- My mentee was more confident and more outspoken.
- My boss put me up for a promotion early.

Qualitative results tend to happen in relationships, and they always involve other people, so I call these **relational payoffs**. They're things that are said, thought, felt, perceived, or experienced, but they're not things that could necessarily be objectively verified in the outside world. Notice how in the last example: "My boss put me up for a promotion early," I'm commenting about something my boss did. It doesn't mean I actually *got* the promotion. If I got it, then it would also be an external payoff: "I got promoted six weeks early." It would be fine to include both in the story: "My boss championed me for early promotion and I got it."

Qualitative results like these are great when you struggle to find measurable ones. But pairing them together is even more effective. You want to give the listener a big payoff, so don't limit yourself to only one kind of outcome. In fact, in the best cases, you can include all three.

Finally, we come to **personal payoffs**: the changes that happened inside you. Some examples:

- This was the first time I was able to lead a project by myself.

- This experience was meaningful to me because it showed me that I can add much more value than was expected of me.

- I dramatically increased my confidence in my analytical abilities.

- I got much better at managing client relationships as a result of this experience.

- I learned how to code like a pro despite having no formal training.

You might even share the knowledge you gained: "I learned that the best way to influence people is to schedule a meeting before the meeting," for example, or "I realize that I was the biggest obstacle to my own success, and that has transformed the way I step up to huge opportunities." It could even be a philosophical result, an internal epiphany: "I gained a lot more insight into how the corporate culture worked and that it's the kind of place where I need to speak up more."

In any case, personal growth is an incredibly important part of your professional career. Anyone who is interviewing you is interested to know how you've grown and developed, so don't overlook these results as part of your story. Consider also including some emotion at this stage. As I mentioned in Chapter 6, there are two important places to include your feelings: when you are faced with extreme conflict and when you succeed in overcoming it. Here are some examples of ways to share your positive emotions as part of the story's happy ending:

- I was so proud that . . .

- It was so rewarding for me to experience . . .

- What I loved most about this was . . .

- To this day, when I think about this accomplishment, I feel . . .

Written Exercise 8.2:
Identify the payoffs.

Expand upon all the different kinds of positive impact that resulted from your accomplishment in your success story. Include external, relational, and personal payoffs.

Payoff Pitfalls

I see two common mistakes in happy endings: people *not* sharing the concrete and measurable results of their journeys or *not* sharing their own positive emotions about them. You might be tempted to downplay this part of the story for fear of seeming full of yourself. But avoiding the appearance of arrogance is the whole point of the Four C's framework and the Hero's Journey approach to personal storytelling.

Once you've shown me you at your worst—when you battled a conflict that threatened to overwhelm you, and how intimidated you felt by the challenges—I'm no longer judging you. Now I feel that I *am* you: I'm sharing in your struggle because you're mirroring my own. So if you deprive me of the payoff, I'll feel incredibly shortchanged. It's actually a dangerous move not to save the best for last when you're telling stories. Just think about *The Sopranos* series finale, and then don't do that.

THE STRATEGIC "WE"

There's a lot of confusion about the word "we." Let me give you an example of a really bad way to use the word "we" in your story. Imagine I'm answering this question: "Tell me about a time you managed a complex process." I know you're probably getting sick of hearing different versions of this story, but now that you know this one already, pay particular attention to what doesn't work about this version.

> Well, it was my first consulting project, and my team at BCG was helping manage the post-merger integration of two consumer goods companies. The timeline was tight, and we had to coordinate the activities of 10 different business functions to make sure that nothing was left out in the transition. If we forgot anything, we'd risk not realizing synergies and making the whole deal worthless.
>
> So we set up a project management office (PMO), scheduled several meetings, and used Excel to manage all the different line items we needed for the transaction services agreement. The clients were all doing this in their free time. In other words, there was only one dedicated PMO employee so we had to be really strategic about timing and communication.

We worked hard to ensure everyone bought into all the changes and ideas at each step through buy-in meetings and town halls. In the end, the contract was a success and the merger went off without a hitch, garnering praise from the CEO, and I learned a lot about client management.

OK. Now ask yourself these questions:

- Do you know what I did, personally, in that story?
- Can you see the impact that I personally had?
- Do you feel like you know me, trust me, or want me on your team?
- The answer to all of these questions is most likely a resounding *no*.

A lot of people "we" themselves in interviews thinking that it will make them seem less full of themselves. The logic goes like this: "If I focus on the team and share the credit with them, then I won't be seen as smug." But in fact, using "we" instead of "I" backfires immediately and has the opposite effect.

At best, it leaves the interviewer with a vague impression of who you are because your actions are hidden behind the smokescreen of "we." The interviewer only wants to know about you. "We" is a fictional character. It's an anonymous mass. Just think about all the ways we use "we." It can mean you and me. It can mean me and an indeterminant number of others. It can mean the entire human race. So, at best, "we" will confuse the listener and obfuscate the impact.

At worst, he will think you're taking credit for the work of others. After all, *you* are the one being interviewed; *you* are the one he posed the question to. If you bring other people into the equation, it will look like you have to take credit for other people's part of the story because you don't have enough to say about your part. Bad idea. We're each navigating our own individual Hero's Journey, after all.

Now look, I know—and so does your interviewer—that nothing in this world happens without collaboration. And you'll most likely need to bring up coworkers and your team, like my Lenny story. But the point of an interview is to discover your role, your impact, and your experiences, not that of your team. Your team isn't the one being interviewed; you are. So make sure you and only you take ownership of the conflict, choices, actions, and accomplishments that were truly yours.

What Makes You Uniquely You

Defining your conflict and the choices you've made will automatically help you do this. This is where you're truly unique. How you navigated this or that conflict will be different from what anyone else would have done in your shoes. So really make sure to define your conflict and not just the project's conflict or the firm's conflict. Drill down to your own personal challenge.

Here's an example of what I mean. Let's say the project is to re-vamp your firm's sales process. The project objective is to redesign the process, roll it out, and train everyone by June 1st. The conflict that the whole project team and even the company at large is facing is that this is an unprecedented level of change management, and there's a lot of time pressure.

But none of this is specific to you. Your specific role is to train managers on the new process and get them to train their sales reps. If you drill down to your challenge and look closer, you'll remember, hy-pothetically, that there were two specific managers who insisted that the old way was better and refused to comply. That's the challenge that you faced: getting two industry veterans on board with a new process and change initiative.

When the conflict is poorly defined, it's hard to grab onto the story. It's really hard to tell it in a powerful way. Imagine this is your conflict sentence: "I wanted to see the project succeed but I had to overcome change management challenges and time pressure, so I de-cided to . . ." It's going to be hard to clarify your choices and build a po-tent story because the challenge is so generic and all-encompassing: it wasn't *your* challenge on this project so it gives no insight into your Hero's Journey. Remember that the power of story is in specificity.

Let's look at a well-defined personal conflict. "I wanted to com-plete manager training successfully and with a 100% adoption rate, but I had to overcome resistance from two specific managers who didn't want to change. So I decided to take a tailored approach to these two managers." Then you elaborate on your approach. This is a much more engaging story because the two older employees will come alive in the interviewer's imagination, and she'll recall instances in her own professional life in which she encountered a similar distrust of innovative ideas in the workplace.

> ### Written Exercise 8.3:
> ### Clarify your conflict.
>
> Go back to your conflict sentence from Chapter 6 and ensure that you've pinpointed your personal conflict—the specific challenge you faced in the process, not the group's or team's challenge (unless you were the official team leader).

Where "We" Works

There are two places that you can use "we" effectively, and that's really in the beginning and the end of the story: The conflict and the choice need to be all about you, but the context and the change can include others. They don't have to, but they can if it's appropriate to your story. If you want to use the word "we" (or "team") to show inclusion of the team, the places to do that are at the beginning, in the context section, like this:

- We had six weeks to finish the project.
- Our client was having serious problems.
- My team was behind schedule.
- We were asked to . . .

But immediately after that, you want to home in on your role:

- My role was to . . .
- I had been tasked with . . .
- It was my job to . . .
- The burden of _____ fell on my shoulders.

Then you could also use "we" at the end in the change section:

- In the end, we finished the whole project on time.
- Ultimately, the project succeeded and we were all so relieved that . . .

- We met the client requirements and . . .
- The team was able to . . .

Introduce the team success at the end, but still be sure to home in on your unique success and results, what you learned, what you're most proud of, what was particularly important to you, and what you personally achieved in that experience.

Let's go back to my example. "Tell me about a time you managed a complex process." Here's the improved version, focusing on me:

> It was my first consulting project, and my team at BCG was helping manage the post-merger integration of two consumer goods companies. My job was to draft the contract that would dictate the hand-off of key business processes post-merger. The timeline was tight, and I had to coordinate the activities of 10 different business functions to make sure that nothing was left out in the transition. If I forgot anything, the company might not be able to realize synergies, making the whole deal worthless. So the stakes were pretty high.
>
> As part of the project management office, I established a process to track and measure all of the different business processes that had to be handed over after the deal closed. I used Excel to manage all the different line items I needed for the transaction services agreement. The clients were all doing this in their free time; there was only one dedicated PMO employee, so I had to be strategic about timing and communication.
>
> I worked hard to ensure everyone bought into all the changes and ideas at each step through buy-in meetings and town halls. *I also helped the dedicated PMO lead influence the team to complete their assignments on time.*
>
> In the end, we did it! The contract was a success and the merger went off without a hitch, garnering praise from the CEO. I learned a lot about client management, and we all felt an incredible sense of accomplishment at having achieved something so huge so fast.

How about now? Do you know what I did? Can you see the impact I had? Do you feel like you know me, trust me, want me on your team? Hopefully, the answer is yes, or at least much closer to yes than it was before.

One other thing I want to point out about this example is that I used the same basic experience to answer a very different question. In Chapter 6, I focused the story on my relationship with Lenny because that was the part of the project that mattered most to me. This story answered a different question. Lenny was only mentioned in passing in this story (the *italics*) because the question was about managing a complex process—the conflict and choices/actions centered on process management challenges. In the next chapter, I'm going to show you how to turn one experience into multiple stories by focusing on different conflicts within the experience.

VIVID MOMENTS

What makes stories relatable is the time-space reality they're based in and the emotions they evoke: the more real they seem to the listener, the more they will connect with him. When I understand that the story you're telling me happened last week, it's much more real than if it just happened "sometime." If I knew you were in your office, then I'll picture you there. If you tell me your boss, Harold, was giving you a hard time, then I'll form a mental image of what Harold looks like. Even knowing that he's a man gives me a place to start imagining.

Remember, storytelling is telepathy at a certain level. So you want to help your interviewer imagine what things looked, smelled, tasted, felt, and sounded like as if he were there himself. Now, don't go overboard—one or two specific vivid moments in your stories will make a big difference in their emotional impact.

A vivid moment happens when the interviewer can see, almost like he's watching a movie, what happens in the story.

If you go back to my story about Lenny, the vivid moment happened during that difficult meeting:

> There was a turning point in one session where Lenny was delivering some information about our process, and Mike, a longtime antagonist of Lenny, stood up and asked a snarky question, attempting to undermine Lenny's authority. And Lenny, for the first time, had a great response. Mike sat down. He was quiet. The whole mood in the room changed, and the project after that was much smoother sailing. Lenny was in charge.

Notice that I actually showed you what was happening in space and time. This is what will bring the listener into your experience. Since stories happen in space and time, the vivid moment is triggered by reference to space and time. Here are some sentences that have a vivid moment cue:

- I still remember the moment when . . .
- I was sitting at my desk when I realized . . .
- I checked my phone at 2 am and found . . .
- We were all sitting around the conference table . . .
- Sue came up to me after the meeting and . . .
- When I heard the news, I actually sat down and cried, laughed, tore the paper up . . .

That last example illustrates a complete vivid moment—time, space, and emotion. There is always latent or expressed emotion in a vivid moment whether you use emotional words or not.

Now if I had wanted to, I could have really amped this up. Like so:

> We were all sitting around the company's biggest conference ta-
> ble like we did every Wednesday at 10. And it was a usual meet-
> ing: Lenny was presenting, and the others were sort of listening
> and waiting for the time their function was discussed so they could
> give an update or a challenge. When Lenny came to Mike's function
> (he managed supply chain), before he even finished discussing the
> first slide, Mike rose to his feet and began challenging the rationale
> behind Lenny's timeline.
>
> But Lenny was ready this time. He shot down Mike's comment
> with a perfect rebuttal. Mike stood there a little slack-jawed, more
> stunned by Lenny's confidence than his answer. Mike sat down and
> stayed quiet. The whole mood in the room changed. It was a turn-
> ing point.

The very best vivid moments are focused on times of intense conflict. Remember the idea of a climax? I provided vivid details when I
recounted how Mike challenged Lenny because it was a turning point
in the drama—the climax. The villain was at his worst, and the hero

was prepared. The darkest and most challenging moments will be the best for connecting the interviewer to your experience—if he can see what you did when things were at their worst, he will be able to trust you on his team.

Typically, your vivid moment will center on the hero, which is you— on your personal actions, feelings, and choices. In the stories you tell about yourself in interviews, you must be the clear protagonist. In my vivid moment, Lenny was the hero precisely because my strategy was to lift him up and bolster his confidence, so the details zeroed in on his actions and feelings.

Now take note that your vivid moment doesn't have to seem terribly climactic or even particularly dramatic: this was just a meeting with people talking. Nothing special. But if you relate moments of great challenge in your story, it will create dramatic tension for the listener, focusing her attention, increasing her empathy with you, and inviting her to share your happy ending.

Written Exercise 8.4:
Brainstorm some vivid moments.

Now back to your success story! Brainstorm any and all points in the story that you could use to illustrate a vivid moment. Examine moments of conflict, challenge, negative emotion, or turning points. Come up with a few options and then play with telling the story a few different ways with different vivid moments.

GREAT VILLAINS

Sometimes the challenge is someone else. No doubt about it, some people suck. And even if they don't suck, they sometimes complicate our lives unnecessarily.

But if I say, "My boss is a jerk," then who looks like the real jerk? Me, of course.

The rule about opinions also applies to others. No one cares what you think about yourself. And no one cares what you think about others, either.

When the conflict in your story is posed by one or more persons, describing their actions will let you present them as the story's antagonists without making the interviewer think you're a gossip, a backstabber, or the b-word. In other words, don't say stuff like this:

- My boss was a micromanager.
- My officemate hated me.
- This particular client had a manipulative way of communicating.
- John was a total flake and never kept his word.

Adjectives, opinions, descriptions, and the internal states of others are off limits. Instead, focus on their actions. Here are some rewrites:

- My boss would ask to see the model I was working on each day at 4 and 10 pm.
- My officemate would frequently lock the door when I was outside and then listen to loud music on his headphones. He could never hear me knocking.
- One member of my team, let's call her "Sally," had sent three different emails to the team airing her grievances about certain coworkers. A few people asked me to speak with her about it . . .
- This client of mine, let's call him "Jerry," canceled three appointments at the last minute and failed to show up for two others.

Notice how when I show you the actions of the other people, you are able to draw your own conclusions about how manipulative, flaky, or jerky they are. I get to reveal the conflict without making myself look bad. Focus on sharing the actions of others, and you can tell the truth about them without making anyone uncomfortable. And notice how I gave the troublesome people pseudonyms. This just adds an extra level of courtesy and respect.

Don't shy away from conflict that involves the inconsiderate actions of others, but make sure to describe their actions rather than your opinions about them so the listener continues to empathize with you rather than viewing you as the villain instead.

Written Exercise 8.5:
What did the villains do?

If your success (or failure) story has one or more persons whose actions blocked your success—antagonists—take a moment and brainstorm what actions of theirs you can relate in the story to illustrate the challenge they presented, rather than describing them as jerks.

Interview Hero Secrets in This Chapter:

- Add high stakes to the beginning half of your story to keep the interviewer on the edge of his seat.

- There needs to be an amazing payoff at the end of the story to reward your listener for paying attention: it's why we can't stop listening to stories. So don't shy away from including awesome results at the end.

- Avoid answering questions with "we." At best the interviewer will come away with a very vague idea of the role you played in your stories, and at worst he'll think you're taking credit for the work of others.

- Include vivid moments so the listener can visualize the story. Details are key: time, place, weather, sounds, and images all help paint a picture of your experience so the listener can step into your shoes.

- When discussing the "villains" on your Hero's Journey, avoid name-calling and opinions. Instead, show your antagonists' actions in an objective way, so that *you* don't end up looking like the jerk.

Get Your Stories Ready for Showtime

All of us invent ourselves. Some of us just have
more imagination than others.
—CHER

PREPARING FOR GAME DAY

ection III of the book is all about every other kind of interview question. The preceding three chapters gave you the chance to construct some Epic Stories. But since Behavioral Interview questions are omnipresent and so difficult to answer thoroughly and gracefully on the fly, this chapter is dedicated to helping you prepare all your stories (or at least several) so that you will be ready to encounter virtually any behavioral question that comes at you.

As a reminder, behavioral questions can look like this: "Tell me about a leadership experience," "Tell me about a time you led a team," or "Tell me about a challenging professional relationship, and how you navigated it." The questions are limitless.

The infinite permutations of questions an interviewer could ask are enough to make your head spin. As you can imagine, there's a good chance you'll get asked questions that you haven't practiced or seen before. But the good news is, you don't have to be prepared for every question, and you don't need to memorize the answers. In fact . . .

DON'T YOU DARE MEMORIZE

If you haven't already, go to Google and search for "behavioral interview questions"; then scroll through some of the examples you'll find. One glance will show you that it would be nearly impossible to fully prepare for them all.

The three major interview pitfalls that I see clients fall into are these:

1. Not preparing enough (you're already solving that problem if you're reading this book)
2. Memorizing answers
3. Not quite memorizing answers, but over-rehearsing

I know you've heard that practice makes perfect, so why, you might ask, are memorizing and over-rehearsing such bad things? Well, remember, how the interviewer *feels* about you is more important than what he thinks. You need to pass the Airport Test. You need to make a genuine human connection. And if you memorize or over-rehearse, you're going to risk seeming robotic, or even worse, smarmy and overly polished. You know that guy who has the perfect answer for any question? He just doesn't feel sincere.

But memorizing will backfire immediately in another really important way. Consider these questions:

- Tell me about a time when you took ownership of an outcome.
- Tell me about a time you led a team under difficult circumstances.
- Tell me about a time you coordinated several others to a shared outcome.
- Tell me about a time you led a team and what you learned.
- When did you overcome a challenge within a team?

These are all subtly different questions. And these are just five of the infinite array of questions you will find if you Google "behavioral interview questions."

When you memorize an answer, you box yourself into one specific version of the story. And that's going to cause all kinds of problems for you in the interview. For instance, if the interviewer asks a different question from the ones you've memorized, you'll have to try to cram one you've memorized into that question, which you can imagine isn't going to work very well. Like shoving a square peg into a round hole.

Or, you're going to have to make up a completely new story on the spot. And that's really the worst-case scenario, because you'll have to think through the story while you are talking—at best you'll have to stumble through a half-baked answer and at worst your confidence will be destroyed.

SQUARE PEG, ROUND HOLE

Let me make this crystal clear. Imagine that you formulated a story about a key experience and memorized an answer to this question: "When have you overcome a challenge within a team?" Now imagine that I ask you this: "Tell me about a time you took ownership of an outcome." And imagine that your best example of taking ownership is the same experience about which you memorized the team conflict story.

If you're telling me about a time you took ownership of an outcome, you're going to want to include details about the complex situation (context), establish the fact that no one had stepped up to take ownership, and describe your decision process to step up and own it, including your concerns and fears about doing so (conflict). Then you'll want to delineate all the steps you took once you stepped up to steer the project to a good outcome (choice). And then finally, include any details about challenges you faced after you took the lead. The takeaways are going to be all about the benefits and the experience of taking ownership (change).

It's unlikely that you would have included all of these details, or maybe even any of them, if you had formulated a story about overcoming a challenge within a team and memorized it word for word. Because overcoming a challenge within a team doesn't necessarily entail taking ownership, it doesn't necessitate stepping up to lead. It doesn't necessarily have anything to do with learning how to manage when you're uncertain and unclear whether you're in the position to do so.

If you give the interviewer an answer to a question that doesn't perfectly match, he's going to think you're not listening to him. Even if he doesn't notice that you've only kind of, sort of, answered his question, he's going to be left with the feeling that you didn't fully connect with each other. To really connect with the interviewer, you need to answer his specific question.

Again, there are just too many questions to prepare fully for all of them. Instead, you just need to learn how to tell a story (check!) and then practice several different ones (coming up) so you get comfortable with your ability to improvise your Epic Stories that directly answer your interviewer's specific questions. These two fundamental skills—storytelling and spontaneity—will make you successful at all Behavioral Interview questions. The best news of all is that if you learn them now, you'll have them at the ready for any future interview or professional evaluation you will face. So let's get to it!

Here's how to get ready for a Behavioral Interview so that you can improvise your answers.

Step 1: Do a Success Inventory.

Step 2: Explore your stories.

Step 3: Know what to expect.

Step 4: Map your stories.

Step 5: Outline your stories.

Step 6: Practice a little.

THE WHOLE PROCESS

Before I guide you through each step, let me just give you the big picture. In Step 1, the Success Inventory, you're just going to free-form brainstorm all the accomplishments you can think of. It's fun and inspiring. Then you'll choose your five to ten most important ones.

In Step 2, you'll dig deeper into the details of each of those top accomplishments and then map them to various values that employers seek.

Step 3 is about doing some research. I'll touch on research in this chapter, but it's so important that I've dedicated all of Chapter 13 to it.

After you know what kinds of questions you are most likely to get in the interview and what you need to account for vis-à-vis your experience and the job description, you'll make some choices about the priority stories and character traits you want to put forward in the interview, and then you'll outline those stories. Those are Steps 4 and 5.

And finally, in Step 6, you'll practice your stories a little bit, so that the framework is embedded in your long-term memory and you're ready to improvise new stories on the fly.

Let's get to it.

Go grab the workbook if you didn't already: **careerprotocol.com/ih**.

Step 1: Do a Success Inventory

First, you're going to create your "A-List," your accomplishment list. This should be fun. It's your chance to take a walk down memory lane and remember every success you've had so far in life, both big and small. Saving a cat stuck in a tree even though you were afraid of heights, getting better at chess, earning a promotion ahead of your peers, or expanding your sense of self-confidence over years of effort— everything counts.

Write down everything that comes to mind. Don't censor yourself. Later, you'll select a few choice items from the list that seem most important to you. But for now, your goal is to make this list exhaustive with as little as possible left out.

Tip: If you find this exercise intimidating, just timebox it. Block off 30 minutes to complete the first seven written exercises below. A time of 30 minutes should give you a rich list to play with for the later steps, and you can always add more later. Work fast, don't think too hard, and write everything down. OK, set your timer!

Written Exercise 9.1:
List your professional achievements.

Write down what you've accomplished so far at work and in your career. Include entrepreneurial endeavors, internships, summer jobs, and part-time work—even being CEO of a lemonade stand at the age of seven— leave nothing out!

Some people like to work backward: starting with recent accomplishments. Others like to work forward in time, beginning with summer jobs in high school or even earlier endeavors. If you get stuck, try a different approach. For now, order doesn't matter. Just write down everything that comes to mind.

Be sure to include the softer more "human" accomplishments. Don't just stick to the successes that can be measured. Making a difference in another person's life, no matter how small, is noteworthy.

Here are some arenas of accomplishment at work to help jog your memory. Use these prompts to help you identify where you achieved something—a desired outcome.

- Helping others, mentoring, or coaching
- Communicating effectively with clients, colleagues, supervisors, or direct reports
- Managing complex processes
- Analyzing data, situations, or strategies
- Generating creative insights
- Solving persistent problems, big or small
- Going above and beyond
- Getting your job done well with limited resources or time
- Creating opportunities for others to participate or shine
- Taking the initiative to launch something new

Written Exercise 9.2:
List your academic achievements.

Write down any memorable academic accomplishments.

This could include high grades on tests, admission to tough schools, degrees you achieved, papers you published, certifications, academic awards, scholarships, or anything else that was meaningful to you in your academic life.

Written Exercise 9.3:
List your community and extracurricular achievements.

Now consider your extracurricular life. Write down every accomplishment you've achieved outside work: community service, sports, special-interest groups, hobbies, religious activities, cultural activities, or clubs. When in doubt, just include it here.

Consider accomplishments related to:

- Initiatives you started
- Projects you completed
- Games, contests, competitions, awards, honors
- Positions you were elected or appointed to
- Change you facilitated
- Innovative ideas you convinced others to adopt

Written Exercise 9.4:
List your team accomplishments.

Write down achievements in any arena of life where collaborating with, motivating, managing, organizing, and/or leading at least one other person was a meaningful part of the accomplishment.

There may be some overlap with these accomplishments and the ones you listed above. That's OK. Note down anything new that comes to mind.

Written Exercise 9.5:
List your personal achievements.

These are the accomplishments that happened between you and yourself. Things like losing weight, learning a new skill, becoming a better public speaker, rebuilding an important relationship with a family member, etc.

Again, there may be some overlap with this list and the others. That's OK. List any new achievements that have meant something to you, even though they might not register on the "resume radar."

Now set these lists aside for at least a few minutes.
Get up and get a drink of water. Stretch a little before completing the next exercise.

Now look at your lists holistically.

Written Exercise 9.6:
Identify and list your insights.

Take just a few minutes to draw out any insights you had while making your A-lists. What do these accomplishments say about you? What insights have you had about yourself and what you value? Do you have more achievements in one area than in another? Does any aspect of your lists surprise you? Whatever insights come to mind, just write them down.

As you extract insights, be sure to also take a moment and pat yourself on the back. Look at all the amazing things you've achieved. Look how you're dedicating your time and energy to things that matter to you. Appreciate how far you've come in life so far. There is always more to achieve, but it's refreshing to pause and admire what you've already managed to accomplish. I recommend you do this from time to time even after you finish this book.

OK. Now it's time to prioritize.
Choose your top five to ten accomplishments from all of your lists above. It's not that the others don't matter. It's simply that you're going to choose the ones you want to look at more closely and eventually speak more frequently about in interviews.

Don't just choose the five to ten you think are the most impressive. Choose the ones that are *truly most important to you*. Self-expression is key. Your goal is to talk about stuff that you actually care about, not just stuff you think others care about.

Written Exercise 9.7:
Select your Greatest Hits.

Write down your top accomplishments. Choose no fewer than five and no more than ten. Include accomplishments from at least three of the five types of successes you brainstormed—don't just stick to professional accomplishments. To the best of your ability, rank them in importance so you have a sense of your most important successes to date.

Step 2: Explore Your Stories

This part is the most rewarding, revealing, and important. It's time to expand upon your Greatest Hits and dig deeper into some of the details. You already know that stories take place in space and time and that concreteness and vividness are key to inspiring the listener. The "art is in the details," so to speak.

For the most part, the details of our experiences are buried away in long-term memory, so now is the time to recover them. I like to say that details are like your paint palette. They're the colors you're going to use to paint a picture of your life for the interviewer. If you can't remember the details of your experience, that picture isn't going to be very pretty: you're not going to be ready to improvise or tell Epic Stories.

This is where I made a lot of mistakes when I was preparing for interviews. I didn't take time to reflect on the experiences I had. I thought, "Hey, I know my resume. I *wrote* that resume. I know all my bullets. I know all my achievements."

But when I was in that McKinsey interview where I was forced to tell a roughly 10-minute story about a single line item on my resume, it all fell apart because I couldn't remember the specifics. Was it Dave or was it Peter who was harassing me in that one meeting? Wait, was this the time that I decided to resolve it by sending emails or did I make a phone call? Did I schedule a meeting? How exactly did I overcome the conflict in that experience? It was very hard to remember those details on the fly.

You need to reminisce before the interview. You've got a finite list now; you've got ten or so experiences you're working with, so with each of them, the first step is to stop and think through the details. You'll do this once and then leverage your work for every other interview you ever have after this.

Answer the questions below as they relate to your Greatest Hits. Again, timebox it. Spend no less than 30 minutes and no more than 60 to complete this exercise for all of your Greatest Hits.

Written Exercise 9.8:
Explore the stories.

Answer these questions for each accomplishment in your top 10.

a. **Describe the accomplishment like you are telling a friend about it.**

b. **What challenges did you face in the process?** (Use the three types of conflict to refresh your memory and flesh out the details.)

c. **What choices did you make to overcome the challenges?** (Include your thought process, strategy, and key actions.)

d. **What were the positive changes?** (Include the external, relational, and personal payoffs, including what you learned and how you grew through the experience.)

e. **What was most meaningful to you about this accomplishment?**

Here's an example, so you can see the kind of detail that will be helpful as you begin turning these experiences into stories that you tell professionally:

a. **Describe the accomplishment:** I managed an international recruiting effort to hire 10 expat staff to support the new and growing need for English support. I ended up only hiring the six people I felt were qualified, but all of them stayed till the end of their contract and all but one of them renewed.

b. **The challenges you faced in the process:** I had never done anything like this before; it was a complicated task, and I had no budget. Management put total faith in me, and I didn't want to disappoint by hiring ineffective people or having them quit shortly after joining. I was in Korea at the time, a difficult culture for expats with no real commitment to the country. I didn't know at first how to screen candidates or what to evaluate.

c. **How you overcame the challenges:** I used my own common sense and my understanding of the job to craft a job description and hiring criteria. I prioritized two criteria: writing ability as assessed in the cover letter and history with/interest in Korean culture. I posted the job on two international job boards and interviewed the small handful of candidates that met my criteria. I made offers to only the six people I felt were qualified and would be committed to the job. I got management's sign-off on each candidate and on my rationale for hiring only six instead of the requested 10.

d. **The positive changes and results:** All six hires completed their term, and five renewed their contracts. I got a raise and a promotion after this project and increased my self-confidence in my job. I validated my ideas about employee recruiting and retention and boosted my confidence and my profile within the organization.

e. **What was most meaningful about this accomplishment:** The fact that I came up with an approach that really worked and that I figured out how to produce high-quality results with no real experience with this process. I was proud of my creative problem solving and of my insightful ideas about how to evaluate future employees.

Step 3: Know What to Expect

Before you can decide which stories to highlight, out of all the possible ones you could tell, you need to understand which questions you're most likely to get in the interview. This means you need to have done some research. Read Chapter 13 and execute the research tactics I recommend there before your interview, but here is a partial list of all the things you will ideally do before a job interview in ascending order of difficulty. The ones at the bottom are also the most valuable.

1. Read the company LinkedIn description: this is the company's messaging to future employees, and it can reveal valuable insights about corporate culture.

2. Read the company website and do a search on "corporate values." Many firms publish their mission or a set of well-defined firm values.

3. Check out the company profile and employee testimonials on career websites such as vault.com, glassdoor.com, monster.com, etc.

4. Search "What to expect in interview at COMPANY" to see if there is any publicly available information about the kinds of questions you should expect. Some firms make information widely available.

5. Read the job description in detail to get a sense of the qualities and experiences the interviewer will ask you about.

6. Speak to people who currently work at the firm or who have worked there in the past and conduct in-depth informational interviews; ask them what to expect.

Do as many of these as you can before the interview (but, again, be sure to engage with Chapter 13 for much more in-depth research advice) and assemble a list of expected questions and qualities. For example, if you're interviewing with Amazon, the firm has published its 14 Leadership Principles. It's a very safe bet the interview will touch upon one or more of these values. Even if the interviewer doesn't ask about the principles directly (e.g. "Tell me about a time you learned and were curious"), he or she will expect you to reflect them in your answers. You'll want to think about how your accomplishments and experiences demonstrate that you are aligned with these values and how you can highlight them in your stories.

Step 4: Map Your Stories

After you've explored your stories and decided which qualities your target company or school is going to ask about, it's time to build your story map.

Here's what it looks like. I've included a template for this in the workbook, so be sure to go here: **careerprotocol.com/ih** and download it if you haven't already.

Your Story Map

GREATEST HITS	Leadership	Teamwork	Overcoming Challenge	Creative Problem Solving	Initiative and Resourcefulness	Upward Management	Persuasion	Process Management	Mentoring and Teaching	Data-based Problem Solving	Steep Learning Curve	Creativity and Innovation	Calculated Risk-taking
1													
2													
3													
4													
5													
6													
7													
8													
9													
10													

(YOUR GREATEST HITS — THE QUALITIES YOU WANT TO HIGHLIGHT)

Take your Greatest Hits (your five to ten most important life experiences) and write them in the first column. Be sure you have at least five or six, but depending upon how many questions you expect, up to 10 may be required. Take, for example, an MBA interview with a school alum. You're not likely to get more than five or six behavioral questions in such an interview, and typically you won't get more than two or three. So, five or six stories may be enough. But for a set of post-MBA McKinsey interviews, where you know you'll need one to two different stories for each of four or five interviews if you make it to the final round, you'll likely want 10 experiences from which you can construct more than 10 stories.

Once you've logged your experiences, decide which qualities each experience reveals about you. I've given you a head start here with several qualities that frequently show up in MBA and job interviews: leadership, teamwork, overcoming challenges, creative problem solving, and so on and so forth. Start with the ones that I've provided, but be sure to add any additional qualities you expect from your target company values research. Go beyond the obvious questions and be sure to include the ones that you know to expect.

When you're done, your story map is going to look something like this:

YOUR STORY MAP

GREATEST HITS	Leadership	Teamwork	Overcoming Challenge	Creative Problem Solving	Initiative and Resourcefulness	Upward Management	Persuasion	Process Management	Mentoring and Teaching	Data-based Problem Solving	Steep Learning Curve	Creativity and Innovation	Calculated Risk-taking
1 Getting early promotion	✓	✓	✓	✓	✓	✓		✓	✓	✓	✓	✓	
2 Leading team testing process	✓	✓	✓		✓	✓	✓	✓				✓	✓
3 Supporting diversity initiative	✓	✓	✓	✓	✓		✓	✓	✓				
4 Completing the model on time			✓	✓	✓					✓	✓	✓	
5 Finishing the ultramarathon	✓		✓										✓
6 Helping Sarah get a job	✓			✓	✓				✓				
7 Etc													
8 Etc													
9 Etc													
10 Etc													

Example

Take the highlighted example above, for example: leading the team testing process. This is a really robust experience because it demonstrates multiple desirable qualities and abilities. A lot of times you'll find that some of your most important experiences reflect multiple qualities, sometimes even all of them.

I've decided that this experience reflects leadership. There was a teamwork component. I definitely had to overcome a challenge. I showed initiative and resourcefulness in getting my job done. I had to manage upward because my boss was giving me a hard time. I had to persuade other people. I used process management to make sure that the team got everything done on time. I had to climb a steep learning curve. I used creativity and innovation in coming up with solutions to some of our roadblocks. I used calculated risk-taking when I had to make a few important decisions.

Be sure to think about any and all qualities that each of your experiences exhibits, because you're going to prepare a few different stories for your most important experiences. In the process of completing this template, reflect on the meaning of these characteristics and concepts. Think about what the words mean to you. For example, what does leadership really mean to you?

What does leadership really mean?

- Is it making decisions and running the show from a position of authority?

- Is it setting a vision for an outcome for a given project and inspiring others even if you're not involved in the execution?

- Is it guiding others through a process and being fairly heavily involved in their work; strategizing, work planning, delegating to others, and troubleshooting what they do?

- Is leadership more about mentoring others that you may not have any positional power over?

- Is it about influencing a group of people toward a specific outcome despite being the lowest member on the totem pole?

- Is it championing your own ideas despite having little influence on the decision makers?

You see, all of these explanations could define leadership. There isn't necessarily a right answer to this question. There's just the answer that you choose. As you're thinking about which of your stories reflect leadership, be sure to spend some time thinking about what leadership actually means to you, and how you want to present your version of leadership within the story.

It's something I recommend you be really overt about and include as part of your story. Something along the lines of, "Well, to me, leadership means influencing a group of people toward a specific outcome, whether or not I have any positional power." This shows self-awareness, it helps guide the story, and it creates a connection with the interviewer because he's getting a clear glimpse into your values.

Step 5: Outline Your Stories

Now you're going to outline stories that reveal the desired qualities. Remember the framework: context, conflict, choice, and change. To outline a story, I recommend you use bullet points. Remember—as I've said all along—you don't want to memorize your answers. So writing your answers out like essays is probably not going to help. Instead, you want to construct bullet outlines for each story.

Let's take my Lenny story, the transaction services agreement experience that you've read about a few times from different perspectives. Here is what the leadership story outline might look like for that experience:

Context

- First project: eager to prove self
- PMI for CPG

Conflict

- Tight timeline, unruly team members
- Team doubted Lenny; no ownership

Choice

- Strategy: coach Lenny to succeed
- Actions: pre-meetings, cheerleading

Change

- Merger success
- I got a good review
- Lenny got promoted

I used abbreviations above because the bullet outline is just for me. It's meant to be a blueprint for the story, and I'm going to memorize just this blueprint. You might even write out your story outlines by hand; that typically makes them even easier to remember later.

My outline above fits the version of the story you read before that focused on empowering Lenny to own the process. But what if I want to use this experience as an answer to a question about process management? I'm going to need a different outline because that would be an entirely different story. That one would focus on a different conflict and different actions:

Context

- First project—eager to prove self
- PMI for CPG

Conflict

- Had to coordinate activities of all functions (finance, manufacturing, supply chain, et al., + legal)
- Complex and no experience

Choice

- Strategy: shared doc to guide the process and use meetings to drive action
- Actions: spreadsheet turned to legal doc, group meetings to stay on top of things, 1:1 sessions with troublemakers

Change

- Merger success
- I got a good review
- Process was fairly seamless

The Lenny story highlights leadership and teamwork, whereas this outline highlights process management. It was obviously a challenging process because there were a lot of people involved. My strategy was to create a shared document to guide the process, and then I decided to use meetings to drive the outcome. My actions were to create a spreadsheet that we later turned into a legal document. I had group meetings to stay on top of things. I scheduled one-on-one sessions with troublemakers. In the end, the merger was a success. I got a good review, and the process was fairly seamless.

Notice how Lenny doesn't appear in this story, because although Lenny was really important to what I'm most proud of here, he wasn't actually that involved in the process management choices that I made and how I executed that part of the project. As you're thinking through your experiences, you'll quickly notice that the same experience can work for different stories. Where an experience is important and significant to you, you're likely going to prepare more than one outline to talk about that experience.

Now, remember that Epic Stories come from well-defined conflict and choices, so spend time looking closely at these aspects of your experience. What makes the two stories above different from each other is the conflict and the choices I made. The context and the change between these stories are virtually identical. If you try the same experience in a few different stories, you'll see how easy it can be to tailor a single story to different questions.

Step 6: Practice a Little

Once you've outlined your stories, it's time to practice a little so you can get comfortable with your stories—comfortable enough to improvise when the time comes. The idea is to take these outlines and make them yours, so that you can tell the stories in an inspiring way that's new every time. This is like the exercises or the drills that you do in sports or martial arts. You do a little bit of exercising so that you have the memory—the muscle memory, the experience of doing the move *well*—so that when you're on the playing field, you can improvise and respond to the curve balls that come at you. This way, when the interview goes off script, you can feel confident in the knowledge that you can be spontaneous while still telling an Epic Story.

So what does "practice a little" look like? Here we go, step by step:

1. Grab your outline.
2. Imagine your interviewer asks you a specific question, e.g., "Tell me about a time you led a team under difficult circumstances."
3. Tell the story out loud and time yourself. (Feel free to consult your outline the first couple of times you practice.)
4. Repeat Step 3 two to three times until you feel comfortable you have the flow of the story in mind.
5. Repeat Steps 2 and 3 again a day or two later from memory without looking at the outline.

The idea isn't to get this perfect. You're practicing so that you can memorize the *flow* of the story; to have the repeated experience of going through the steps of the story so that you know the territory well and can draw upon that memory in the interview.

Once you've memorized your bulleted outline, another great way to practice is to tell your stories to a few different types of people. Talk to your mom, talk to your boss, talk to a friend. If you can't improvise with them in person, then you can always pretend. You can always imagine that you're talking to your mom and think about how you would tell your mother this story. And then how would you tell this story to a friend; how would you tell it to the CEO of a company in your industry? Think of all the different ways you would change how you tell the story, depending upon the person you're talking to.

This is going to give you flexibility so that you can really improvise appropriately no matter what kind of person shows up to interview you.

When you explore this framework and practice it over and over again, you get to the point where you can start to make up stories on the fly. You'll need to prepare less and less for each subsequent interview because you'll have become so good at telling stories and mapping stories to the framework. You will have internalized and owned this skill.

PREP TWO FAILURE STORIES

Once you've prepped your success stories, I recommend you also choose two failures to work with. Just pick two that come to mind—don't overthink it. Choose ones that are in the distant enough past that you can demonstrate real improvement since. Avoid any that touch upon ethical issues or immaturity, such as treating others with unkindness or engaging in ethically questionable behavior. Then answer these four questions for each failure:

Written Exercise 9.9:
Explore failures.

Describe the failure like you are telling a friend about it.

1. What was the nature of the conflict you faced?
2. What mistake can you take responsibility for?
3. What was the impact of the mistake or failure?
4. What did you learn, and how did you grow through this experience?

Once you've explored the failures, build your outlines and practice a little.

Context
-
-

Conflict (The failure, mistake, and impact)

-
-

Choice (Actions you took to improve and grow)

-
-

Change (Growth and later success that resulted)

-
-

A WORD ABOUT TIMING

There is no real rule about how long an answer to a single question must be. Many will tell you that two minutes is a good benchmark. Others might argue 30 seconds is the limit. What's most important is that you're engaging the interviewer in a story that captures his attention and gives him real insight into the kind of person you are. If that's happening, then a long story or a short story will work.

That said, it's not a bad idea to practice telling stories within a finite time limit because it will ensure that your interviewer has enough time to handle all of his or her considerations and will reduce the likelihood that you'll get too bogged down in any one answer.

A good benchmark for an Epic Story (i.e., an answer about success or failure to a behavioral question) is two to four minutes.

A GOOD TIMING BENCHMARK

	CONTEXT	CONFLICT	CHOICE	CHANGE
min	0:30	1:00		0:30
max	1:00	3:00		1:00

Practice telling your stories within this time limit and you'll feel good about fitting everything into the conversation without sacrificing rich detail. The interviewer may want to probe into the specifics and ask follow-up questions, and if he does so, that should be considered a good thing! But construct your stories in the two- to four-minute range assuming that you won't be interrupted. Take on the responsibility of telling the whole story as you want it to be known and let the interviewer decide if he wants to know more about any part of it.

UM AND UH AND, LIKE, BODY LANGUAGE

There's a lot of advice out there about how to manage the 90+% of your communication that's nonverbal, including your body language, vocal tone, and use of filler words such as "um," "uh," "like," "actually," "kind of," "sort of," etc. While it's true that these nonverbal aspects of communication have a huge impact on the listener, the way to make sure you do them well is *not* to go to work on them directly.

During business school, I was forced (or at least strongly encouraged) to videotape myself being interviewed. The tape was then dissected and each gesture and vocal anomaly criticized for my benefit. Though I actually grew up in the theater and at the time was even somewhat of an expert on body language and vocal variety, this session obliterated my confidence. It made me paranoid about every minute detail of my physical appearance—and I didn't have the best self-confidence in that department to begin with. Even worse, it concluded with the advice that I needed to "watch my hand movements" and concentrate on "eliminating filler words from my speech." That in turn further distracted me in interviews.

Rather than focusing on connecting with my counterpart, I was worried about my hands and voice. I was squandering precious mental energy judging and evaluating my every move in my mind instead of focusing on inspiring the interviewer with my stories.

The advice to "work on your body language and tone" is a little like saying "You're a little bit ugly, so focus on being prettier." It's not really actionable, and it makes you feel terrible. If you want a beautiful tree, don't work on the leaves; pay attention to what's going on at the roots. The root of ineffective body language and excessive use of filler words is confidence—or lack thereof. For most of us, watching a videotape of ourselves will exacerbate insecurity, and nitpicking gestures and vocal choices will give further fuel to that critical voice in our head that threatens to sabotage interview performance.

So my advice for improving your body language and eloquence is to focus on the actions that give you more confidence. Practicing answering questions the way I outlined above is going to help you improvise in a concise and confident way. It's going to reduce the probability that you'll ramble and go off the grid, and it's also going to reduce your ums and uhs and other filler words.

Your body language will naturally exude confidence and comfort when you're fully present in the conversation, which you'll do more readily when you feel good about the inspiring stories you're telling. So be sure to think about outlines—just general structures for key questions. And then practice a little. You can practice in the mirror; you can practice in the shower; you can practice with friends and family. But don't tape yourself, and don't invite feedback on the minutiae of your communication style. It won't improve your confidence, and that's the most important thing for you to nurture and safeguard as you approach interview time.

If you've got a lot of time before your interview, then consider experimenting with your vocal range and quality. I recommend a great TED Talk by Julian Treasure called "How to Speak so That People Want to Listen."[1] He breaks down all the components of voice and gives you some ideas to play with. And though Amy Cuddy's work on power poses has seen some controversy, her TED Talk still offers some useful gestures to play with to uplevel your body language.[2] Approach these as experiments and play: have fun choosing your personal form of expression that best fits who you are.

PITFALLS

Before I end this crash course on Behavioral Interviews, I want to remind you of a few pitfalls that I hope you'll be able to avoid.

First, don't memorize your stories. I mean it. Even if you're not a native speaker of English, even if you're shy, even if you're worried about stumbling and umming and uhhing the day of the interview. You'll do much better if you write out key bullet points and memorize the outlines so that you can improvise the details, the word choice, and the story itself. This is what's really going to allow you to connect with the interviewer and not come across like a robot. Many clients tell me that this one change alone radically transforms their interview performance.

Likewise, if you're just trying to remember an essay you wrote or the cover letter you submitted and recount that in response to a related question in an interview, you're going to come off like a robot because you don't write the way you speak. This has the added disadvantage of making you seem distracted and unfocused because you will inherently be trying to recall your exact words in the written piece. That will take you out of the present moment and out of connection with the interviewer (hopefully this highlights yet another reason why writing answers out in full and trying to memorize them is a bad idea). So please don't repeat your essays or cover letter.

Finally, make sure you think through the details. If the details aren't top of mind, the story is going to be weak. Even worse, you're going to exhaust all of your mental energy and presence, and destroy your charisma, trying to remember details while you're telling the story rather than focusing on painting a vivid and evocative picture of your experience.

Interview Hero Secrets in This Chapter:

- Don't memorize or over-rehearse your stories; you're going to risk seeming robotic.

- There are just too many Behavioral Interview questions—no one can prepare for all of them. Instead, focus on strengthening your storytelling skills so that you can improvise and spin a yarn spontaneously.

- Create a Success Inventory of your Greatest Hits accomplishments so you'll know which main stories or themes you'll dip into for your answers—like an artist's palette.

- Create a story map of your most important life experiences, and create bulleted outlines using the Four C's that match the qualities each experience revealed about you.

- Only practice telling your stories out loud a few times to become familiar with them and to time yourself. Tell the same stories to people of various ages, backgrounds, etc., to force yourself to improvise and see how it feels.

- Feeling confident with your story outlines will boost your confidence, and that ease of delivery will be evident in your voice and body language. Don't sweat the small stuff like posture and inflection; just focus on your stories and the rest will take care of itself.

SECTION III

Values and Vulnerabilities

*Each morning when I awake,
I experience again a supreme pleasure:
that of being Salvador Dalí.*
—SALVADOR DALÍ

Hopefully by now you're well on your way to storytelling mastery. You can use storytelling in almost any interpersonal context—far beyond interviews—to entertain, connect, and relate to other humans. And now you know how to tell inspiring stories about any experience—even crushing failures—that will uplift and inspire you and your listeners.

Well done!

But we still have a few things to do to prepare us for that interview. Even though you understand behavioral questions, they constitute only part of the interview; there are additional question types to prepare for.

1.	Chitchat While You Are Sitting Down	⇒ Breaking the Ice
2.	Walk Me Through Your Resume	⇒ The 30,000-Foot View
3.	Behavioral Questions	⇒ Your Past and Behavior
4.	Point-Blank Questions	⇒ Your Values and Vulnerabilities
5.	Why Questions	⇒ Your Future
6.	What Questions Do You Have for Me?	⇒ The Interviewer's Experience and Advice
7.	Your Thank You Note	⇒ Appreciation

REVIEW OF THE SEVEN STAGES OF THE INTERVIEW

In this section, I'm going to show you how to approach question types 2, 4, and 5. The Walk-me-through-your-resume question opens the discussion and invites an executive summary of your life to date. We'll tackle that all-important question that creates your first impression in Chapter 11.

Then in Chapter 12, I'll talk about future-based questions that often begin with the word "why." Why do you want to work for our company? Why do you want an MBA? What are your goals (the why is implied)? These questions require you to share desires, goals, and your imagination.

Point-blank questions encompass almost every other line of inquiry you'll encounter that deals with the past or the present of your life, questions such as "What's your greatest strength?" and "What should I be concerned about in your candidacy?" Since this area of inquiry is so vast and requires a different strategy from behavioral questions, let's start with these in Chapter 10.

But all of these questions probe even deeper at what makes you you. They invite you to share your vision and vulnerabilities. They invite you to let the interviewer in on the secret joys of being yourself. Let's follow Salvator Dalí's example and get to the bottom of what's so awesome about being you.

Point-Blank Questions

Be yourself. No one can say you're doing it wrong.
—CHARLES SCHULZ

POINT-BLANK QUESTIONS

These generally look something like this:

- What's your greatest weakness?
- Why should I hire you?
- What is one bad thing your boss would say about you?

Do you know? Could you answer these questions off the top of your head? Would your responses make you worry that no one would hire you? How would you react if I put you on the spot right now and forced you to answer?

If this line of inquiry evoked even a trace of anxiety in you, then you understand the challenge of point-blank questions. They put you on the spot and force you to answer sometimes—but by no means always—uncomfortable questions.

People make two big mistakes when answering point-blank questions. First, they go on the defensive. It's easy to do! I've been caught like a deer in headlights more than once by these types of questions. The question is fired at point-blank range (hence the name), so you don't have time to think or the luxury of two to four minutes to get your point across. Being forced to answer tough questions so directly often makes people feel a little bit like they're under attack, so they become reactive to the conversation and to the interviewer, and that sabotages the rest of the conversation.

The second mistake people make is just simply answering the question. "What's my greatest weakness? I'm a perfectionist." Though the question is point-blank, it would be a mistake to give a similarly point-blank answer. Not just because you risk failing the Airport Test, but also because you're squandering a tremendous opportunity to reveal how awesome you are. Most point-blank questions are investigating your values and vulnerabilities, so they're a chance to share openly and deepen the human connection growing between you and the interviewer.

In this chapter, I'm going to give you some frameworks, tools, and strategies so you can make the most of these fascinating questions.

WHAT MAKES THESE QUESTIONS DIFFERENT

A story question, or behavioral question, is easy to identify. It begs a story: "Tell me about a time you led a team," or "Describe an experience in which you overcame a challenge." Point-blank questions, on the other hand, require a direct response. Because they're more pointed and frequently probe deeper values and personality traits, they often come after behavioral questions in the interview—after the interviewer has given you the chance to talk about your past experiences and to share a little bit about what you've accomplished so far.

You'll know you're in point-blank range when you're asked to respond fairly directly to an inquiry about you, your character, your values, your weaknesses, or your life. Here are just a few examples:

- What do you do in your free time?
- What kind of leader are you?
- What's your biggest weakness?
- What are three words your boss would use to describe you?
- What are you reading these days?
- How do you know you've had a successful day?
- What do you think about net neutrality?

And the list goes on into infinity. As you can see, the interview gets a little bit more up close and personal with these questions. They're designed to reveal your beliefs and your values. But they also put you on the spot a little bit—asking you spontaneous or surprising questions that require some thought. As a result, these questions also help the interviewer gauge how well you can maintain your poise and confidence under pressure.

You won't use the Four C's or tell a full story with a beginning, middle, and end. Indeed, your response will be much more concise, typically taking 30–60 seconds—much less time than for behavioral questions. So you need to cut right to the chase: there's no time to lay out the context and the conflict. Simply give a direct answer to the question.

SHOW, DON'T TELL

But it would be a mistake to just stop with a single-sentence answer for a few reasons. First is the Airport Test. Confident Humility, the Friendship Mindset, and enthusiasm are still in effect: you need to be forthcoming and frank in your response. But recall from Chapter 6 that you also need to do your best to avoid adjectives and opinions when talking about yourself. Instead, wherever possible, *show* your values and vulnerabilities instead of just telling the interviewer about them.

Let me give you a quick example:

Question: What's your greatest strength?

Wrong Answer: I'm a great communicator.

Airport Test fail, right? An interviewer couldn't help but doubt this claim and find you arrogant to boot. If you're like most people, you wouldn't feel very good giving an answer like this. And that's a very good sign!! It means you're not actually arrogant.

Here's a tip that's worth the price of this whole book: if something doesn't feel good, don't do it. Your bad feelings will tell you it's not a fit for who you are. Listen to your gut.

Here's a better approach that's just as direct but goes beyond the "tell" and engages a little bit of "show."

Question: What's your greatest strength?

Better Answer: I work really hard to communicate well, and I spend extra time and effort on this. For example, last week a member of my team sent me an email that really confused me. It seemed like she had ignored my instructions. But I gave her the benefit of the doubt and asked where she was coming from. Turns out she hadn't understood my instructions at all, so I took the chance to clarify. She did a great job once she got it, and I learned a better way to communicate with her in the future. I always believe communication is 100% my responsibility, and it helps me create harmonious teams.

This second version takes only about 30 seconds of interview airtime, but notice how much more it achieves than the first answer. It shows values, it shows a character struggling, it reveals what she does in difficult situations, and it makes a connection with you. You could easily imagine yourself in that situation—or in the situation of the confused team member! You're going to want to work with someone like that; someone who is committed to nonreactionary, effective communication. Airport Test pass.

The opportunity of these questions is to share your experiences and your character as vividly as possible, to evoke emotion and connection. When you approach these questions with an intent to vividly reveal your life and your values, you shift the dynamic. You're not simply reacting to the interviewer, and you're not merely giving your judgments and assessments; you're sharing your experiences—and that's always endearing, and it will feel good for you, too!

STRENGTHEN YOUR CORE VALUES

Let's consider a few different types of questions that typically appear in this point-blank section. The first I will call values questions. Questions like this:

- What is your greatest strength?
- What's your leadership style?
- What makes you the right person for this job?
- What do you bring to the table that no one else does?

- How will you be remembered in this job?
- What would friends say about you?

And lots more. These are the questions that get at strengths, abilities, and values. You'll know them when you hear them. Don't give in to the temptation to give a curt, opinion-based answer. Storytelling Rule #1 applies whenever you are talking about yourself: we want actions, not opinions.

How do you apply this piece of advice when the question is fundamentally asking you for your opinion? Well, naturally, I have a framework for you, and here it is. There are three parts:

POINT-BLANK QUESTIONS

THE ANSWER	A VIVID EXAMPLE	THE CONCLUSION
• Sum it up in one sentence	• Show one clear moment that shows *how you act*	• Learning, improvement, or belief that shows *how you think*

The first step is to sum up the answer in one sentence. Just give it to your interviewer. What is your greatest weakness? What is your greatest strength? Just answer the question, but don't stop there. Next, give a vivid example. Present one clear moment that shows how you act. Refer to the "better answer" above for a clear example of what this looks like.

And then there's the conclusion. This is the learning, the improvement, or the belief that shows how you think. It puts the period on the sentence and brings the answer back to your values. Here's another good example:

Question: What's your leadership style?

Answer: Well, I would say that I strive to be a compassionate leader. (THE ANSWER) For example, I once stayed up all night with a team member who was struggling to understand the firm's spreadsheets to make sure she could complete her tasks and learn the process for next time. (THE VIVID EXAMPLE) I found that it makes the experience much better for me and everyone else if we can understand each other's perspectives, especially on difficult projects. (THE CONCLUSION)

Here, I've given the answer. I've provided a specific example of what that behavior, value, or quality looks like *in action*. And then, I've revisited the question by showcasing what values are revealed by the vivid example I just gave. It shows how I think and what I believe. And it shares my experience rather than touting my opinions. The example and the happy ending give you a chance to understand me at a much deeper level than if I had just stopped with, "I would say that I strive to be a compassionate leader."

OPINIONS VS. EXPERIENCES

It's important to notice the word choice in the first sentence of the answer above. The question was, "What is your leadership style?" In the answer, I talked about the kind of leader that I *strive to be*. I did that on purpose. This furthers your Confident Humility because it acknowledges the fact that living up to any value is a never-ending journey—nothing in life is static or fixed, and you are either growing or shrinking, expanding or contracting, advancing or atrophying.

I show myself striving to be a better person—this evokes the feeling of the Hero's Journey, and you are back to empathizing with me as a character in an epic drama as opposed to reacting to my judgment and trying to assess whether or not you agree with it. Opinions evoke argument and disagreement; vivid details inspire connection and empathy.

KEY CONFIDENT HUMILITY PHRASES

Here are some more words that share experiences:

- I strive to be . . .
- I try to be . . .
- I make it my goal to . . .
- I like to think that I am . . .

- It's very important to me to be . . .
- I hope other people would say . . .

You can find your own phrases that communicate Confident Humility; these are just some examples to play with. But notice how different each of these feels than hearing, "Hey, I'm a compassionate leader! Everybody says so!"

Using these Confident Humility phrases creates connection with the listener because we can all relate to the experience of striving, having a goal, believing we're a certain way, trying to uphold a value, and caring about the impression we make on others. When you're talking about your strengths in these point-blank questions, you have a golden opportunity to reveal your values. And you do that by sharing experiences, not opinions.

GRACIOUSLY AVOID COMPARISONS

Now, you're going to encounter some tricky questions like . . .

- What makes you the best person for this job?
- What do you bring to the table that no one else does?
- How are you going to be better than your teammates?
- Why should I hire you?

These questions seem to evoke a comparison. If you've got a competitive streak like I do, you might be tempted to tackle these at face value and go in touting why you are better than others. But that would constitute a major Airport Test fail. Naturally, if you go on and on about how you're better than other people, it's going to be very hard to show that you're also humble (or likable). So, try to avoid comparisons.

Here are some ways to do that:

- Well, I can't speak about anyone else, but I'd like to think that I . . .
- Well, I hope that I am . . .
- Here's what I'm most excited to contribute . . .
- The reason this job is the perfect fit for me is . . .

- I strive to be . . .
- I'm sure there are a lot of other qualified candidates,
  but what I bring to the table is . . .

Avoid commenting on your competitors whenever possible and instead direct the interviewer's attention to you and your experience. Notice how the sharing experience words were brought out with these phrases. This mandate is doubly important for MBA or other grad school interviews. Though you're ostensibly competing with everyone else for a spot in the class, each program prides itself on a collegial and cooperative student culture. If you're willing to be so ruthless in interviews, that won't bode well for your future as a member of a collaborative community. So don't judge yourself and don't judge others—just vividly share your own experiences.

A caveat: this strategy will be right 99.9% of the time. That said, there are a few firms with cutthroat cultures where insulting your competitors is actually expected and desired. If you uncover this in your research, you may decide to ignore the advice above. But before you do that, ask yourself this question: do I *really* want to work in a place where I'll have to watch my back and where demeaning others is rewarded? If the answer is yes, then proceed. But you always have a choice. It probably feels better to you to work in a place where you will be treated with respect and kindness. So displaying that same treatment of others in the interview will help ensure you land at a place that aligns with your values.

YOUR BEST SHOT AT MAKING
A GENUINE HUMAN CONNECTION

Let's talk about vulnerability questions. Most people dread the weakness questions most of all, but when you show self-awareness about areas of possible improvement and have a plan of action for self-development, you win even more trust in the interview than if you deny having weaknesses in the first place. We're all human in the end, and we all need to confront weaknesses to grow and learn.

These questions are extremely important because vulnerability is what makes you human. In Chapter 7, I gave you tools that will help you talk about failure, so hopefully you're looking forward to utilizing those!! Likewise, don't be afraid of admitting a weakness, even if it's in the present tense! Just like failure questions, questions about vulnerabilities and weaknesses are a critically important moment to be human, to connect, and to reveal your emotional intelligence, self-awareness, and maturity. You'll earn more points talking about failures, mistakes, and weaknesses than you will talking about successes.

Almost everyone feels uncomfortable with the subject of weakness, so most likely your competitors will punt. They'll give weak answers. They'll dodge the questions. But whatever they do, they're probably not going to deeply reveal their humanity to the interviewer in this moment. But you *will*, and it will give you a competitive edge like no other. If you've been practicing failure stories, this should be easy.

Here we go. Here are some questions:

- What is your biggest weakness?
- What is the toughest feedback you've ever received?
- What's something you've learned through failure?
- What would your boss say is your worst quality?
- What is one thing you would change about yourself?

We're going to use the same framework to answer questions about vulnerabilities in a vivid way. First, give the interviewer the answer. Sum it up in one sentence. Then, give a vivid example. Show one clear moment that shows how you act and how it impacts you. And then the happy ending—the remedy and evidence of improvement.

TRY BEING HONEST ABOUT VULNERABILITIES

THE ANSWER	A VIVID EXAMPLE	THE HAPPY ENDING
• Sum it up in one sentence	• Share one clear moment that shows *how you act* and *how it impacts you*	• The remedy and evidence of improvement

MAKE YOUR WEAKNESSES WORK FOR YOU

All right, so here's an example:

> **Question:** What is your biggest weakness?
>
> **Answer:** Well, I would say that I can be too detail-oriented some-
> times. (THE ANSWER) For example, I was once building a giant
> model to predict the market size for a medical device and I just got
> completely lost in the numbers. When I finally came up for air and
> shared what I found with my manager, he pointed out that I really
> needed to frame the data in terms of the big picture. Ultimately, I
> had to go back and redo a lot of things, and I regretted wasting
> time. (THE VIVID EXAMPLE) But now that I've realized this weak-
> ness, I always make it a point to outline my analysis before I jump
> in and to always cross-reference my findings with the big-picture
> question at least a few times a day. On my last project, I finished my
> analysis much faster using this approach. (THE HAPPY ENDING)

You may recognize this story as the same one I referenced in the
failure chapter: the time I toiled away for days without my manager's
input. I chose the same story not for lack of other examples of failure
or weakness. Ha!! But rather to demonstrate both how the same experience can fit multiple questions and how weakness questions and
failure questions differ in approach even with the same subject matter. This weakness vignette reveals yet another aspect of that experience and where I struggled. But it's framed here not as a discrete
failure that happened once, but rather as a weakness that persisted
through time and one that I have to continue to be mindful of. In an
actual interview, I recommend you choose different examples if you
are asked both a failure and a weakness question.

WHAT IF THERE'S NO HAPPY ENDING YET?

That said, in the example above, I'm completely honest about the
weakness. I'm showing a true moment of human vulnerability, but I'm
also including the happy ending. I'm showing how I've taken concrete
action to improve on this and how my performance is indeed getting
better. It's always best to give examples that show how you've learned
from your mistakes and demonstrated at least some improvement. In

other words, examples of past weaknesses—stories where the happy ending is already apparent.

But sometimes you're going to get questions about *current weaknesses* that have a genuine present-tense impact on your future. Questions like:

- What is something I should be concerned about in your profile?
- What do you expect to struggle with in this job?
- Why is your GMAT or GPA so low?
- Which weaknesses are you still working on?

Basically, these are questions that force you to confront a current weakness or something that might impact your future success. Now, remember Storytelling Rule #8: *all stories have a happy ending.* If it doesn't seem like it, that's because the story isn't over yet.

Well, as it happens, sometimes in interviews you've got to talk about a story that isn't over quite yet. It's raw. The weakness is alive and well. It's still there with you today. We don't have a happy ending to bookmark the experience and provide perspective yet. But don't be afraid of these questions either. Like I've said, these are key moments for you to differentiate yourself in the interview.

THE WIMP FRAMEWORK

You want to tackle questions like this using the WIMP framework. And here it is.

THE WIMP FRAMEWORK

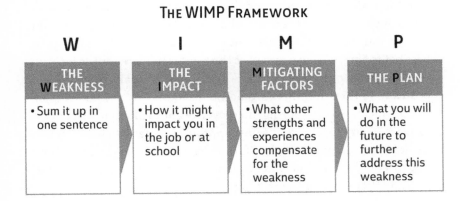

W	I	M	P
THE WEAKNESS	**THE IMPACT**	**MITIGATING FACTORS**	**THE PLAN**
• Sum it up in one sentence	• How it might impact you in the job or at school	• What other strengths and experiences compensate for the weakness	• What you will do in the future to further address this weakness

You start with the weakness. Sum it up in just one sentence. Then, talk about the impact, how this weakness *might* impact you on the job or at the school that you're applying for, showing that you've done some research and know what to expect. Then, talk about mitigating factors. What other strengths and experiences compensate for that weakness? Then, finally, show that you have a plan, what you will do in the future to further address this weakness.

Here's an example.

> **Question:** What is something I should be concerned about in your profile?
>
> **Answer:** Well, you might notice that I have only three years of experience in strategy and the job description calls for five. (WEAKNESS) I can imagine this will force me to climb a very steep learning curve very quickly. (IMPACT) However, I believe I have what it takes to do this job because in those three years I worked at a strategy consulting firm, and most of my projects were in this industry. I've had deep exposure to the primary strategic challenges I'll need to tackle in this role such as supplier relationships and ever-changing international market dynamics. (MITIGATING FACTORS)
>
> Still, I plan to use my first 30 days to quickly get up to speed through conversations with the rest of the team. I also hope to use the first initiative I tackle to do a deep dive into the other issues the company is facing, putting in substantial hours to develop the grounding I need to manage the rest of my responsibilities. (PLAN)

In this answer, you can see that the candidate is self-aware about her limitations. She's done the work to figure out what mitigating factors still make her a strong candidate, but she's humble enough to admit that she's still not there yet. She has a plan, and she's going to hit the ground running to tackle that weakness on the job. This is your best bet for presenting yourself as the right candidate for the job.

Almost no one will have 100% of the desired qualities for a given position. If they did, there would be no room to grow and the job would quickly become boring. Employers want to offer growth opportunities to employees, so it's only appropriate that you won't match the job description perfectly. Show them that you've thought about this carefully and already have a plan to use the role to improve yourself, and they will most likely want to work with you.

PERSONAL QUESTIONS

The last kind of point-blank question you might be asked is what I call *personal questions*. Questions about your free time, about what you're reading, where you get your news, a person you admire, and even discussions about current events. Now, these are questions that you really don't want to overthink—just act natural and answer the question. But wherever possible, give insight into your values.

Here's what I mean:

> **Question:** Who do you admire?
>
> **Mediocre Answer:** I really admire Thich Nhat Hanh. I've read all his books, and I saw him speak twice.

But this doesn't reveal very much about you, your beliefs, or even why Thich Nhat Hanh is interesting to you. Instead of that, why not try something more like this:

> **Better Answer:** I really admire Thich Nhat Hanh. I've read his books, and I particularly appreciate his views on seeking inner peace and unconditional love as the path to the greatest success.

Or . . .

> **Another Good Answer:** I really admire Thich Nhat Hanh. I've personally tried to implement his guidance on inner peace and unconditional love in my day-to-day life. I'm still struggling with it, but I've found that it's really helped me navigate challenges more gracefully.

In the mediocre answer, you just got the "what," the point-blank response. It's Thich Nhat Hanh. In the second two answers, you also got the "so what?" You got a glimpse into what admiration looks like in the speaker's *values* in the first answer and in her *experiences* in the second answer. Try this out. Whenever you can, don't miss a chance to share your values in an interview.

But these ideas are useful beyond the interview, too. You can use the tools of excellent communication in your daily life: when you're talking to your friends, when you're answering questions with people that you're just getting to know, or when you're talking about how your day went. Share experiences and values. It just feels good to communicate and connect based on what matters!

YOUR PERSONAL DEVELOPMENT PLAN

And speaking of tools that are useful beyond interviews, did you notice how that WIMP framework is actually a tool to cultivate your own personal development? You can use it not just to answer questions about weaknesses, but to assess them and build your personal growth plan. Here's what that looks like.

> **Step 1:** Take stock of the weakness. Name it. Pinpoint it. Figure out exactly what the weakness is that you're currently dealing with.
>
> **Step 2:** Then, assess its impact. How is it affecting you in your job? How is it holding you back? And how do you think and feel about that impact? Be honest with yourself.
>
> **Step 3:** Take stock of your mitigating strengths. What other aspects of your professional or extracurricular life, your skill set, and your qualities and abilities are offsetting this weakness? Which of those strengths and abilities might you be able to use to overcome or sidestep this weakness?
>
> **Step 4:** Then, develop a plan. First decide if you actually want to improve in this area. You're great just as you are, so you don't have to change! But if you're like most ambitious careerists, you love the feeling of growing as a person. So if this is a weakness you're going to tackle, then decide what you're going to do about it in the future. How are you going to grow? Whose feedback do you need? What kind of coaching might you seek? Do you want to take a class? Figure out how you're going to achieve improvement in this area and then implement a plan.

You can use this framework to communicate weaknesses and growth strategies to colleagues, peers, and superiors. Try this out when you're preparing for a performance review, when you need real advice or honest feedback, when you're trying to enlist a new mentor, or when you want your boss's support for a promotion. Tell them the weakness, its impact, the mitigating strengths you're leveraging, and your plan of action. Ask for their input and support. You might be surprised by people's eagerness to help when you take the initiative to be self-aware about shortcomings and develop a concrete plan to tackle them. You make it easy for them to contribute to your success.

Being great at interviews is ultimately just being great at communication. Don't just use these tools to get the next job you're seeking or to get into business school. Use them to be a more effective professional in every aspect and at every stage of your career.

Interview Hero Secrets in This Chapter:

- Show, don't tell. Don't resort to descriptions and adjectives. Instead, give a concrete example of your awesomeness in action.

- Try using phrases like "I strive to be," "I try to be," "I like to think that I am," or "It's very important to me to be . . ." when describing your qualities, because they share experience instead of giving your opinion.

- Graciously avoid comparing and contrasting yourself with your competitors. Instead, navigate questions that beg comparison by gracefully using phrases such as: "Well, I can't speak about anyone else, but I like to think that I . . ." or "I'm sure there are a lot of other qualified candidates, but what I bring to the table is . . ."

- Don't be afraid of divulging your weaknesses. You'll earn more points by talking about failures, mistakes, and weaknesses than you will by talking about successes.

- When you answer personal questions, make sure to address the "So what?" Don't just answer with one sentence, but reinforce your answer by explaining why—*why* is Martin Luther King, Jr., your personal hero? This will say a lot about you.

Walk Me Through
Your Resume

Find out who you are and do it on purpose.
—DOLLY PARTON

WALK ME THROUGH YOUR RESUME

O K. Now let's take a step back and go to the beginning of the interview. Up till this point, we've been talking about the guts of the interview—the juicy stories, the past experiences, the values and vulnerabilities—the stuff that tends to make up the bulk of the conversation. So now that you know everything that comes *after* the Walk-me-through-your-resume question, let's back up and address the introductory questions.

Most interviews start with a question like this:

- Walk me through your resume.
- Tell me about yourself.
- Walk me through your timeline.
- Tell me the short story of your career.
- Sum up your career in a nutshell.
- What led you to apply for this job?
- How did you get here?
- What's your story?

All of these questions invite you to give the interviewer a 30,000-foot view of your life and career. It's like seeing earth from an airplane; you get a panoramic shot of the landscape all at once. You have a chance to show the interviewer your entire career in a period of about two to four minutes. That's how we're going to start the conversation.

What's the purpose of these types of questions? Well, they're very practical. They're just to get you and the interviewer settled into the conversation. It's early; you don't really know each other very well. The interviewer probably didn't prepare very well for the conversation, so he needs an easy place to get started. You need a little bit of time to warm up. It also orients the interviewer to the big picture of your career. Now he has a sense of where he might want to probe, and even if he's not going to use this time to decide where to probe, it gives him an understanding of how your career has unfolded to date, so that he can later map your specific experiences onto your timeline.

THE QUESTION REALLY, REALLY MATTERS

But don't disregard these questions just because they're softball openers. In fact, I would argue that "Walk me through your resume" is *the most* important interview question. It's a make-it-or-break-it moment in your interview, because 90% of the time, it's the very first question. It typically takes a person about seven seconds to form an opinion about someone else. Your answer to this question gives the interviewer another two to three minutes to really make up his mind about how he's going to relate to you.

But even beyond your first impression, this is a golden opportunity to take ownership of the conversation. It's the first step in your relationship with the interviewer, so it's your chance to establish how you want to be known to this new professional friend. A lot of people don't see it this way and therefore blow off this question. Or even if they take it seriously, they approach it from the wrong angle. They reuse an old personal introduction or just go mechanically through their chronology. Even worse, I've seen people use their resume as a visual aid and then point by point explain everything on it.

If you don't have an inspiring answer to this question that gets you excited to talk about who you are, then you set the interview off on a reactive foot—you're just reacting to the interviewer instead of creating the connection on your own terms. If you want to elevate your confidence from the first moment, crush the Walk-me-through-your-resume question.

FRAMEWORKS, OH MY!

You've learned the Four C's, the three-part point-blank question framework, and the WIMP format for interviews. For the Walk-me-through, however, there isn't really a one-size-fits-all approach. I'm going to present, not one, but eight different frameworks for you to choose from and even the tools to invent your own. You have to be self-aware and choose the perfect one for you. If you've done the work in the previous chapters, you're already well on your way to knowing how to set up the big picture of your career to date. When you can open that conversation with a clear narrative about your career and why you're there, it's so much easier to make a connection and win the interviewer's trust and respect. And if you do, the rest of the interview is going to go much more smoothly.

The two most common forms of this question are as follows:

1. Walk me through your resume.
2. Tell me about yourself.

I like to think that "Walk me through your resume" is more squarely focused on your career, whereas "Tell me about yourself" is broader; it might include aspects of your personal life or your background. But the truth is, you can approach these questions the same way and show the interviewer exactly what you want him or her to see based on your background, your values, your priorities in the interview, and the position you're applying for.

When people answer these questions, they usually explain their life chronologically in terms of the choices they've made and why they made them.

FRAMEWORK 1: THE WHY LINE

Chronological Choices and Motivations Approach

- **Intro:** Tell a bit about your college, your major, and why.
- **Job #1:**
  - › Why
  - › Key learnings and contribution(s)
- **Job #2:**
  - › Why
  - › Key learnings and contribution(s)
- **Job #3:**
  - › Why
  - › Key learnings and contribution(s)
- **Conclusion:** Why you are so excited to be interviewing with the target firm or business school

WORKS BEST IF YOU HAVE WORKED IN VARIOUS COMPANIES

This framework is a chronological "choice and motivation" approach. It's really up to you where you start, but for most people, this doesn't stretch back before college, assuming you are more than a couple of years out of school. Your opening sentences can include a bit about college and/or a little about your background—where you're from and/or your culture. You talk about your major and why you chose it. Then you introduce your first job and explain why you took it. Maybe you add some key learnings or contributions or achievements from that job. Then you move on to the second job, explaining why you took that one, and so on and so forth until you get to the end. (If you're *in* college, then start with why you chose your school and course of study before moving on to primary extracurriculars and internships.)

I like to think it's a good idea to end any introductory question with a conclusion that ties the story to the present moment. It shows that you're proactively thinking about the future and excited about the current opportunity, and it further connects you to the interviewer. That's why he's talking to you after all, to learn how you fit with this opportunity! So if you choose this framework, you might end with why you're so excited to be interviewing with a target firm or business school as an extension of the choices and motivations that have brought you to this present moment.

LET ME WALK YOU THROUGH MY RESUME

So that you can see what this looks like, let me give you an example. When I was interviewing for business school, my Walk-me-through went something like this:

> I chose to major in philosophy because I fell in love with the discipline in the first class I took. I just loved working with concepts and ideas, testing them for reason and logic, and then drawing meaningful conclusions based on thinking. Studying philosophy really taught me how to think for myself.
>
> That's part of what enabled me to make a radical choice for my first job. I realized toward the end of college that my education, though robust and edifying, had failed entirely to expose me to the cultures, history, and philosophies of the rest of the world outside the West. This felt incredibly wrong to me, and I figured that the best way to remedy it was just to move east. To go live in one of these unknown cultures and learn through immersion. I chose Korea because it was the most unknown to me of the far east Asian cultures.
>
> My first job was teaching preschool English. Every day, small swarms of three- to five-year-olds would come into my little schoolhouse room, and with no instruction or guidance, it was my job to help them learn to speak English. This experience really taught me how to own a process and how to be responsible for the development of others. I invented my own curriculum and testing system to gauge their progress and ensure they were actually gaining ground. Then I parlayed that experience into a job teaching business English at the college level, and this further challenged my creativity and teaching skills: college students and preschoolers have very different criteria for attention and engagement.
>
> I fell into my job managing human resource strategy at KPMG by chance. Through a series of introductions, I became friends with the head of financial services at a major local firm. I started out

doing English training and expat recruiting projects, and when the firm was granted the new local license for a KPMG partnership, there suddenly was a lot more work to do to get the firm operating at international business and English standards.

That opened the door for me to get involved in some much more interesting work. I helped revamp the firm's marketing materials. I recruited many more expats to support English language operations at the company. I created English and communication training programs for the firm's now 700 employees. And most importantly, I helped draft the company's five-year strategic action plan. In the process, I exerted a lot of influence on how the founders of the firm thought about employee satisfaction as one of the metrics of success. They were exciting and exhilarating times.

And this is why I'm applying to business school. I've learned so much and had an impact. I realize that the business world is where I want to spend the rest of my career, but I feel that I've maxed out the impact I can have without some more formal business training.

The Why Line approach works really well if you're applying to business school. And it works especially well if you've worked in several companies and made multiple decisions throughout your career. If you've only been working in one company before your interview or if you've never had a full-time job, this probably isn't going to be your best framework. Likewise, if you're interviewing for a job that's very different from what you've done before, this might be the worst possible approach.

Imagine if I were interviewing for a product management role in a tech company and I walked the interviewer through my resume according to the above answer. Don't you think the interviewer is going to rule me out right away because I show no exposure to or affinity for the tech industry, no experience with customer management, and no ability to manage a complex process such as developing a product? No, this answer would not work at all in a whole range of other interview circumstances, and if I indeed were interviewing for a product management role in tech, I'd need to try a completely different approach that highlights completely different skills and experiences so as to connect with that specific interviewer.

I can't tell you how many people I've coached who started out walking me through their resume using this framework when they were applying for a job that was radically different from the ones they had held to date. That's a big mistake because it calls attention to the fact that you're less qualified for this job owing to your unrelated background.

Think about this: your recruiting manager doesn't really care why you did the things you did. MBA admissions directors might be interested in your motivations and career choices to date, which is why people frequently learn this approach during MBA admissions interviews. But MBA or any other graduate school admissions directors aren't evaluating your competence, skills, or experience vis-à-vis a *specific* job like a hiring manager would be. They're looking for a diverse cohort of good people: your motivations and choices are a huge factor in their specific calculus. But if I'm a recruiting manager, I don't care why you did the stuff you did in the past. What I want to know is this: what's in it for me in hiring you or even listening to you? Do you fit with my company? Are you going to perform in the role I'm asking you to do?

Consider this definition of good communication:

GOOD COMMUNICATION HAPPENS HERE

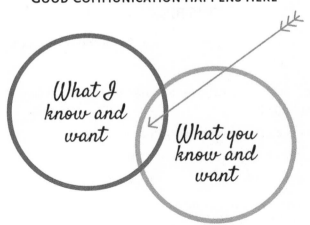

Your answers to each question, and especially this one, should resonate with your interviewer's wants, objectives, and knowledge base.

Remember this guy? We have to take his interests and feelings into account.

If your introduction connects with the firm, the role, and your interviewer, then he's going to like you. You're starting the interview off on the right foot, because you're showing him that you resonate with the qualities he's looking for. It's not because you're showing him that you're awesome. It's because *you're speaking directly to his concerns.* This is good communication. This is how you win hearts and minds. You talk about the intersection of what the listener knows and wants and what you know and want.

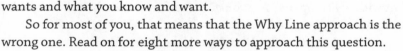

So for most of you, that means that the Why Line approach is the wrong one. Read on for eight more ways to approach this question.

HOW TO GET READY FOR THIS BIG QUESTION

When you're preparing to answer a complex question, your process has four steps:

1. Reflect on your values and characteristics that you want to highlight.
2. Choose a framework to organize your response.
3. Outline your answer according to the framework.
4. Practice a lot.

So we're going to do the same thing here for "Walk me through your resume." But with this one, you're going to practice a *lot* more, because it's virtually guaranteed that you're going to get this question, and it's critically important that you answer it with confidence and that you own your narrative from the get-go.

Here's the process for getting ready for the Walk-me-through:

Step 1: Reflect

Your first step is to reflect on some key themes in your career—key principles and philosophies that have guided you, and key strengths you've used to chase your dreams. Decide what your priorities are vis-à-vis this interview.

Step 2: Choose Your Framework

Then you'll choose a structure that allows you to highlight the most important features of your career to date as they relate to the company and role you're interviewing for. Bear in mind that you may use completely different frameworks if you have two interviews on the very same day, depending upon which company and role you're interviewing for, and by which employee. Choose the framework at the intersection of what you know and want and what the interviewer knows and wants.

Step 3: Outline

Then you'll outline your answer—just like you did for Behavioral Interview stories, but according to the Walk-me-through approach below that you choose.

Step 4: Practice a Lot

Then you'll practice more than a little. You still don't want to memorize your answer, but you want that outline to be fully emblazoned in your brain so you can confidently and eloquently walk your interviewer through your resume with aplomb while still being spontaneous.

No time like the present! Let's go through these steps together now.

REFLECTING UPON KEY THEMES AND VALUES

These exercises build on the Success Inventory and the questions you answered in earlier chapters, so be sure to grab the workbook here if you're starting on this page: **careerprotocol.com/ih**.

At this point, you've explored all the rich details behind your successes, as well as facets of your strengths, weaknesses, values, and personal qualities. So now you're going to take a step back and look at the big picture. Take a moment and review your Greatest Hits list and the details of your experiences. Then complete these written exercises.

Tip: As always, don't think too much. Just write down whatever answers come to mind.

Written Exercise 11.1:
Themes and values

1. Which accomplishments inspire you most? What are you most proud of?

2. Do you notice any themes or recurring patterns in your accomplishments?

3. Which **outcomes, results, or impact** have been most meaningful to you?

Now it's time to clarify your secret sauce: what you bring to the table that will enable you to add value to any company, team, or project. These next questions invite you to consider your strengths. Given what you learned as you explored the details about your successes, what can you conclude about your strengths? Feel free to be as braggy as you want here. No one else needs to see it.

Written Exercise 11.2:
Strengths

1. Which **skills** and **abilities** have you most relied on to achieve success?

2. What would you say are your three greatest strengths *as a professional*?

3. What are your intrinsic values? What are three to five things you would never change about yourself *as a person*, unrelated to external accomplishments or validation from others?

Bonus Exercise: Ask your friends, family, and colleagues how they would answer these questions. What would *they* say are *your* greatest abilities, strengths, and values, and write them down too.

Now that you've identified your strengths and most important values, it's time to decide your priorities for this specific interview.

Written Exercise 11.3:
Personal priorities

1. What are the three most important things you want other people to know about you?

2. What if you could only choose three accomplishments to sum up your whole life to date? Which three would you choose? (Pick the ones you care most about, not the ones you think others would find most impressive.)

3. If you had to choose only one accomplishment to sum up your career, which would it be?

4. What are the top three things you want to make sure this specific interviewer knows about you?

5. What is the single most important thing you want to make sure this specific interviewer knows about you?

HERE'S AN EXAMPLE BASED UPON MY PERSONAL ANSWERS:

Exercise 11.3: Priorities (Angela's Example)

1. **What are the three most important things you want other people to know about you?**

   › I love working with and empowering other people, and I will seek to do this no matter what my job is.

   › I value communication, and I will always work hard to communicate clearly and understand others.

   › I love to learn and will languish if I'm not being creatively challenged on a regular basis.

2. **What if you could only choose three accomplishments to sum up your whole life to date?**

   › Moving to South Korea when I was young and building a whole new life speaking a foreign language.

> › Getting a job in consulting and then transitioning into a role supporting women and recruiting that was much truer to my passions.

> › Writing this book. It has taken me 20 years to finally finish something at a book scale. (I've started about six books and eight screenplays but never finished one till now.)

3. **If you had to choose only one accomplishment to sum up your career, which would it be?**

> › The Korea accomplishment really tells everything you need to know about who I am, what I'm made of, and what I value.

4. **What are the top three things you want to make sure this specific interviewer knows about you?**

> › I'll seek to uplift everyone around me.

> › I love learning and will seek ever steeper learning curves wherever I can find them.

> › I'm loyal to impact and great ideas, not to processes or protocol—I can be counted on to be creative but not to toe any kind of line.

5. **What is the single most important thing you want to make sure this specific interviewer knows about you?**

> › I'll seek to uplift everyone around me.

Beyond your personal priorities, it's useful to think about the key features of your candidacy that are most relevant to this specific interview. So be sure to engage with Chapter 13 so you can do some company research and analyze the job description vis-à-vis your strengths and gaps.

MAKING CHOICES

Once you've done that, you'll want to make some choices about what you want to call the interviewer's attention to.

Written Exercise 11.4:
Priorities for *this* interview

1. Which three of your professional experiences or accomplishments are most relevant to this role?

2. What one to three key transferable skills do you need to highlight from your background?

3. Which one or two weaknesses or experience gaps do you need to proactively mitigate with a discussion of related strengths, alternative skills, or a growth plan?

4. What are the top three things you want to make sure the hiring manager knows about you vis-à-vis your fit and enthusiasm for this role and company culture?

5. What is the single most important thing you want to make sure the hiring manager knows about you vis-à-vis your fit with this role and company culture?

Once you've made some decisions about the messages you most want to convey and have done some company research, it's time to build your Walk-me-through.

Below I've outlined several different ways to walk someone through your resume. Choose the framework that best introduces your career or educational history in roughly two to four minutes. Some frameworks are chronological, others work backward, and still others discard time as an organizing principle altogether. It all depends on what you want to highlight and what you'd like to conceal through omission.

FRAMEWORK 1: THE WHY LINE

I described this one earlier in this chapter. It's everyone's default setting. It's worth considering, not because it's likely the best option for you, but because it can help you understand what almost everyone else will do in their Walk-me-throughs.

Chronological Choices and Motivations Approach

- **Intro:** Tell a bit about your college, your major, and why.

- **Job #1:**

  › Why

  › Key learnings and contribution(s)

- **Job #2:**

  › Why

  › Key learnings and contribution(s)

- **Job #3:**

  › Why

  › Key learnings and contribution(s)

- **Conclusion:** Why you are so excited to be interviewing with the target firm or business school

> WORKS BEST IF YOU HAVE WORKED IN VARIOUS COMPANIES

Some examples of who this is great for:

- The tech engineer turned product manager interviewing for another product role at a competitor. She would explain a bit of her technical background, then explain the transition to product management and her new learnings, and then connect all that to the role she's interviewing for.

- The English teacher turned curriculum director interviewing for a school principal role. He would show his progression through the ranks of academia and why he wants to move ever upward in the system.

- The MBA applicant who is following a linear and predictable path: accounting to corporate finance pre-MBA and continuing her trajectory in corporate finance at a more strategic level post-MBA, for example.

FRAMEWORK 2: THE BACKWARD TIMELINE

Work Backward from Your Most Recent Role

Work backward, sharing your **highlights**.

- In my most recent role I have . . .

    › Share one key accomplishment and/or learning at Career Co.

- Before that I was . . .

    › Share key learnings at Job Co.

    › In addition, I . . .

- **Conclusion:** Now I want to join your company/pursue an MBA because . . .

The Backward Timeline emphasizes your most recent experiences. If what you're doing right now is most important to elaborate on and you want to lead with that, try this framework. You're going to talk first about your most recent role, sharing one or more key accomplishments or learnings. Then you'll say, "Before that, I was . . ." and talk about what you were doing before. At the end, you'll circle back around to the present moment: "I want to join your company/pursue this MBA because . . ." It's similar to the Why Line, but it just goes backward instead of forward, and it puts your most recent experience up front so that you can spend more time talking about that and really put the emphasis there.

Some examples of who this is great for:

- The actor turned sales manager who's interviewing for a new sales position. He'd emphasize his sales experience and then just mention that previously he was a paid actor for several years.

- A private equity associate who's been working on healthcare deals and who's interviewing for an operational role in a healthcare company. She would just mention that she spent two years in banking prior to private equity, but those skills are significantly less relevant to the role she's applying for, so she would speak much more about her recent work.

- The MBA applicant who wants to transition into marketing and who recently had the chance to dabble in marketing at her consumer finance company. She would spend half of her Walk-me-through talking about her most recent projects and then just briefly outline her trajectory leading up to that project.

FRAMEWORK 3: THE HIGHLIGHT REEL

A Thematic Approach

- **Intro:** Establish two to three key themes in your career to date *related to known aspects or values of your target firm and role.*

- **Theme #1:**
  › Key learnings and contribution(s)

- **Theme #2:**
  › Key learnings and contribution(s)

- **(Optional) Theme #3:**
  › Key learnings and contribution(s)

- **Conclusion:** Why you are so excited to be interviewing with the target firm

---

Our third framework, the Highlight Reel, isn't chronological. Instead, you're going to pick two or three themes to frame your life and/or career to date. These themes will help you align your demonstrated values with those of your target firm. Here are some examples of themes:

- Cross-functional team management

- Designing new processes

- Teaching or mentoring

- Delivering results under time pressure

- Driving insights with analysis

- A passion for the customer experience

- A love of creative problem solving

These are just a few examples. Look back on your career and think about some of the core themes that have really embodied your choices and all of your accomplishments. Work with the top two to three things you want to make sure your interviewer knows about you as a starting point. Then end with why you're so excited to be interviewing with the target firm (but remember that the middle part isn't chronological).

You might say, "I like to think that my career can really be summarized by two themes—helping people communicate more effectively and empowering teams to do better work. I discovered how important communication is in my first job, but in my current role, I focus on fostering effective collaboration with my teams using transparent communication. For example . . ." By laying out your core themes and tying them into aspects of your experience, the interviewer learns what is important to you.

Some examples of who this is great for:

- Any radical career switcher, because it calls attention to your transferable skills and values while deflecting attention from your eclectic or unrelated work history.

- The MBA applicant who is making a very big shift post-MBA. Say someone aiming to transition from nonprofit management to strategy consulting would use this framework to highlight themes that align with consulting: collaborative teamwork and a love of strategic problem solving, for example.

- On the flip side, a strategy consultant transitioning into nonprofit management might use the Highlight Reel to focus on two at-work themes (such as his love of problem solving and multiple projects that focused on operational challenges) and then use the third theme to talk about his extensive community work that relates to the organization at hand.

FRAMEWORK 4: THE SINGULAR FOCUS

> ### Focused on One Core Theme
>
> Choose **one core theme** and highlight it in each role.
>
> - **Intro: I would say that most of my career has centered on____. In my first job I . . .**
>   - › Share an example of how you____.
> - **In my most recent job, I focused on . . .**
>   - › Another example
> - **Outside of work, I . . .**
>   - › An example of how this theme manifests outside of work
> - **Conclusion:** How will you be able to continue to do ____ in the new company or through an MBA

An alternative approach to the Highlight Reel is to choose just one core theme in each role you've had to date. You can make this chronological or not; it's up to you. You would start by saying, "I would say that most of my career has centered on (theme)."

Some examples:

- Understanding technology
- Simplifying and improving processes
- Empowering others to excel in their own work
- Creating opportunities for marginalized people
- Applying rigorous financial processes to achieve better bottom-line outcomes
- Advancing technology in the healthcare space

You can make it as specific and detailed as you want, but make sure that it reflects a quality relevant to the firm and role and a quality that's important to you. Make sure that the value aligns with the company, the team, and the role you're going to be playing. Then share some examples of how that theme has reflected itself throughout your career. Conclude by explaining how you'll be able to continue acting on that theme in the new company or through an MBA.

This framework works great for the same situations I outlined for the Highlight Reel, but it's especially effective for people who've either had a long career to date or held many jobs and roles, not all of which are directly relevant to the current position. It allows you to highlight just the most important feature of your career vis-à-vis this interview.

FRAMEWORK 5: THE GROWTH INVENTORY

> ### Highlight Your Key Learnings So Far That Are Relevant to the Role
>
> - **Intro:** I think of my career as being marked by three major phases of my professional development.
>
> - **Step 1:**
>   - › In my first role, I had to learn . . .
>
> - **Step 2:**
>   - › Leveraging skills I learned in my first role, I then had to get up to speed on . . .
>
> - **Step 3:**
>   - › But none of that helped me figure out how to . . .
>
> - **Conclusion:** What kind of growth and learning makes you most excited about the current opportunity

GREAT IF YOU LACK KEY JOB REQUIREMENTS BECAUSE IT SHOWS YOU ARE SCRAPPY

The Growth Inventory is another great framework for career switchers. But it's especially great when you're underqualified for the job, because it gives you a chance to show how you learn. It also proves that you're scrappy. You might start by saying, "I think of my career as being marked by three major phases of professional development." This is only one way to start. You could also start by saying, "I've learned a lot in my career," and go from there. But the idea is that you're putting the emphasis on things you've learned.

For instance, what core skills and lessons did you acquire in your first job? What about in your second job? And so on and so forth. The interviewer should notice increasing skills and abilities if you take the chronological approach. Then you want to conclude by talking about what kind of growth and learning makes you most excited about the current opportunity. Again, highlight key learnings that are relevant to the role you're applying for.

Consider using this framework if you lack key job requirements, because it really shows that you're a scrapper—someone willing to work hard to prove yourself worthy of the role. It shows that your orientation toward life is one of personal growth. If you use this approach, the interviewer will see that you're ready to learn and grow in the new role.

FRAMEWORK 6: THE THICKENING PLOT

Highlight Key Turning Points on Your Career Path

- **Intro:** I would say my career has been marked by three major turning points.

  SUPER SELF-AWARE ANSWER

- **Step 1:**
  › I started doing _____, but in this first role (learning and/or an accomplishment) I discovered **INSIGHT 1** . . .

- **Step 2:**
  › This led me to (different company or role) doing____. And here, I (learning and/or accomplishment) and eventually realized that **INSIGHT 2** . . .

- **Step 3:**
  › Then I finally had **INSIGHT 3** when I was doing____ . . .

- **Conclusion:** Why all of those insights have led you to this company and role and why this is the perfect next step

---

The Thickening Plot is one of my personal favorites because it gives you the chance to show self-awareness and mindfulness about the kind of person you are. Instead of focusing on growth, you focus on turning points and insights. At step one, you might say something like this: "I started out teaching English. In this first role, I taught children and I managed the lesson plan over the course of an entire year. I was responsible for their learning and progress. The most important thing about this role, though, is that it really showed me that I care about the growth and development of others. Every single role I've taken since then has manifested this passion in some way."

Next, go on to step two: "This led me to a different company (or role) doing something else." Now you want to talk about the insight you had in this job, and how it led you to your next step. Again, you can have two or three insights here, and make sure that you highlight how each role incorporated the previous insights and moved you closer to the ideal role and impact for you.

Finally, explain why all of these insights have led you to this company and this role and why this is the perfect next step. I love this framework because it creates a singular cohesive narrative (like the Hero's Journey!), and it shows how self-aware you are. It emphasizes that you're someone who is striving to know yourself better and make better choices.

Use this framework only if it accurately reflects your career and the current role. Think carefully if this is the right one for you. It's not a good one to fake. You should make sure to use it only when you can authentically connect the job that you're applying for with insights from your past career to date.

FRAMEWORK 7: PARALLEL LIVES

Include Significant Aspects of Your Extracurricular Life

- **Intro:** Establish two or three key areas of your life.

- **(Optional) The backstory:**
  - › Key elements of your pre-professional life

  > GREAT IF THEY SAY "TELL ME ABOUT YOURSELF"

- **Step 1: In my professional life . . .**
  - › Key learnings and/or contribution(s)

- **Step 2: Outside of work . . .**
  - › Community, entrepreneurial, or extracurricular life: key learnings and/or contribution(s)

- **Conclusion:** How your target firm will let you continue growing on each of these important dimensions

This framework breaks your life into two segments, the personal and professional. The backstory is optional: you might start by talking about your pre-professional life, your upbringing, or college. It would only make sense to include that information if it's relevant to the rest of your story or this role. For example, if you're an immigrant and your extracurricular activities have centered on supporting immigrant communities, then your background is relevant.

One key thread of the Parallel Lives framework is your professional life. Here you're going to talk about the key learnings and/or contributions in your career. This part can be chronological or thematic, but you'll talk first about your professional life, then move on to your personal, entrepreneurial, or community life. This is a great one to use if you're asked, "Tell me about yourself," or if you have significant community or entrepreneurial accomplishments, especially ones that might not be fully captured on the resume. Be sure to conclude by talking about how you see your target firm fostering your growth in both of these important parallel lives.

FRAMEWORK 8: MEETING YOUR DESTINY

When Your Career So Far Was Building to This Role

- **Intro**: I am so excited to be speaking with you today because this is my dream job. My career to date has given me the precise skills to contribute in this role.

- **Step 1:**
  › In my first role, I gained _____ (skill or experience relevant to the role)

  ONLY USE THIS ONE IF IT'S TRUE!

- **Step 2:**
  › Later on, I developed (skill or experience relevant to the role)

- **Step 3:**
  › And most recently, I have been working on_____ (skill or experience relevant to the role)

- **Conclusion:** It's really a dream come true to be interviewing for this job, and I'm excited to have this conversation.

Use this when the job you're applying for is truly one that you've wanted for a long time. You could start with something like this: "My whole career to date has been leading me to this role. I am so excited to be speaking with you today because I think/feel that I've spent the last X years amassing the precise skills that will allow me to contribute in this role." Then proceed to highlight three core skills/experiences that have prepared you for this opportunity. You do not need to touch on every role; just highlight the most relevant experiences: that could be just one project within a specific job, or it could have to do with company culture and soft skills—you decide which elements of your past have most prepared you for your dream role.

Only use this one if it's really true. I once worked with a client who wanted to work for Google. She had wanted to join Google after her MBA because of the company's ability to expand economic opportunities in certain developing economies that she was passionate about. Instead, she drifted around multiple smaller tech companies across the gamut of technologies that Google deals with: telcos, internet service providers, and software as service startups. She had applied for a job at Google three times prior. When she showed up for her first interview this time around, she had a 50-page deck outlining her personal strategic plan for Google's expansion in her chosen geography. This approach to the Walk-me-through was the only one that made sense for her: it was a dream job she had been working toward for years.

She got the job.

FRAMEWORK 9: INVENT YOUR OWN

YOUR FRAMEWORK
Invent Your Own!! Make It Yours!

- **Intro**: Invent your own.
- Typically, you will want to have two to four steps or sections to the story.
  - › **Section 1**
  - › **Section 2**
  - › **Section 3**
- **Conclusion**: Wrap it up in a way that ties to the company and role at hand.

I've given you eight different frameworks to work with, and one blank template to do with as you see fit; so now you have several different ways to think about introducing yourself in an interview. These days, when I talk about myself, I never introduce myself the same way twice. I don't even have a framework anymore because I've been doing this for so long. Each time I talk about myself, I invent my introduction in the moment based upon the person I'm talking to and what I'm talking about. So, once you've used a couple of the other frameworks a few times, try inventing your own.

Don't just go with the default framework that you're comfortable with, and don't even use any of the eight above if you think you can create one that's better for you. Try experimenting with your own innovative Walk-me-through. Take a real point of view on what your life is for and what it means to you, and then construct your answer around that: slice and dice experiences into two to four sections that allow you to account for your most significant achievements and meaningful learnings. Make sure you conclude by connecting the Walk-me-through to where you are in this current moment. Connect it to why you're excited to be applying to this business school; why you're excited for this job opportunity. Make it yours. Use two to four minutes as your timing benchmark and have fun!!

Let me give you a few more tips as you set out to craft the perfect Walk-me-through.

KEEP IT POSITIVE

I recommend that you focus on the positives because negativity doesn't sell. So if you left a job because you had a bad boss, or you got fired, or you got laid off, or you just got bored, leave that out! This is a mistake I see people make all the time when they go with the Why Line framework when instead they should be choosing the Highlight Reel or the Backward Timeline. Think really carefully about whether the reason *why* you did something is all that relevant. And then if you decide it *is* relevant, make sure you reveal only the inspiring reasons. Here's an example of what I mean.

> **No:** I was let go of my first consulting job as part of a mass layoff. But I was ready to leave anyway, so I joined the marketing team of Consumer Co.

Yes: I joined the marketing team of Consumer Co. after consulting because I had always loved consumer-facing projects and it was a natural step to focus on the consumer experience.

The second one omits the reason she left consulting and instead focuses on the reason she was excited to join Consumer Co. These are both 100% true. The Walk-me-through isn't the time for TMI, or to tell the whole truth, or to air your dirty laundry. If you include the sordid details of your career in this first answer, the interviewer is going to assume the worst: either that this layoff is the best story you have to offer and it only gets worse from there or—perhaps even more damningly—that you have no emotional intelligence or self-censorship ability. All communication is essentially editing, so point the listener to what you want him to see and leave the rest out. Keep it positive.

But beyond avoiding negative details, it's important to express your enthusiasm in a concrete way. For example, share what you loved about your work, what you've enjoyed so far, the projects that excited you, what you appreciated about the company or job or even your co-workers, and other positive aspects of your career to date. Don't just say, "I really loved the work I was doing." Instead, say, "What I really loved was designing a work plan and then executing it on a timeline of my own choosing." Your descriptions here not only lend your excitement authenticity but also give you an opportunity to slip in some of your personal values. You didn't just like XYZ. You liked XYZ because it allowed you to (insert a statement about your values here). This last sentence tells the interviewer so much more about you. It's vivid, and it will evoke your own (and therefore the interviewer's) enthusiasm.

PRACTICE DOESN'T MEAN AIMING FOR PERFECTION

Once you've chosen a framework, create a bulleted outline just like we did for point-blank questions and behavioral questions and then practice it. I recommend practicing this response a little more than the others because it will, without a doubt, come up. Still, resist the urge to memorize: that will make your answer sound cardboardy, overly scripted, and therefore disingenuous. And don't practice it so much that you accidentally memorize it. One way to ensure this doesn't happen is to practice the same outline with different words every time. Try walking your mom, your boss, your hairdresser, and your college friend through your resume.

Practice it just enough so that the outline is in your long-term memory and it feels comfortable and familiar. But again, please, please do not memorize. I know you're going to be tempted to ignore my advice on this one because you know you're going to get one of these questions. But resist!

TAILOR YOUR APPROACH EVERY TIME

If you're interviewing for a marketing job today and a product development role tomorrow, your answers should be different. If you're talking to a big tech company today and a small tech startup tomorrow, your answers should be different. Even the framework you choose in these cases could be different. The further away your experience is from the role you're interviewing for, the more creative and thoughtful you need to be in your choice of framework to call the interviewer's attention to what you want him or her to take away about you. Your Walk-me-through should showcase industry, company, and role fit, so don't recycle the same Walk-me-through for every job. Take the time to think carefully about how best to make that first connection with your specific interviewer and his firm.

Just think about this: you might get an interviewer who is an HR manager, who just joined the firm last week and is only two years out of college. Conversely, you might interview with a partner of the firm who's got twenty years of experience in the industry. Don't you think you're going to introduce yourself a little bit (or a lot!) differently to those two people? You have to. You're trying to make a connection. You're trying to communicate with them on their level. So, don't memorize your answer. Outline it and then practice enough to solidify the outline in your memory.

I also recommend that you play with a few different frameworks so that you can begin to be flexible and enjoy introducing yourself on your own terms. No matter what approach you choose, I encourage you to get creative. Talking about yourself is always about self-expression, so genuinely express yourself! *You* are what makes you awesome. There is no one else like you in all the universe throughout all of time. And that's your competitive advantage: you're one of a kind!!

So introduce yourself your way and find the approach that really inspires you. The best-case scenario is that you'll inspire yourself while walking the interviewer through your resume, and that enthusiasm is infectious!

Interview Hero Secrets in This Chapter:

- The interview will begin with a Walk-me-through-your-resume question. This is your chance to take ownership of the conversation. Don't blow this off: choose a framework that helps you shine from the first moment.

- Whichever framework you choose, make sure your answers resonate with the interviewer's wants, objectives, and knowledge base. Good communication happens when your interests and the interviewer's interests coincide.

- There are four steps to answering a Walk-me-through-your-resume question: reflect upon your values and principles, choose your framework, outline, and practice. Practice these types of answers more than the others because you know for a fact that they'll come up.

- Keep the Walk-me-through positive: draw the interviewer's attention to what you want him to see, not the stumbles and setbacks. There will be time for those later.

- Tailor your answers for different audiences. You never know who your interviewer will be. Will he be a fresh hire about your same age, or a senior executive your parents' age? Think about how your story will connect with all different types of people.

Why Do You Want This Job?

Do not do what someone else could do as well as you . . . Care for
nothing in yourself but what you feel exists nowhere else.
And, out of yourself create . . . the most irreplaceable of beings.
—ANDRÉ GIDE

WHEN YOU'RE NOT THE
BEST CANDIDATE FOR THE JOB

Let me tell you about a time I was chosen for a competitive job despite being *the least qualified* applicant. Now you already know that I famously failed to get a summer internship during my MBA in my chosen field: consulting. That was a tough year for everybody. It was just after the dot-com bubble burst, and companies had cut back on MBA summer internship budgets. So faculty members at the University of Chicago Graduate School of Business allowed MBA students to apply for their faculty research internships.

It was a very competitive process, because as MBAs, we were competing against PhD students who were far more qualified to conduct the intense statistical analysis the jobs entailed. There was only one internship I was interested in, and it was with Professor Mike Gibbs. He's an awesome guy and at the time (and now) was one of the leading thinkers in the field of organizational economics. His intern would need to collect publicly available corporate performance metrics and then run regressions and other statistical analyses against that data combined with a huge dataset of employee satisfaction surveys collected across hundreds of publicly traded companies. The hypothesis was that increased employee satisfaction yields stronger corporate market performance. I would need to use pretty sophisticated statistical software that I had never even heard of at the time. But it was a groundbreaking study, and it was directly related to the very reason I had decided to pursue an MBA in the first place: to forward the movement toward greater happiness at work. So I applied.

During the interview, Mike asked me what analysis I had done in the past and what qualifications I had for this job. I confessed. "Well, I'll tell you what: I got an A in statistics, but I've never done anything like this before. I applied to business school because I wanted to help people be happier at work, though, so this project is directly in line with my personal passion." Then I told him all the classes that I'd taken that were associated with that subject matter and shared some experiences learning new and difficult subjects quickly. I continued, "I know I'm going to have to work hard to get up to speed on the software, but I'm not worried about that because I'm truly passionate about this position."

I got the job despite the fact that I was the single *least* qualified applicant. Literally every other candidate had more directly relevant experience than I did. He later told me he was taking a risk in hiring me, but that he couldn't resist because we shared the same passion. He trusted that I would learn the ropes quickly because I genuinely cared. The other applicants had more skill, but they weren't pursuing the opportunity because they had a personal stake in the research themselves. Man, I had to work hard that summer to impress Mike and make his investment in me worth his while. And that meant that I did even better work as a result. In the end, it was win-win for both of us.

WE WORK HARDEST WHEN WE PERSONALLY CARE

Not every hiring manager will make the same call Mike did, but you can bet that employers understand the dynamics of personal incentives. They know that people work harder when they have a personal vested interest in the outcome or impact of their work. They know that top performers are usually well-aligned with their sense of purpose in a given job. And they know that if you have a selfish interest in what you're doing, you'll naturally work harder and smarter.

This is why interviewers ask about your future. If they can get a glimpse of your vision, they can draw conclusions about how well-aligned the opening is with what you really want for yourself. They need to get a sense of your desires.

This is often the last part of the conversation because it's the most intimate. Desires cut right to the core of who we are. Think about it; aren't there wishes, dreams, and wants you've got that you've never told anyone? Or maybe you've shared them with only one or two really close friends or family members? Our desires are closest to our hearts and therefore the absolute most vulnerable thing to talk about. Even more vulnerable than weaknesses and failures—because our desires have not yet come to pass. Wishes and wants are in the magical realm of the future—they live in our imagination and in our hearts—two very precious places that we keep mostly to ourselves.

QUESTIONS ABOUT FUTURE DESIRES

Let's look at some questions about what you want and why. For MBA programs, they can look like this:

- What are your short-term goals, and what are your long-term goals?
- Why do you want an MBA?
- Why is now the right time to pursue an MBA?
- Why do you want to go to our school?
- How will attending this program help you achieve your goals?

For job interviews, it's just a variation of these same questions.

- Why do you want to work for our company?
- Why do you want this job?
- What about this role appeals to you?
- Where do you see yourself in three, five, or ten years?

These questions all talk about the future; they connect directly to your values and your desires. This is where the interviewer is beginning to picture you working at his company, joining his school, or collaborating on his team. It's when your relationship is starting to move to the next level from something casual and theoretical to something concrete and plausible.

As you look at answering why and want questions, your keys to success are enthusiasm and concreteness. The interviewer needs to know that you're inspired by the possibilities his firm or school would provide. And he needs to know that you have an accurate sense of what the program or job offers and how that fits with your personal objectives. Crushing this part of the interview can help you make up for any number of weaknesses in your profile because it enables the interviewer to really picture you succeeding in the role. He won't be able to get that image out of his head as he considers who he'll advocate for when it comes time to make a final decision.

HOW TO GET READY FOR THESE QUESTIONS

So, how can you convey authentic enthusiasm about a job or a school? You may think this is easy, but it's also an easy answer to fake. Everyone will have thought about this, and everyone will have planned an answer. Most of them will be boilerplate and flattery. Stuff like:

- I just love your product and I really want to help it succeed.
- I love the firm culture because it's so collaborative.
- I've spent my career building sales skills and now I just want to apply them to a product I like.

Answers like these are generic and pandering. To the interviewer, they will feel hollow at best and disingenuous at worst because they lack concreteness and true passion. If you're dialing it in, the listener will feel it. Enthusiasm is unmistakable: when it's real you just know it.

So just like we did for the other core question types, we need to do a little digging into your genuine wants and passions before you can build a great answer to this question. You need to believe that this job is going to give you something you truly want. If it doesn't, then don't apply in the first place.

So, let's start with the self-awareness building blocks for all questions about the future, motivations, whys, and wants. Here they are:

- Your vision for your career—what do you want in the long term and why?
- Your needs for your next steps—what do you need to gain from this next opportunity that will help you get closer to your long-term objective?

- How your needs align with this opportunity—what does the company or school offer that fulfills your short-term wants and needs?

OK, so clearly a necessary step to be able to answer these questions effectively is figuring out what you really want in the first place: we need to be a little bit selfish before we begin preparing our answers to these questions. Here are a few exercises to help you home in on your long-term vision.

YOUR LONG-TERM VISION FOR YOUR CAREER

First, let's build your Career Bucket List. This list helps you think and dream big; it's what keeps you moving into the future and strategizing in the medium term. The long-term part of your plan should always be pie-in-the-sky dream stuff, like where do you see yourself long term? Where do you see yourself in 10 years or 15 years? What do you want to achieve before you retire?

In thinking about your long-term vision, you want to focus as much as you can—be as specific as possible—but aim high. Long-term goals should be lofty and ambitious. You should ideally have no idea how you're going to make them happen. It's a wish list.

Written Exercise 12.1:
Create your Career Bucket List

Long term in my career, I want to . . .

1. Lead _____ (what do you want to have ownership of?)

2. Achieve _____ (what do you want to accomplish?)

3. Learn _____ (what knowledge and expertise?)

4. Experience _____ (what experiences do you want to have?)

5. Impact _____ (what kinds of outcomes and results?)

6. Work with people who _____ (what kind of people and culture?)

7. Be _____ (what do you want to be able to say about yourself?)

8. (Add anything else you envision for your career long term . . .)

BE HUMAN CAPITAL GREEDY

Now, given that those are your long-term ambitions, think about what you need to gain next. Rome wasn't built in a day, and you won't achieve your Career Bucket List next year. So you need to be both a long-term visionary (that's what the last exercise was for) and a short-term pragmatist (thinking strategically about what next steps will move you in your preferred long-term direction).

In other words, I recommend you prioritize learning in your next job. Choose the position and seek the opportunities that will most expand your experience, skill set, and knowledge base. This is the currency you will cash in on later in your career.

During my MBA, I wrote a paper about the long hours MBAs end up working in consulting firms and investment banks when I took Nobel laureate Gary Becker's PhD Human Capital Economics class. My coauthor and I found that consultants and bankers make less money per hour than their general manager counterparts immediately after business school. Cash payments tell one story, but there is another very important form of compensation we earn at work: knowledge.

Consider two kinds of knowledge capital—specific and general.

- **Specific Human Capital** evaporates when you leave the company. Stuff like how to use the billing system, where the copy machine is, political chains of command and communication.

- **General Human Capital** follows you for life—critical thinking skills, Excel modeling, PowerPoint storyboarding, effective meeting management, etc.

The power of general human capital is why an MBA costs so much these days and why people will continue to pay for it. The knowledge capital you build in those two years in most cases pays off. It's also why, post-MBA, people love management consulting despite its notoriously challenging work-life balance—because consulting pays way more general human capital than do most other roles, increasing your potential for long-term earning and success.

The amount a company will be willing to pay you is a function of how much your human capital is worth to the company. Especially early in your career, make sure you're getting paid in general human capital. It's more valuable than cash in the beginning because it's the base upon which you will build the rest of your career.

In your career, I recommend you go beyond your duties to cultivate your knowledge capital: earn your wisdom. Be general human capital greedy. Make sure you're climbing a steep learning curve and developing yourself. Enlist mentors to help you grow, and seek cultures where apprenticeship is part of the business model.

And then, when facing a job search or an interview, create your own Developmental Objectives List. Think about what your next role or educational opportunity will give you that gets you one or two big steps closer to your vision. What will it allow you to learn and experience and what skills will it give you the chance to develop that you can bank on for the future? Work backward from your big, shiny future and figure out what you really want from the next year or two of your career. Be as concrete and specific as you can.

Written Exercise 12.2:
Build your Developmental Objectives List

My next job must . . .

1. Give me the chance to learn _____ (what knowledge and expertise?)

2. Help me to develop _____ (which skills and abilities?)

3. Enable me to experience _____ (what experiences do you want to have?)

4. Allow me to impact _____ (what kinds of outcomes and results?)

5. Permit me to work with people who _____ (what kind of people and culture?)

6. (Add anything else you must get next . . .)

MAP YOUR NEEDS TO THIS OPPORTUNITY

In your answers include a little bit of you and a little bit of the target companies or schools—so it's important that you know about them and how they fit with your needs. Hopefully, you already know this from your research. If not, the next chapter is all about research.

To decide which of their offerings is most exciting to you, you can work backward from what you want to gain to what they offer. Think about your goals, and then do research against those objectives. If you want to build quantitative skills, find classes and clubs that help you build those skills at your target MBA school. For a company, learn about the company's mentoring and training in this area and how much your job will require these skills.

Alternatively, you can work forward from the role or school you're recruiting for.

Written Exercise 12.3:
Your selfish interest in the role

Think about it: in the job you're applying for . . .

1. How is this role an interesting stretch for you?

2. What will you learn in the first 90 days?

3. What skills are you excited to develop in this role?

4. What experiences most interest you in the job?

5. What plan do you have to quickly fill any experience gaps?

6. And what part of the job are you most excited about?

Select the two to three aspects of the company, culture, role, and job tasks that are most meaningful to you and exciting vis-à-vis your developmental needs and objectives and then organize your answer according to the framework below.

YOUR FRAMEWORK FOR WHY AND FUTURE QUESTIONS

These questions have an even simpler framework than the rest, just two steps:

YOU + THEM

In your answer to each question about future goals, include a bit about your selfish motivations and a bit about what the company or

WHY DO YOU WANT THIS JOB? 233

school offers. For longer answers (such as listing out multiple reasons why you want to work at the company or attend the school), be sure to organize each part of the answer into two to four "buckets."

Let's look at some examples.

Questions about goals:

- What are your short-term goals, and what are your long-term goals?
- Where do you see yourself in three, five, or ten years?

   Answer for a Job: *(Function or industry related to the role you're applying for)* is my field of passion, so I anticipate building my trajectory within it. Longer term I hope to *(something concrete from your Career Bucket List)*. [YOU] I am particularly excited about this role because it will give me the chance to *(one to three things this job will give you from your Developmental Objectives List)*. [THEM]

   Answer for a Grad School Interview: *(Function or industry you've identified as a passion)* is my field of passion, so I anticipate building my trajectory within it. Right after I graduate, I expect to do *(target role in type of company you're most interested in today)*. Longer term I hope to *(something concrete from your Career Bucket List that would follow naturally from your short-term goal)*. [YOU] I am particularly excited about your school because it will give me the chance to *(one to three specific school offerings that match your Developmental Objectives List)*. [THEM]

Notice how these answers proactively segue into what excited you about the role. This isn't necessary, but it shows that you're proactively thinking about why you want to be there and how the opportunity connects to your future.

I don't recommend you copy these examples verbatim. Just observe the construction of the answer and how simply it can come together to match both your needs and the company's (or school's) offerings. Choose your own words and really make the answer yours.

Now let's look at questions about why you want this opportunity:

- Why do you want to work for our company? Why do you want this job? What about this role appeals to you?

- Why do you want an MBA? Why do you want it now? Why our school?

Your answer to these questions will follow the exact same format as the ones above: YOU + THEM.

Here are two examples:

Answer for a Job: *(Function or industry related to this role)* is my field of passion, so I anticipate building my trajectory within it. In my next role, I am really hoping to gain *(one to three things from your Developmental Objectives List)*. [YOU] I am particularly excited about this role/company/team for three (or two or four) key reasons.

- First of all . . .
- Second . . .
- And finally . . .

(Walk through two to four aspects of the job description, team, role, or company culture that fit directly with your Developmental Objectives List). [THEM]

When you construct the last half of your answer, be sure to make it very easy for the listener to follow by including signpost words such as "first of all" and "second." Ideally, you'll have multiple reasons, and if you organize them in your speaking, the interviewer will be able to retrace your steps and recount them later if he is asked to do so.

Answer for a Graduate School Interview: I am applying to business school because I hope to transition/build my career in the direction of *(function or industry of passion and item from your Career Bucket List)*. So I am looking to my MBA program to give me *(two to three things from your Developmental Objectives List)*. [YOU] I am particularly excited about your school for three (or two or four) key reasons.

- First of all . . .
- Second . . .
- And finally . . .

(Walk through two to four aspects of what the school offers that fit directly with your Developmental Objectives List). [THEM]

Notice how both of these answers include a glimpse into your vision. If you've already talked about your longer-term vision, there is no need to discuss it again. But if it hasn't yet been covered in the conversation, outline it before you talk about why you're excited about the opportunity. This will make your reasons more credible and relatable.

If you're excited about a job or school, there will likely be far more than three or four reasons you want to end up there. So work to "bucket" your inspirations into categories. For example, for business school, you might have three key areas: the school's curriculum and academic offerings, the community, and the extracurricular activities. Or perhaps you'd focus on the school's leadership development opportunities, the chance to gain quantitative analytical skills, and the prospect of building lifelong friendships with bright, likeminded individuals. Then group all of the things that excite you into those buckets, like so:

The school's curriculum and academic offerings

- Classes A and B
- Professor X

The community

- The campus and location
- The alumni network
- The people you've met so far in your research

The extracurricular activities

- The top two clubs you plan to join
- Other offerings outside class that relate to your needs

Your reasons for wanting a job could be organized into similar categories: aspects of the job, the corporate culture, and the people you'd be working with. Or, alternatively, the company's product, the learning and advancement opportunities, and the chance to collaborate with likeminded people. How you divide your answers and choose the buckets is up to you; just make sure you're organized so that the listener can easily follow you. And, as always, write up your outlines and practice a little, and you're good to go!

Interview Hero Secrets in This Chapter:

- Being a less qualified applicant is not a deal-breaker. Hiring managers know that people who have a selfish interest in what they're doing will naturally work harder and smarter.

- Before pursuing any opportunity, take time to understand your developmental objectives: what do you want to learn, develop, experience, and impact?

- Make your answers to questions such as "Why do you want this job?" personal and concrete. Give a selfish answer that shows you have a vested interest in a future with the company.

- Map your needs to the opportunity. Include a little bit of you and a little bit of them, so be sure you know how this opportunity specifically fits with your personal learning and advancement objectives.

- Structure multifaceted and complex answers in an organized way and then give verbal cues so the listener can follow, such as: "I have three reasons . . . first . . ."

SECTION IV

Getting Ready for the Main Event

Care about what other people think and
you will always be their prisoner.
—LAO TZU

So far, this book has been about the soft stuff: getting to know yourself better, storytelling, envisioning and inspiring the future, and creating a meaningful connection with the interviewer. That stuff takes up the lion's share of this book because it requires the most time and thoughtfulness, and it will drive 80% of your success in interviews (and in life too!).

Still, there are practical matters to attend to: you need to research your target companies and opportunities thoroughly. You need to know what to wear. You need to get yourself ready for showtime. All of this is important because being prepared will give you a competitive edge, and *feeling* prepared will give you confidence. So in these last three chapters, I will walk you through:

- How to efficiently research a company and the job itself

- How to get ready for game day

- How to manage your confidence before, during, and after the interview

Research a Company in 30 Minutes Flat

To pay attention, this is our endless and proper work.
—MARY OLIVER

COMPANY RESEARCH!!!??? WHAT A DRAG!!!!

That's what I always thought. I don't have a terribly organized mind: I see possibilities far more than I notice realities. And the idea of exploring and cataloging a lot of information about the vast universe of career options out there and then organizing that information and making sense of it did not, let's say, inspire me.

I made some blind career choices as a result. I didn't look closely enough inside myself before embarking upon my career journey. If you've completed the exercises earlier in this book, you've already done WAY more toward that end than I did when I was in your shoes. I also didn't look closely enough at the important facts about the various options to make informed decisions about where to dedicate my efforts. That's kind of crazy when you think about it. All we've really got in this life is our time. That's very literally what life is made up of: years, months, days, minutes. It's our right, privilege, and even duty to invest those hours in work that's meaningful to us.

But it's hard to do that without some real information about what these jobs actually are, what the companies actually stand for, and what working for them would actually look and feel like. That's why you've got to get good at research. Fortunately, I've since discovered some secrets to make it much easier for you to get 'er done.

Though I frame the tools of this chapter as a way to prepare for interviews, I highly encourage you to use at least the first 30-minute quick research process to screen companies and decide if you want to apply to them in the first place. It will ensure you're only pursuing opportunities that harmonize with your values and align with your personal impact and learning objectives.

DON'T BOIL THE OCEAN

I used to teach test prep for MBA and JD applicants: in other words, the GMAT and the LSAT. In order to qualify to teach these tests, I needed to achieve a 99th percentile score on each test. The LSAT was the trickier of the two for me because it tested things like reasoning, reading comprehension, and linear logic. I could do all these things, I just couldn't do them fast enough under pressure in a room full of 100 other anxious people trying to do the same. It took me three tries to do it, and a very surprising technique helped me succeed.

Reading comprehension had always been my Achilles heel— again, because of speed. I like to take my time when I read and absorb every detail—this goes double if I'm reading something I find interesting. I never found conducting research easy, because I'd just get lost in the information and take forever to find the conclusion. This is also part of why philosophy was challenging for me—I was drifting in a vast sea of ideas. On the LSAT, I had a really hard time completing reading comp quickly, especially because the passages were often heady and jargon-laden things on subjects I was unfamiliar with and uninterested in.

But the company I worked for had a great technique to teach speed reading comp, and it worked like magic. The idea is that if you're just "reading," then every piece of information—every single word— is just as important as the next. The passage is like water—a single uniform mass where every part is connected to every other part. It was impossible for me to read faster with this approach because I'd have to process each new piece of information with respect to every other piece of information in the passage.

But if instead of just "reading" the passage, you approach it with the intent to answer one or two very specific questions, then the experience transforms: you're no longer absorbing information; you're hunting for something specific. You're not wading in the ocean; you're making a beeline for the other end of the pool. You no longer have to connect all the different pieces of text to all the other different pieces of text; instead, you're connecting each thing you read only with your central question.

Now you might think this would cause you to read less carefully and absorb less information overall in the time it takes you to read the passage. But much to my surprise, the exact opposite was true. When I was hunting for an answer to my question, the entire passage made much more sense. I could suddenly comprehend the big picture and the details of things—like complicated scientific analysis linking trilobite fossil composition and climate change—in half the time it used to take me despite the fact that I have no knowledge of climate science or any inclination to learn it. It turns out that hunting for meaning is a much more efficient way to learn than just "reading."

I only wish I had figured that out in high school. Or during my MBA when I was tasked with company research. So many hours wasted . . . but now you can take advantage of this method in your research!

TAKE A TARGETED APPROACH TO RESEARCH

The basics about your target company should be easy to identify. Things such as where the firm is located and whether it has offices in different geographies you're interested in and the nature of the position you would be interested in (e.g., entry-level analyst, senior consultant, etc.). Even salary info can be found through websites such as Glassdoor.com and Transparentcareer.com. But all of that information will just help you decide if you want to apply for the job in the first place; it won't help you differentiate yourself in the recruitment process or perform well in your interview.

When people attempt to research companies, the two biggest questions they have are "How do I know where to start?" and "How do I know when to stop?" The research process can truly seem infinite these days, especially now that the worldwide webs have created what is—from our human perspective at least—an infinite amount of information to parse through. So let's bound our research very tactically by targeting only four very specific questions:

1. How do this company's values align with yours?
2. How is the company positioned in its market vis-à-vis its competitors?
3. What should you expect in the interview?
4. How do you stack up against the job description?

If you're applying for admission to a graduate program, then just substitute "school" for "company" in all four steps, with the fourth being "student profile" instead of "job description."

If you can answer all four of these questions, you'll be ready for that interview. Now I'm going to show you how to answer those four questions in 30 minutes flat—what I term the 30-Minute Research Plan. Follow the next four steps to complete your research. I will tell you what to do with each piece of information afterward. The workbook has templates to help you keep track of your research, so go get it here at **careerprotocol.com/ih** if you *still* didn't do so.

Step 1: How Do This Company's Values Align with Yours?

The first step is to look at corporate values and what companies look for in recruits. This takes two simple steps. First, Google this:

"COMPANY NAME core values"

Within the first few links, you should find something the company has published about its guiding principles. If this search doesn't bring up good results, try also:

- "Corporate values"
- "Corporate philosophy"
- "Guiding principles"
- "Mission statement"

Most organizations will have information related to their beliefs, philosophies, and values on their websites. If this search reveals nothing useful, then one last angle is to try:

"What does COMPANY NAME look for in hires/recruits"

This will bring up any articles that have been published by third parties on the subject, as well as anything relevant the company has published. You might also want to search "How to get a job at COMPANY NAME," "How does the COMPANY NAME hire," and "Key attributes of COMPANY NAME employees." All of these should bring up information about qualities and principles the firm considers important.

Written Exercise 13.1:
List corporate values.

Record what you find in your Google search in the "Corporate Values" column of the worksheet. This is the quickest step. Don't think about what you're finding; just write it down. *Try to complete this in five minutes.*

As a final step in the values search, check out the company's LinkedIn profile and see how it is positioned to potential employees. Then check out two or three of the companies that "People also viewed." This will be a start to the competitor list. Compare what your target says about itself vs. what its competitors say: their LinkedIn summaries are quite helpful in distinguishing subtle differences in values. Record any additional insights this gives you.

Step 2: How Is the Company Positioned in Its Market vis-à-vis Its Competitors?

To understand how a company is positioned in the market, you just need two things:

1. A list of its closest competitors
2. An understanding of what matters in this market: what makes a company successful in producing and selling its products or services vs. competitors

You've already got #1 from your LinkedIn research. If you look up Google's company profile in LinkedIn, the "People also viewed" list includes Amazon, Apple, Facebook, and Microsoft. These are Google's direct competitors in the platform war of the 2010s.

Hopefully, you already have an understanding of #2, because you're applying for a job in a field that you either already have experience in or that you've had an interest in and therefore have some knowledge about. At the very least, you need an understanding of who the company's customer is. Is it a B2C company (business to consumer)? Does it sell its products to individuals like you? Are you part of its target market, for example? Or is it a B2B company (business to business)? In other words, does it make most of its money from selling to companies?

Google and Facebook are interesting examples because though their users are individuals like you and me, the vast majority of their revenue comes from companies that pay for advertising on their platforms. To understand your target company, start with a description of who its customers are.

Written Exercise 13.2:
Do a customer assessment.

Take two minutes and write down who your target company's primary customer base is. Define it as clearly as you can.

Next, see if you can assess how your target company stacks up against its competitors. Use one of the famous business assessment frameworks taught in business school to organize your ideas. For example, you could use Porter's Five Forces[1] to understand industry dynamics. If you're applying for a strategy or operations role, this would be a great place to start:

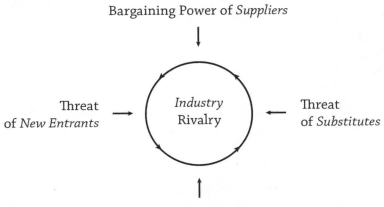

Bargaining Power of *Suppliers*

Threat of *New Entrants* — Industry Rivalry ← Threat of *Substitutes*

Bargaining Power of *Buyers*

But if you're starting from scratch to understand your target company and/or you're still quite early in your career, then I recommend you work with the 4P's marketing framework to build your basis of understanding.

PRODUCT + PRICE + PROMOTION + PLACE

	Your Target	**Competitor 1**	**Competitor 2**
Product: What are the core relevant products or services of each company, and how are they different?			
Price: How does each firm price its core products?			
Promotion: How does each company promote its products or services? (What different media does each use? How are the brands different in advertising and marketing materials?)			*(continues)*

	Your Target	Competitor 1	Competitor 2
Place: Where are the products or services actually purchased? (Online? In stores? How does the buying experience differ?)			

Written Exercise 13.3:
Do a quick competitive assessment.

Take eight minutes to jot down the differences between your target company and two to three of its competitors. If you're starting from scratch, use the Four P's dimensions of marketing.

Step 3: What Should You Expect in the Interview?

Back to the Googles for this one. Now you want to Google . . .

"COMPANY NAME interview process"

You can also try: "How to get a job at COMPANY NAME," "How does COMPANY NAME interview," and "COMPANY NAME hiring process." Many firms make this information completely transparent on their websites. Try looking at Glassdoor.com, Vault.com, PoetsandQuants.com, and other sites where employees talk about their recruiting and working experiences as well. Especially if you have or want an MBA, PoetsandQuants.com will have a ton of useful insight about target companies.

You're looking for information about how many interviews you should expect, with which kinds of people (hiring managers, HR professionals, partners, your direct manager, your teammates, etc.) as well as what kinds of questions will be asked. If there are technical components to the interview such as case interviews, skill tests, personality profiles, drug tests, background checks, required references, or any other component that goes beyond a series of conversational interviews, now is the time to avail yourself of that information so you can begin preparing.

Note what to expect.

Make notes on what you should expect in interviews with this firm and if there are any other components of the recruiting process to prepare for. Again, do not process or do anything with this information; just write it down. *Try to finish this in under 10 minutes.*

Step 4: How Do You Stack Up against the Job Description?

For this step, all you need is the description of the job you're applying for. Print it out and grab two colored pens. Most job descriptions consist of a series of preferred qualifications and experiences and then include a list of the tasks, required skills, and responsibilities of the role. With one color pen, you're going to put a checkmark next to the qualifications and experiences you have. With the same color, put a checkmark next to the tasks, skills, and responsibilities you have direct experience with in your career so far.

With the second color pen, put an "X" next to the qualifications and experiences you do not have and the tasks, skills, and responsibilities you have no direct experience with. *Complete this in five minutes.*

Mark up that job description.

Use two color pens to "✓" the experiences, qualifications, and skills you have and "X" those you don't. *Try to finish this in under five minutes.*

If you're applying to grad school, then instead of measuring yourself against a job description, look at how you line up with the student body: years of work experience, grades, test scores, community service, demonstrated leadership, etc.

WHAT TO DO WITH THIS INFORMATION

In 30 minutes, you've answered the four key questions. Here is how you want to use this information to enhance your interview preparation.

1. How do this company's values align with yours?

Be sure to prepare for behavioral questions related to these core values. But go beyond direct questions about values and create stories that reflect the company's leading principles. For example, if I were interviewing with Amazon, and I know that one of its core values is "Invent and Simplify," then when I tell the story about creating the transaction services agreement for the post-merger integration of the two consumer goods companies that I told in Chapters 6 and 8, I will want to choose details that reflect inventing and simplifying the process. I might even go so far as to use those exact words.

2. How is the company positioned in its market vis-à-vis its competitors?

Use this information to inform your answers to future-based questions (highlighting what is unique about this firm in the marketplace and why, therefore, you're particularly excited to work there) and to help you formulate meaningful questions for the interviewer (asking about nuances of the company's strategy, marketing, or operations vis-à-vis its competitors).

3. What should you expect in the interview?

Let this drive any additional preparation you need to do beyond everything I'm covering in this book. If there are technical tests, case interviews, or coding reviews, you will need to get ready for those. But also let your research guide your story-preparation focus. For example, if you learn that the company or school conducts fit interviews that are 100% behavioral—in other words the interviewer will ask only one or a few "Tell me about a time when" questions, then you will know you need to go deep in preparing for those but you will be able to spend less time on the rest.

4. How do you stack up against the job description?

The items in the job description you checked are your strengths, while the X's are your growth opportunities. Show enthusiasm when you discuss why you want this opportunity for the strengths (checks) you will get to leverage and the new skills and abilities (X's) you will get to develop. Consider also crafting some WIMP answers if you have one or two big holes in your experience profile that you think the interviewer will be concerned about.

ADVANCED RESEARCH

In 30 minutes flat, you can get enough information about a company to know whether it aligns with your values, how it competes and recruits, and how qualified you are for the job. Those key pieces of research are helpful for passing the first phase or a phone screen and for ensuring you're prepared even for advanced interviews. They're also incredibly useful for deciding whether or not to apply to work at the company in the first place.

But for certain opportunities, you might want to do some advanced research. The more you advance in your career, the more your future employers will expect you to know about their firm and its place in the market before they consider hiring you. So here are a few tools for advanced research.

GET MORE INTIMATE WITH THE FIRM AND THE INDUSTRY

Stay on Top of the News

It's a great idea to be up to date on any big news about your target company—this is truer the more senior you get and the more specialized your career becomes. For your first or second job, some of this will be overkill. Choose only a couple of these to do if you're very early in your career.

Do a Google search on press releases or just "news" related to your target. For public companies look at earnings releases and their most recent annual report. Even better, set up a Google alert for your target companies and their key competitors. Read industry trade publications and websites. Follow industry developments on your regular news sources. Subscribe to newsletters. Attend conferences and industry events. All of these will keep you informed about the industry you're planning to enter and the companies you're going to interview with.

Do a SWOT Analysis

SWOT stands for "strengths, weaknesses, opportunities, and threats." It's just a simple way to contrast your target company with its competitors and understand how it's positioned in its market. Here's your template.

Written Exercise 13.6:
Use the SWOT template.

Complete this template for your target company based on your research and reading.

Top 2–4 Competitors	Your Target Company vis-à-vis Each Competitor	
	Strengths	Weaknesses
Opportunities and/or Threats the Company and/or Industry Will Face in the Next 1–5 Years		
Opportunities	Threats	

- What are the company's and brand's strengths vis-à-vis competitors?
- What are its weaknesses vs. those of competitors?
- What opportunities will the broader industry encounter in the next one to five years?
- What opportunities will the company have?

- Likewise, what threats might lie ahead for the firm or its broader industry?

These last two questions are particularly important in this era of disruption. What would Barnes and Noble have done if it could have truly anticipated the success of Amazon? What would Blockbuster have done if it had taken Netflix seriously? What will be the thing to disrupt your target company's position? Can you imagine what it might look like? Spend some time thinking about it.

Use The Company's Stuff

If it's a company that sells directly to consumers (instead of business to business), be sure to come with informed opinions about its offerings.

> ### Written Exercise 13.7:
> ### Do a product assessment.
>
> Use the company's stuff. Answer these questions.
> - What do you like about it?
> - Where is it clearly superior to competitors?
> - Where is it inferior?
> - How might it be improved?

PRIMARY RESEARCH: INFORMATIONAL INTERVIEWS

Informational interviews are one of the most powerful tools you can use in your recruiting process. They allow you to build relationships with people at your target firm while gaining valuable firsthand insights about the company, its culture, and how to succeed there. If you do them well, it might even increase your chances of getting the interview in the first place. And certainly, if you're applying for very competitive opportunities, having insider information will give you an edge.

YOUR SEVEN-STEP PROCESS FOR CONDUCTING AWESOME INFORMATIONAL INTERVIEWS

1. Get introduced

You can skip this step if you have already met the person you're interviewing. But if you're in an active job search, you may need to approach strangers and people you haven't met yet. If that's the case, email the stranger directly only as a last resort. Try instead to use your network to get introduced directly to people who work in the firms you're interested in by people who already know you. Once someone has agreed to an informational interview, there are a few key things to remember.

2. Respect their time

People are busy, so keep it brief. Ask for 20 minutes to talk. Recognize that you may have to conform to their schedule, so propose a few specific times and ask them to give you some alternatives if your proposed times don't work. The phone will work best for most people, so don't propose coffee or a live meeting unless you're confident they can meet you in person without extreme inconvenience. Then make sure you're ready to get everything you need in those 20 minutes. If they want to extend the conversation, that's up to them.

3. Do your research

Speaking directly with someone at a target firm is a rare opportunity for primary research. So don't ask basic questions that you could find answers to on the internet. Start with the four core questions outlined in the 30-Minute Research Plan above and do this before your informational interview.

4. Know what each firm has to offer

Don't just research the firm; research the individual to whom you will be speaking. Use LinkedIn and the company website to familiarize yourself with your interviewee's basic information—title, tenure with the firm, career trajectory prior to this role, etc. This is critical to asking great questions. For example, if you think you'll be interested in a position in the finance department of this particular company, and your interviewer is on the marketing team, he will likely not know much about the challenges a finance associate will face. That said, he'll know plenty about corporate culture, firm success factors, and the interview process. Leverage the expertise of the person you're talking to and show respect for his time by asking him questions he's able to answer.

5. Set the context

Do not neglect this step. Before you jump in and begin firing off questions, let the person know who you are first. Introduce yourself. Be brief, but provide a little bit about your background, where you are in your career, and what you hope to get out of this conversation. You could use a brief version of one of the Walk-me-through frameworks to construct your introduction. People want to be useful to you, and you make it much easier for them to do that when you tell them what you want and need.

6. Ask great questions

People like to talk about their experience, and most people like to give advice. These are also the two topics that will make your informational interview most valuable. It might even be worth your time to create an interview guide for your conversation. You'll get much more valuable information if you ask questions that are easy to answer and require robust answers. So instead of asking "What is your job like?" consider asking something like "Describe what your work life looks like in a typical week."

Some topics to explore:

Firm culture

- How would you characterize the culture of the firm?
- How do people collaborate and work together here?
- What values are emphasized in teamwork?
- What kind of people have not been great fits at this company?
- What would you suggest I do to learn more about the firm's culture?

The work itself

- What does a day in your life look like? What percentage of your time do you spend in meetings, on email, on the phone, working on the computer, traveling, etc?

- What aspects of the job have you struggled with most? What aspects of the position I'm applying for do people tend to struggle with most?
- What do you find most rewarding about your work?
- What problems have you been most passionate about solving?

Success criteria

- On what key dimensions are you evaluated on your work? What key dimensions is the position I'm applying for evaluated on?
- What are the three core skills without which you could not have succeeded?
- What are the key development areas you're working on now?
- Do you have any advice for me on core skills or qualities to develop that would make me a better candidate for the position I'm interested in?

This isn't an exhaustive list. These are just a few ideas to get you thinking about what you want to know. But notice how most of these questions center on the interviewee's own work and the "what" of the job. This enables the individual to expand upon his or her own experiences rather than just giving opinions, which may or may not be relevant to your own job search.

7. Give the connection a future

This is the important last step in any conversation. Create an opportunity for follow-up. This is as simple as asking for something or offering something. For example . . .

> **An Ask:** I would really appreciate if I could follow up with you in the next several months to see if you have any openings on your team. Would that be all right? If you think of a position that would be a good fit for me, please let me know.

> **An Offer:** I read an article last week that reminded me of the challenges you described in your job. I'll send it to you when I get back to my office.

Then make sure you actually follow up as you promised!

Use this tool when you're researching new jobs, when you're actively searching for your next role, or when you'd just like to get to know someone and his work better. It's a great first step in developing professional friendships, and it's an essential component of advanced interview research.

Interview Hero Secrets in This Chapter:

- Use the process in this chapter to get enough information about a company to know whether it aligns with your values, how it competes and recruits, and how qualified you are for the job in 30 minutes.

- Target your research on a few key things to streamline the process: the organization's values, its position in the market, interview expectations, and how you stack up against the job qualifications.

- Use your analysis of the company's position in the market to help you formulate meaningful questions for the interviewer (about nuances of the company's strategy, marketing, or operations vis-à-vis its competitors).

- Use research to discover whether the interview process will include technical tests, case interviews, or coding reviews, and be sure to prepare for those too.

- Show enthusiasm for aspects of the job that leverage your strengths as well as those that represent developmental opportunities for you (aka, skills and experiences you don't yet have).

- Conduct informational interviews to get insider company information and cultivate relationships before you apply.

Get Ready for Game Day

If you are always trying to be normal,
you will never know how amazing you can be.
—MAYA ANGELOU

Finally, feeling prepared is your invincibility cloak in this process. If you've done everything right leading up to that conversation, you're going to feel strong, confident, and ready to knock people's socks off. Inner confidence will allow you to relax, be yourself, and focus on the Friendship Mindset. If you're doubting yourself because you didn't do all you could do to prepare for this important opportunity, you're going to have a hard time relaxing and connecting.

Here's a step-by-step guide to preparing for that interview so you can walk in there ready to enjoy the conversation.

DAYS AND WEEKS BEFORE THE INTERVIEW

Before your interview, do your research, prepare your stories, and practice a little. You can't prepare for absolutely everything, but you want to prepare for as much as possible so that the curve balls and unexpected questions that seem to come out of left field won't surprise you. We'll talk about how to handle those curve balls in the next chapter. If time is limited, I recommend you focus on preparing answers to these questions:

1. The Walk-me-through tailored for this firm, role, and interviewer.

2. Questions you know for sure will come up.

3. Questions you're *worried* about—do not go into the interview dreading any question that has come up in your research. If you're worried about it, craft an answer you're proud of so you look forward to it instead.

4. Any other questions that seem important to you.

LET GO OF YOUR BODY LANGUAGE AND TRAIN YOUR MIND INSTEAD

People sometimes worry about body language. I've read a lot about it that I think is hogwash. In my years of coaching clients for interviews, I've found that attempting to change body language by working directly on the body language itself is at best a waste of time and at worst entirely counterproductive. I explained why in Chapter 9. Even if you're super confident about your appearance, I don't recommend videotaping yourself or spending time focused on your gestures to control your mind-body connection.

Think about it: it's not like there are two other people in the interview answering the same exact questions so the interviewer can analyze your body language and compare it with theirs. Likewise, your interview isn't being recorded on video so that someone can go back and harp on your movements entirely out of experiential context. Body language is something that affects us at an emotional level. It's not intellectual. We respond to body language based on how it makes us feel, so it's highly unlikely that your interviewer is meticulously analyzing your body language and thinking, "Oh, you know, she should have gestured bigger." Or "If only she were taking up more space in the chair." It doesn't really work like that.

Trying to improve your body language by going to work directly on your body language is like trying to improve the quality of fruit by covering it in sugar. You actually ruin the fruit in the process. If you want delicious fruit, you need great soil.

As I said before, however you naturally move when you're comfortable and relaxed is probably fine. What you don't want to do is come off as overly aggressive, nervous, or shy. And no matter how much you rehearse better gestures, if you *feel* defensive, nervous, or shy, your body language and nonverbals will show it. So, the secret to successful body language is maintaining your confidence. It's remaining calm and collected so that you don't feel defensive, or like you want to run and hide. If you feel that way, it'll reflect in your body language, and there won't really be much that you can do to prevent it. So instead of worrying about your body, pay attention to your thoughts and feelings. Rest assured that a confident mindset will be communicated through your body naturally. Your body language will take care of itself.

All of this goes back to Confident Humility. If you end up in a freaked-out state of mind during the interview, your body language is going to reflect it. So instead of worrying about what your body is doing, do whatever work you need to do on your stories, on your research, and on your Friendship Mindset. That's what will create iron-clad confidence. You want to project inner peace and you want to have fun. This is really the vibe we're going for, and it will happen naturally when you feel prepared, when you're inspired by who you are, and when you know what you want to say in the conversation.

THE DAY BEFORE THE INTERVIEW

The day before the interview, you want to make sure you're organized and ready to perform. You don't want to leave anything to chance and you don't want to leave any important details for the last minute, because it will inevitably undermine your self-confidence and peace of mind. You want to spend your extra time and energy focused on getting yourself in the right mindset.

Logistics

Figure out where the interview will take place, how you're going to get there, and how long it will take you. Are you going to take a bus, an Uber, or a taxi? Are you going to walk? Plan how much time it's going to take you to get there, and add a buffer—a half an hour to an hour at least. It's fine to arrive early, but arriving late will be a deal-breaker. Even if the interview doesn't dismiss you because you're late, your confidence will be destroyed.

Make sure to bring a printed resume. Admittedly, most interviewers aren't going to need it. That's true for MBA interviews as well as job interviews. They'll typically already have it on file. Even if you aren't asked for a copy, you're going to feel better if you have one.

Sharp Suits or Business Casual?

Look sharp, but most importantly, *feel* sharp. Know what the dress code is. For most opportunities, a sharp suit is your best bet: go business formal when in doubt. But some firms have a shorts and flip-flops dress code, so wearing a suit there might not be a great idea. Be sure to look into this. Do your research. If the information isn't publicly available or isn't communicated to you directly, then ask someone. If there's no way to ask, then use your best judgment. But for most MBA interviews, and for most corporate jobs, a suit is really what you want.

You want to dress in a way that makes you feel good. Wear something that looks good and makes you feel confident. Shoes are probably very important toward this end. In my personal experience, how my feet feel affects how my entire body, how my entire persona feels. Figure out what works best for you.

Be sure to plan this at least one day before, or more if you need dry-cleaning. Lay everything out so that you don't have to think about it the day of the interview. Then the night before your interview, be sure to get enough sleep. You really need to recharge your brain for the challenge of the interview. If you know you need seven hours of sleep, consider aiming for nine. That way, if you're nervous and have a hard time drifting off, you've got a buffer.

Prepare Your Questions for the Interviewer

In Chapter 4, I talked about the sixth stage of the formal interview: the time when your interviewer says, "What questions do you have for me?" Not all interviewers save time at the end for you to ask questions, but when they do, you need to be prepared. Just like the Walk-me-through, a lot of people blow this off. But this part can really solidify your performance: just like the first impression sets the stage, this last impression is what the interviewer will take away with him and remember most. And, as always, he will remember how you make him feel more than he will remember anything else about you. He's spent the last umpteen minutes listening patiently as you told your life stories. Now it's time for you to reciprocate and to shine by letting him shine.

You want to craft meaningful, well-researched questions to further connect you to the interviewer and make an indelible impression as someone he or she can see working with side by side. I talked about a few options in Chapter 4, but I am going back to the subject here, because the time to prepare these questions is in the last day or two before your interview. Incorporate any recent news or current events so your questions are fresh. Imagine who your specific interviewer will be and how you will connect with that person to set the stage for the conversation.

TWO THINGS PEOPLE LOVE TO TALK ABOUT

People love to talk about two things: their experiences and their advice. Now it's your turn to give the interviewer the chance to be enthusiastic. So ask questions that let him talk about what he's experienced. Give him a chance to tell a story. Or give him the chance to talk about what he knows by asking for insightful guidance and advice.

I gave several examples of this type of question in Chapter 4, and here are a few again.

Some experience questions:

- What has been your favorite project here?
- What did you struggle with most in the early days?
- How did you end up in this role?
- What did you do in your first 90 days at this company that you found most edifying?
- What changes do you expect to see happen based on (big recent change at company)?

And here are some advice questions:

- How do you suggest I hit the ground running?
- What are two things I need to know about organizational culture that you had to learn the hard way?
- What changes do you think are coming in the near future that I should be prepared for?

264 GETTING READY FOR THE MAIN EVENT

- What have you found has been the key to success in this role or organization?

Here are some good experience questions if you're interviewing for business school. If you're talking to a current student or an alum, you could ask...

- What has been your favorite class?
- What do you wish you had known before school started?

Here are some advice questions that would also work if you're talking to an admissions committee member who has never been a student at the school herself...

- How do you suggest I hit the ground running?
- What advice would you give me about preparing for summer internship recruiting?
- What changes do you expect to see happen based on (big recent change at school like a new dean or building)?

GOOD COMMUNICATION STARTS WITH COMMON GROUND

Remember, good communication happens at the intersection of what you know and want and what the listener knows and wants. Ideally you know who is going to be interviewing you. If not the specific person, hopefully you'll at least understand the *type* of person you will speak with: an HR representative, a fellow member of the team you're joining, your direct supervisor, etc. Formulate questions that you know the interviewer has the capacity to answer. But also ask questions that allow the interviewer to add value beyond the boilerplate. If you have no idea whom you'll encounter, then plan questions for all the possible scenarios: for example, questions for an HR manager, questions for your direct manager, questions for a senior VP of the firm, etc.

So, "How is Google, and what is Google corporate culture like?" isn't a very intelligent question to ask in this moment. Or, "Does Kellogg offer finance classes?" That's going to show that you haven't done any research. Instead, leverage all the company research you did and the insights about corporate culture and current events you gleaned to engage the interviewer in an interesting dialogue about the future. Such as . . .

- I read about the recent _____ change. How do you envision that changing life day to day around here?

- I am very excited about _____ (aspect of offering at the company or school) because it will give me the chance to _____. I wonder if you have considered implementing _____ (creative new idea related to this offering that would be even more interesting and valuable for you).

- I have so loved using _____ (product), and I wondered if the company had plans to introduce _____ (new product or product revision you would personally like to use).

- Going forward, what changes do you expect to see in _____ to enable the company to achieve _____ (objective the company should be looking toward based on your SWOT analysis) more effectively.

Questions like this will show you've been thoughtful and done your research. They will likely also spark a legitimately intriguing conversation. Ask about topics that you're genuinely curious about, and be sure to tailor your questions to the person you're speaking to. Keep them positive. For example, if the company has recently been dragged through the mud, put a positive spin on it. E.g., "I imagine things have been a bit crazy around here dealing with the recent negative press. How do you envision this development inciting positive changes in the company?" Take some time the day before the interview to get these ready.

THE MORNING OF THE INTERVIEW

All right, it's go time! Be sure to maintain your morning routine. Do whatever you usually do. If you usually go to a spin class at 6 am, do it today, too. Have whatever breakfast you usually have. Your system doesn't need any surprises today.

Coffee and Commute

I'll tell you one of my favorite tricks. Whenever I had important per-formances coming up, even if I was traveling in a strange city, I'd al-ways find the best coffee shop in town to get a latte. You know, the artisanal hipster places where they put milk rosettes on top. This really helped bolster my confidence. I was doing something kind for myself, giving myself something I enjoyed, and taking control of my morning. So, despite all the uncertainty and ambiguity of giving a large public speech or going to an interview, my day always started on a high note that made me feel good.

Of course, you have to budget a lot of extra time to do something like this, but in my case, it was always worth it. It always helped me feel like I owned the day. No matter how it went, the day was mine, and that deeply affected my confidence. Whether you go out of your way to get a special coffee or not, be sure to consume your regular daily dose of caffeine if you're a coffee drinker and be sure to budget extra time into your commute if you need it.

Practice Your Stories a Little Bit on the Way In

Once you've exercised, or meditated, or had coffee—whatever it is you do—it wouldn't hurt to practice an inspiring story or two. Don't go nuts. Don't think through new answers the day of the interview. Don't experiment with new approaches. Just practice telling some of the stories that you already know, ones that really inspire you. You can go over them in your head on the train, out loud in the shower, or talk-ing to yourself in the back of a cab. You might get some strange stares, but what matters is that you're feeling confident and inspired.

Prep Some Ideas for Chitchat

If you're interviewing in a culture that's different from yours, it's a good idea to understand the norms of social distance in that culture before the interview so you can make sure to avoid any landmines in the chitchat part of the conversation. This will help you further impro-vise and create casual conversation without fear of committing a faux pas. Social distance tells us where people draw the lines of privacy, and therefore what's OK to ask about. The closer the relationship, the more trust that exists and the more topics of conversation are available to you. In some countries, it's fine to bring up salary, marital status, family, or age in a first conversation. In others, these subjects are strictly taboo among strangers.

I'm American, and in my experience living on three continents, I've found the American concept of social distance to be the most conservative, so following American norms about social distance will almost certainly be all right regardless of the culture you're entering, but do your own research.

Here's the Social Distance Circle for Americans. The outer circle is stranger-safe. The inner circles are risky to probe during a first-time conversation.

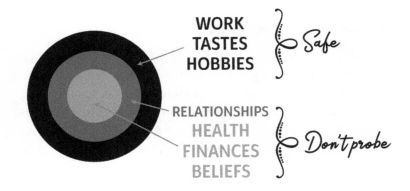

**WORK
TASTES
HOBBIES** } Safe

RELATIONSHIPS
HEALTH
FINANCES
BELIEFS } Don't probe

In the United States, people hold their bodies, health, finances, and beliefs most personal. It would generally be considered inappropriate to discuss body issues, income, religion, spirituality, and politics with someone you just met. These are subjects you want to avoid during interview chitchat. Likewise, you shouldn't inquire about someone's marital or parental status—their relationships. The topics that are generally safe to initiate and inquire about are work, hobbies, and tastes.

Most people enjoy discussing food, films, and fun, for example. Asking about the nature of someone's work and pastimes is also a great place to start. Public common subjects like the weather and traffic are always safe.

I think the best chitchat topics are present-tense phenomena. The weather right now, your commute into the office, the incredible coffee you just drank. We're all sharing this present moment and this current time-space reality, so talking about something that happened in the last half hour or that's happening right now is the easiest entry point into the conversation. As you make your way to the interview, think about two or three things you could start the conversation with if the interviewer doesn't take the reins and draw you into a casual exchange from the get-go.

Here's one last tip: pay attention to positive emotion. Choose a chitchat topic that further lifts your mood. Like how beautiful the lobby foyer is. Or how nice the weather is. Or how kind your taxi driver was. Positive emotion lends itself to more positive connections with others.

Get Happy in the Last Moments before Go-Time

You want to stride into the building, into the interview room, and into the conversation beaming with life and excited to be there. So here are some ways to get inspired in the final moments before your interview.

The first thing you can do is review your resume and remind yourself of how many awesome choices you've made. If you think about it, you care about some pretty awesome stuff, and you have every right to be proud of the life you've lived. You've spent your time investing in causes and outcomes that really matter to you. So get enthusiastic about the choices you've made. On particularly stressful interview days, I'd lock myself in the bathroom for a few minutes with a copy of my resume to get my head in the game. This is especially effective if you end up with multiple interviews in the same day and need to reset after a rough one.

If you meditate or if you work out, you probably have a set of tools to elevate your mood and generate good energy. Music really touches us at a deep level, so I find that music helps set my mood. Find some tracks that get your "life is amazing" energy up and listen to them. It might be something inspirational; it might be something that kind of gets your heart pumping and your toes tapping. Find what works for you.

If you want to try out my personal Interview Mojo Playlist, it's on Spotify: https://bit.ly/InterviewMojo.

You might even consider a pep talk by a close friend or mentor the morning of the big day. I have clients who call me for a pep talk before big interviews because there's nothing quite as confidence-boosting as having someone you like and respect tell you how awesome you are.

But other than chatting with a friend, supporter, or loved one about how awesome you are, I recommend turning off your phone. You should turn it off before you enter the building anyway, so that you can focus on your environment and engage. But I recommend ignoring texts, messages, snaps, and emails all morning before your interview. The last thing you want is bad news from home or work distracting you on game day.

Think about the Big Picture

Finally, think about why you're doing this interview in the first place. What's your broader objective here? Obviously, you want to get the job, but that's just your short-term agenda. What kind of impact are you hoping to have in your career? How are you trying to make the world a better place? What's your life purpose at this stage in your career?

Maybe it's something grand like helping transform the healthcare sector to better serve patients. Or maybe it's something less defined, like, "applying my considerable talents to a team and an endeavor that I find meaningful." Whatever it is, focus on that and remind yourself that your intention is pure, and that you're completely worthy of and able to fulfill it, no matter what happens in this specific interview.

Do What Works for You

You're going to find, probably, several other techniques that inspire you and get you excited about your next interview. The most important thing is that you're feeling excited, confident, and inspired. If all else fails, I recommend watching funny cat videos on YouTube. At the very least, it will lift your mood and remind you that sometimes we just have to laugh at ourselves.

But whatever you do, get happy. Walk into the interview feeling good about yourself, about the opportunity, about who you are, and about the conversation you're about to have.

Interview Hero Secrets in This Chapter:

- Don't focus on your body language: create inner confidence by using the tools in this book instead.

- Take care of interview day logistics ahead of time. Print copies of your resume. Make sure your clothes are pressed. Figure out breakfast, coffee, and transportation the day before.

- Know what the dress code is. Wear a suit unless the company has a very casual dress code. Make sure you feel good in what you're wearing.

- Prep some small talk ideas on your way in. Some safe subjects are the weather, the commute, or the incredible coffee you just had. Anything involving work, tastes, and hobbies is OK.

- Get yourself into a positive headspace before the interview. Figure out the techniques that work best for you.

- Big picture: remind yourself of why you're there in the first place. How are you trying to improve the world? Why are you seeking this opportunity? Build confidence by remembering your intention.

Managing Your Confidence Before, During, and After the Interview

Is life not a hundred times too short
for us to stifle ourselves?
—FRIEDRICH NIETZSCHE

You might have read every word of this book and spent hours implementing all these tips and techniques, doing excellent research, designing brilliant stories and practicing them, dressing up, and getting yourself to a happy space before the conversation. But you're like an Olympic athlete—the circumstances of game day are still out of your control. Surprises that you can't predict or account for may be in store for you. A live conversation is an organic and unpredictable thing. It's like an unchoreographed dance that can go in any direction, changing style from minute to minute. If you've done the work and feel prepared, you're going to be able to enjoy it even if things don't go according to plan. Take, for example, the dreaded poker face.

There are interviewers who adopt a poker face philosophy: they know that it's more disturbing for candidates to face a blank stare than even an angry expression. They'll deliberately withhold feedback—facial expressions and body language—just to see if you crack under

271

uncertainty. I had a few interviewers who diddled around with email while pretending not to listen to my responses. Even though the interviewer may seem unbelievably rude and unprofessional, it might all be part of the plan. Keep that in mind to help you navigate these awkward psychological tests.

But even if the interviewer doesn't deliberately antagonize, mental states are fleeting and fragile. Maybe you're telling a brilliant story, but you suddenly forget the name of that guy who challenged you in a meeting and you stumble. Then, of course, you mentally berate yourself instead of focusing on the rest of the conversation. Or maybe you get a curve-ball question that you just can't answer and then you get stuck replaying it in your mind. Or maybe something the interviewer says reminds you of a stressful situation you're dealing with at work, a situation that you're trying not to think about, and your confidence derails in an instant.

Anything is possible. You can't count on confidence as a steady state—it's fluid and changing. So you need some techniques to get you back on track when the unpredictable inevitably occurs. This chapter will help you take care of your emotional state before, during, and after the interview, no matter what happens.

THE INTERVIEW BEGINS THE MOMENT YOU ENTER THE BUILDING

Assume that the interviewer is evaluating your every move as soon as you arrive on the premises. So, first and foremost, smile. Make eye contact and connect with every human being you encounter once you enter the building. I recommend you memorize the names of each person you meet, especially if you're interviewing with Amazon. Put your devices down (turn off your phone!). Say hello to everyone in the waiting room. Be kind to the secretary. Engage.

Have a good handshake. I recommend you practice this. It's firm. It's conscious. There's eye contact. I can't tell you how many people make a negative first impression with their handshakes. You might be one of them, so take some time to investigate this, get some feedback, and improve. Have someone coach you, or watch YouTube videos and practice. Figure out how to make a firm, positive first impression with that handshake. This will get you off on the right foot (er, *hand*).

DON'T TRY TO BE A MIND READER

During the interview, try not to analyze yourself and your performance. It's hard, but try not to think about how you're doing. Try not to think about yourself at all, in fact. Don't think about your voice. Don't think about your body language. Don't focus on how you're doing. Just focus on what you're communicating. Tell your story. Be present in the story as you're telling it.

Similarly, don't try to assess what the interviewer is thinking. You just never know what that facial expression means. Remember, negative expressions might be feigned to see how you handle the pressure. It might just be angry resting bitch face. It might have nothing to do with how well you're doing. If you get yourself caught up in this game of trying to intuit what the interviewer is thinking, you're going to undermine your confidence. Your telepathy only goes in one direction—you can't read the interviewer's mind, but you *can* plant the seeds of inspiration in your own. So focus on *your* feelings and inspire yourself instead of trying to decipher his thoughts.

Do this by maintaining the Friendship Mindset: this person is already your friend. Facial expression and body language have nothing to do with it. Focus on the vivid details of your story: this is one of the virtues of an Epic Story—it allows you to get swept up in the telling. Let yourself feel passion and enthusiasm for the things you're talking about. Let your enthusiasm be the barometer of your interview success, not the vicissitudes of your conversation partner. This way, you'll enjoy the discussion even if the other person isn't giving you positive feedback or any feedback at all. You'll enjoy being who you are, and your stories and that positivity will shine through.

You really can't go wrong if you're having fun.

CURVE BALLS

If you get stumped by a question, don't freak out. Here are some tools to get through it. Let's talk about the two different kinds of "stumped." The first one is when you get a question that you didn't prepare for, but you can think of an answer if you pause a moment to recollect. The second type of stumped happens when there's a question you can't answer even if you *do* think about it.

If you get a question that you didn't prepare for, here's the process I recommend you follow to answer it on the fly.

Let's say you get this question: "Tell me about a time you had to use data to influence a customer." And imagine this question was nowhere on your preparation radar. Tackle it in five steps.

Step 1: Say, "You know, that's a great question. Let me think about that for a second," and then actually pause and think.

Step 2: While you're thinking, scan your story map and your memory bank for a related experience or answer. If the interviewer is asking you a question that you haven't really prepared for, there's a good chance that it's not going to be on your story map. In this case, you'll need to dredge your memory to find an experience that fits more or less the question that's being asked.

Step 3: I recommend you pick the first experience or answer that comes to mind. You can spin your wheels trying to find the ideal response or the ideal answer, but in my experience, that tends not to improve the outcome. If the first thing that comes to mind is a time you convinced a customer to buy your product by urging him to do competitive research, then run with it. It doesn't showcase your data modeling skills, but it will give you the chance to show how you use information to help drive clarity and influence.

Give yourself permission to work with the first thing that comes to mind. Worst-case scenario, you'll give a decent but mediocre answer to this one question while still getting to the next one with grace and aplomb. A subpar answer can still have impact if you tell it in a meaningful way.

Step 4: Before you start talking, pause and ask yourself, "What does this answer or story say about me? What is the meaning conveyed?" If it's a behavioral question, the meaning is the "change." So in the case of your "influencing the customer by inciting competitive research" example, think about the change. What was the outcome, and what did you learn in the process? If it's a point-blank question, then the meaning is the conclusion—the value the answer reveals about you. In this case, perhaps, you value people having free choice and being satisfied with their decision (even if it means losing a customer for the time being).

The meaning is your endpoint to the answer—what you're working toward—and it's going to help you bound your answer so that you don't ramble or get lost while you're improvising. The interviewer will come away with the knowledge that you have integrity, and that having satisfied, long-term customers is more important to you than a quick sale. That says a lot about who you are.

Step 5: Go. Improvise. Tell the story and answer the question. If you know what the endpoint is, you'll be able to navigate your way through the uncharted wilderness of spontaneous storytelling. Be sure to end with what your answer reveals about you as a person and echo the words of the question to bring it home.

AN EXAMPLE TO REASSURE YOU THAT ANYTHING CAN WORK

I was recording my Interview Hero training program and decided to model this five-step process with an example. Here is what I came up with:

I scrolled through my behavioral question bank and picked a random question. It was one I had never answered before: "Tell me about a time you had to solve a problem in a creative way." I stopped to think and scanned my memory. The first thing that came to mind was this: recently I was trying to make cashew milk even though I didn't have a very good blender, so I needed to add several steps to the process to achieve the results I wanted with the appliances on hand. It was tempting to dismiss an idea like this because it seems so trivial and off the cuff, and honestly, what does cashew milk have to do with work? But I had committed to Step 3: choosing the first idea that matched the question so that I could spend more of my energy telling a great story instead of sifting through the infinite file of experiences in my mind.

So, I moved to Step 4: I paused and asked myself, what does this story reveal about me as I was making my cashew milk? It shows that I'm able to reach a good outcome using imperfect means and that I'm resourceful. That was the endpoint of the story. So, even though this particular anecdote wasn't something I would have planned to talk about in an interview, I had to make it work.

I started telling my trial-and-error story of how I taught myself to make cashew milk with only an immersion blender and a sieve. Instead of acting bashful or humiliated by my less-than-perfect story, I embraced it. I talked about my step-by-step process that involves soaking cashews for many hours, refrigeration, and then going through multiple sequences of blending, using the sieve to get the right consistency. I even shared the recipes I researched online and the ultimate recipe I settled on. I concluded with something like this. "So, in the end, I discovered how to make a great cashew milk and actually use this recipe every week. I really like the fact that I was able to create something awesome without the perfect tools and without using the conventional approach, so I enjoyed the milk much more as a result. I feel like I really earned it—not to mention I saved myself $700 on a really fancy and expensive blender."

Now, this is clearly not going to be your number one story in an interview. Obviously, you're going to prefer professional stories for most questions, or at least more conventional accomplishments. But when you're caught like a deer in the headlights, when you don't know what to say, almost anything you say can work as long as you frame it in a way that reveals something meaningful about you. What's most important is that you find an answer that really works with the question and reveals something about who you are, how you think, and how you produce results, even if it's not a strictly professional story.

This quirky answer has an unexpected bonus. After interviewing umpteen candidates, your interviewer might appreciate a fresh and unexpected take on a question. If you want to practice this approach to knowable curve balls, you might ask a friend to fire some questions at you and practice improvising using this methodology. It really works. Hopefully you won't have to use it too many times in an interview, but it could really save you from an awkward moment.

ALTERNATIVE ANSWERS ARE USUALLY OK

Sometimes it happens that you don't have a perfect answer to a question. No precise experience comes to mind that matches the question. But even when this happens, you can relax if you remember this isn't a test. You won't get penalized for not having experiences that perfectly align with the questions. You *will*, however, suffer the consequences of sloppy communication. Just be transparent and take ownership of the moment—it's much better than making up an answer (this is un-ethical and in fact much harder to do than just telling a true story).

Step 1: Ask for a moment to think.

Step 2: Scan your database for a related experience. Let's say nothing good comes to mind that fits the question exactly, but you can think of something obliquely related.

Step 3: Propose the alternative and let the interviewer confirm it.

Let's imagine I asked you, "Tell me about a time you managed an interpersonal conflict within a team to produce a result." You realize you don't have anything that's a perfect fit. So instead you say: "Hmm, I've only worked on really fun collaborative teams. I don't have any ex-periences like that, but I could tell you about a time when I helped a colleague deal with an interpersonal conflict on *her* team. Would it be OK for me to talk about that?"

Most of the time the interviewer will appreciate your thought-fulness and transparency and let you run with the story. This can win you bonus points for clear thinking and collaborative communication. On the other hand, the interviewer might reject your alternative. She might say, "No, that's not really what I had in mind. Do you have an-other example?" If that happens, then just repeat the steps and try again. If you repeat the process and still nothing comes to mind, then you're in the second category of stumpers. So let's talk about that now.

WHAT IF NOTHING AT ALL COMES TO MIND?

The second type of stumped is when there's a question you can't an-swer even if you do think about it. This shouldn't happen very often if you've read this book. But people are creative, and communication is infinite. As a result, unanswerable questions are still possible, so you want to have a strategy to get you through.

Let's say you go through Steps 1 and 2 above, but literally noth-ing good (or even related) comes to mind. Getting stumped like this is most likely to happen on weirdo curve-ball questions. Stuff like "Why is a manhole cover round?" or "If you were a pizza, what kind would you be?" Or "Explain why the board of directors should fire me and hire you to take my place." There are an infinite number of bizarre questions people can scheme up, so the time will come when you'll be asked a question you have no idea how to answer.

If an answer comes to you, go with it. But if nothing comes to mind, you might say something like, "You know what, you really stumped me, and that's pretty good because I worked really hard to prepare for this interview. Why don't we move on to another question, and I'll follow up with you later if I'm able to come up with a good answer for this question?" and then just keep going.

Don't lose your confidence. You're not expected to know everything, and it's OK if you can't answer a question as long as you do it gracefully and without losing your momentum. There are some interviewers who will force you into a moment like this on purpose because they want to see what you do when you're backed into a corner and don't know the escape route. Think about how many times you got confused in your professional life and had to overcome surprising information and questions you couldn't immediately answer. If you demonstrate that you can navigate this moment gracefully, you're going to inspire a lot of confidence in your resilience and flexibility.

When I delivered case interviews, I would give extra points to people who flubbed a mathematical equation but moved on and finished the case with no loss of confidence. In a way, those people seemed more mature and ready for the job than the ones who did flawless math.

THIS IS JUST A CONVERSATION BETWEEN ADULTS

Whatever you do, keep your cool. If you don't fully understand the question, if the interviewer uses a term that you don't know, or uses a word with a lot of nuances and you're not sure which nuance the interviewer is looking for, just ask. Remember, this is a dialogue, and the idea is to see what it's like to work with you. Just about any boss will tell you that if you don't know something, ask early and get clarification rather than make mistaken assumptions.

If anything goes wrong or seems to be going wrong, remember: this is just a conversation between two adults. No one's going to die. No one's going to be born. The whole world isn't going to change dramatically based on this conversation. Just remember to breathe and keep difficult moments in perspective.

Deep breathing really is a lifesaver. If you notice that you aren't feeling great—you're nervous, you're freaking out—just turn your attention to your breathing for a couple of long, slow breaths and then come back to the conversation. This is helpful if you find yourself experiencing a lot of anxiety in an interview.

IT'S OK TO ASK FOR A DO-OVER

If you flub an answer, just let it go. Stop focusing on the error and shift your attention to the current question or the next one that you're focused on. Forget about the one you messed up and just keep going. This is the right approach for almost all your flubbed answers. But if you messed something up and it's an important question to clarify, then you might want to ask for a do-over.

Here are some ways you could do that. You could say, "Wow, that was not the answer I wanted to give. Can I try that again?" You want to do this with a little bit of humor. You might chuckle a little bit. "You know, I was not happy with that answer. Can I give you another one?" or, "Gosh, as I got to the end of my answer, I realized that it didn't completely match the question that you asked me all that well. I would really love it if I could give it another shot."

Or if the conversation has moved on a little bit and you've answered a couple more questions in between, you might say, "You know, my answer to the question about leadership 10 minutes ago really didn't sit right with me, and it's been nagging me since we moved on. Would it be all right with you if I answered that question again or if I added a little more detail?"

Try this out. The important thing here is that you need to maintain your peace of mind and your confidence. If you give an answer and you find yourself rehashing it in your brain while talking about the next question, your performance is going to suffer. If your mind is somewhere else while you're talking, your answers aren't going to be as eloquent as they could be, and it'll be obvious that you're not present. Your interviewer is going to feel that, and it doesn't feel good. It feels like someone is ignoring you, and it's even worse when the person is talking and ignoring you at the same time.

If you feel like you can't move on from the mistake you've made, try one of the strategies above to hit the reset button so that you can keep moving forward and complete the conversation. Again, this isn't something you want to do every time you fumble something small, but try it out in those rare cases where you feel like you really need it.

THE REMEDY FOR TMI

When you open yourself to spontaneity, you open yourself up to sharing too much information. I'm a nervous oversharer, so I'm often at risk of rambling or accidentally saying things that I don't really want to say when I improvise.

The remedy for this is mapping and outlining your stories (all the work from the previous chapters) so that you know the barriers and the boundaries to begin with. You can always improvise safely within those boundaries and know that you'll arrive at the right endpoint. Memorizing the underlying outline helps a lot too because you know the next point in the story at each step so you won't get too off-course.

But sometimes, despite our preparations and best intentions, something inappropriate or out of bounds slips out. If that happens to you, you can just apologize and say something like, "You know, that answer really got away from me—I didn't mean to share so much information. I apologize. Let's keep moving."

You can give it a little laugh if that feels appropriate. Just act natural. I promise the world isn't ending no matter how much it might feel that way. Chances are, the interviewer didn't notice, so what you probably want to do is just let it go and move on. But if you have really overshared and said something that's borderline inappropriate or that you can tell perhaps made the interviewer a little bit uncomfortable, just note it without drama and keep going. If damage was done, it was done, and you can't go back and fix it. Your best chance of recovery is to do well going forward, so just focus on the rest of the conversation.

If you're worried about how your rambling is perceived, again, just let it go and focus on the story you're telling right now. But if you get caught up in negative self-talk about it because you know the institution values concision (Harvard is one such place)—you might say, "Wow, that was a really long-winded answer! But, you know what, it's because I'm just so passionate about this subject. Let me be more concise on the next one." Or you might say, "You really forced me to think on the spot on that one, and I just got carried away in the answer, didn't I?" If you're rambling, don't beat yourself up about it. Just focus on the conversation and let it go. If that doesn't work, then say something small to acknowledge it. Show self-awareness. Perhaps joke about it a little bit and then keep going, and then make your next answers more concise.

NERVOUS ABOUT BEING NERVOUS

Sometimes the best thing to do is acknowledge your nervousness because the problem isn't being nervous. The problem is needing to *hide* that you feel nervous. You're nervous about being nervous. It's a vicious cycle. You can simply say, "You know what? I'm so excited about this opportunity and it's making me a bit nervous. Let me take a moment to calm down," and then take a couple of deep breaths and move on.

You don't need to do this. Nervousness tends to pass if you leave it alone. But if you feel overwhelmed and you can't concentrate on the conversation, then a small disclosure like this will usually clear the air for you and allow you to go on with your confidence intact.

Keep in mind that just about every single person on earth would be nervous in an interview. Even I would be, and I wrote the book about it!! So instead of being embarrassed about your anxiety, embrace it. It's just part of what makes you human. Interviewers witness candidate meltdowns all of the time—your butterflies are no big deal.

The tactics in this troubleshooting section are probably going to be used in outlier cases. For the most part, you want to get into the conversation and enjoy it. It's like a dance. You can put your foot in the wrong place a couple of times, but the whole thing is still enjoyable, so don't overthink it. Also, don't overthink these troubleshooting items. Just keep them tucked in your pocket for worst-case scenarios. They're only here for emergency situations when you need to restore your confidence in the middle of the conversation and keep it moving forward.

HOW TO GRACEFULLY DODGE QUESTIONS

If you encounter a question that you don't really want to answer, find a graceful and respectful way to dodge it. Here's a question that a lot of people are worried about. "What are your salary expectations?" Most employers won't ask this, but some do, and some can apply quite a bit of pressure. If you've read anything about negotiations, you know that it's probably not best for you to make the first move in this conversation. So you might try something like this:

"You know what? That's a fair question, but I'd really like to pass on that right now. If we feel that this is a mutual fit, then I'm confident we can work together to find an arrangement that works for everyone."

This won't work all the time. There might be times when the interviewer will force you to give an answer, so it's best to do some work ahead of time and determine your acceptable range. The bottom line is that you don't want a job that's not going to pay you what you're worth, so crunch the numbers in advance. But it's typically advisable not to disclose too much about this up front.

If there are any other questions you encounter that you don't really want to answer or that may not be in your best interest to answer, just respectfully ask to move on. "That's a great question, but if it's all right with you, I'd like to pass on it for now." Then just wait patiently for the next question.

WHEN TO LISTEN

I've learned that people will forget what you said,
people will forget what you did, but people will
never forget how you made them feel.
—MAYA ANGELOU

I want to point out that the very last stage of the conversation is about listening. Once you've tackled chitchat, the Walk-me-through, behavioral, point-blank, and future questions, the interviewer will very likely give you the chance to ask him some questions of your own. I've talked about the kinds of questions you want to ask here, and you've hopefully prepared some good ones.

So when this time comes, your job changes radically from speaking to listening. No matter how much you think you bombed the rest of the interview, you could potentially turn it all around when the time comes for you to reciprocate the gift of listening. The spotlight is off you now, so shift your attention from yourself to the interviewer and enjoy the experience of getting to know someone else.

When I interviewed candidates throughout my career, my number one pet peeve was when it came to this point in the conversation, and I gave the interviewee the chance to ask me questions. Far too often I could sense that as I gave my answer, they weren't listening to me. I could tell when they were just waiting for the chance to ask their next question. It was obvious when they didn't react to what I had said and instead just charged right into a new and completely unrelated question. This inattention was an instant red flag for me.

Imagine how it makes you feel when you're talking to someone, you're giving the grace of a generous answer to a question he asked, and he's not listening to you. We've all been there. It destroys all the goodwill that was created in the 30 to 45 minutes you spent telling your stories. So really make the most of this last moment in the interview to solidify the relationship as a reciprocal dynamic. It goes both ways. You shared stories about your life; now give him the chance to share a little bit about his. If something he says piques your interest, ask follow-up questions.

THE SEVENTH STAGE OF THE INTERVIEW

Once the conversation is completely over and the interviewer has answered your questions and signaled that the interview is over, it's time to create a future. Remember that asking for feedback on your performance when the conversation is over is not a good way to end the discussion. Instead, you can ask when you can expect to be notified of results or what the next steps are. That would be an appropriate way to end the dialogue. I also don't recommend that you ask for the job outright (unless you know that "closing" will be part of your job responsibility). Be sure to give a good handshake. Say thank you. Look him in the eye, and then get his card. This is important for the seventh stage of the conversation.

Now you want to focus on the future. We covered the first six stages of the conversation in detail. The seventh stage of the conversation is the future. It's the future of your relationship with the firm, with the team, and with the interviewer. And it starts with thanks. Send a timely thank you note. Send it the same day or the next day at the latest. I recommend you do this within 24 hours. Make it personal, and make it specific but brief.

Don't blow this off or think it doesn't matter. Ideally, you'll be acknowledging an open and fruitful exchange of ideas and experiences. Remember, the word "appreciate" has two meanings:

1. To be grateful for something
2. To rise in value or price

Consider that doing the first causes the second. When you express appreciation toward someone, the interaction (and therefore his relationship with you) becomes more valuable to both of you. Appreciating your interviewer, and the conversation makes it far more likely that this person will want to stay connected to you. Remember the Friendship Mindset: staying connected and making this person a professional friend is your goal anyway. Friendships founded on mutual respect and appreciation are the only ones that can go the distance.

I gave you a thank you note template in Chapter 4, but here's another one:

> Hi Mustache Man,
>
> I just wanted to drop you a note to thank you for your time today. I really appreciated learning more about (FIRM'S/SCHOOL'S) culture and hearing more about your perspective on (thing the interviewer discussed when you asked questions of him/her). It's always a pleasure getting to talk about (thing you discussed in the interview that meant something to you, possibly something personal and not work-related), so thank you for giving me the chance to do so! Really look forward to continuing the conversation. My interest in (FIRM/SCHOOL) has only deepened after our discussion.
>
> Best,
> YOU

This one is 98 words. Of course, you can say more than this, but this will work. Just customize it and make it specific to you and the conversation that you had. Keep it brief. You might also have some follow-ups from the interview. Let's say that you couldn't answer a question and you promised to circle back, or you remembered a small detail that was relevant and you want to include it. Or perhaps you quoted a number and later realized that it was slightly inaccurate and you want to correct it. You can include any or all of this in your thank you note.

For the few times that you meet someone you genuinely want to keep in touch with, try this ending: "I look forward to keeping in touch with you regardless of the outcome of the interview today." You just never know how it might help both of you in the future. If you don't get invited to work at the firm, if you don't get the offer, you can always follow up in a few months and let him know what you're doing, let him know how your career is going. You might ask him if he knows of any other opportunities you might be a good fit for if you don't get the job or ask him to connect on LinkedIn. You can also share articles related to topics that you discussed. Find meaningful ways to keep in touch with people that you genuinely connect with. Don't inundate them with requests but create a reciprocal acquaintance that extends into the future.

I recommend firing off a quick thank you email within 24 hours. If you'd like to send an extra dose of appreciation via handwritten note, feel free to do that after you send the email.

Interview Hero Secrets in This Chapter:

- Remember, when things go wrong, it's not the end of the world. Stay calm and carry on.
- Be kind to everyone you meet that day and remember their names.
- Use our five-step process to tackle tricky curve balls.
- Give alternative answers if you don't have a perfect one.
- Just move on from an accidental TMI; the interviewer probably didn't notice.
- Pass on the question and follow up via email if you really can't think of an answer.
- Don't forget to listen.
- Send an awesome thank you note within 24 hours via email.

Focus on the Future

After the interview, do a download and debrief with yourself. Answer these questions so you can move on from this interview to your next one full steam ahead:

- What questions did the interviewer ask?
- Which ones went well?
- Which ones could have gone better? Why?
- What do you need to do to perform better next time?

Then start training for your next interview. Constrain your debrief to a practical and tactical analysis of what went well and what you want to improve. I recommend that you let go of any other negative thoughts about your performance. It's natural to second-guess yourself. In hindsight, you're always going to think of a better way to answer the questions. But an interview is a live performance. It's really like dancing. You can't revise it once it's done. Once you've taken the step and done the spin, it's over. There's really no point in going over it ad nauseum. And as I've said time and again, the interviewer isn't a robot, so he probably didn't even notice that you tripped up.

Just let it go and try not to drive yourself crazy with second-guessing and scenario analysis. If it helps you recover from a performance you didn't feel good about, remember that the interview is still just one piece of the puzzle. You can get a job without totally crushing the interview. You can get into business school without totally crushing the interview. Even if you *do* totally crush the interview, the company or the school still might offer the position to someone else. Keep it in context. It's just one piece of the bigger picture. Then focus on the future and train for your next interview. Schedule time to complete any follow-up actions to improve your performance next time and then let it all go.

Most importantly, *you survived the interview*! Give yourself a huge pat on the back. No matter how well or how poorly you performed in the interview, remember that this won't be your last. There will probably be many more interviews in your lifetime, so if nothing else, chalk each interview up to experience. This is really the best thing that you can do: integrate whatever wisdom this experience has given you; then shift your focus to the future and to improving for the next time. The Hero's Journey doesn't end until we're dead. And you've got the whole rest of your life to keep shining.

NEVER FORGET WHO YOU ARE

And speaking of shining, I want to leave you with a wish. Two wishes, actually. These are the wishes I have for you. If it wasn't crystal clear to you before you started reading this book and doing the exercises, hopefully it's crystal clear to you now: you are awesome. You've had a positive impact on the world and the people around you. You've tried, failed, and picked yourself up to try again. You've confronted huge challenges and discovered a deeper meaning for your life. You've made choices, you've grown, and you've become more of who you want to be—who you were meant to be.

If you ever feel like you're not "all that," remember, *that's* the illusion. You are incredible and powerful and free. There is a lot of information out there telling you that in order to be happy or fully actualized you need to be more, better, and different. That you need to channel Elon Musk or Steve Jobs or that guy who runs ultramarathons through Death Valley if you want to be a successful person.

Not that productivity tips aren't useful. But you don't have to work so hard to make yourself happen. Just as you are breathing without thinking about it, you are awesome without having to try. I wish you would consider measuring success by how good you feel, not by how well you measure up to some imaginary ideal in your head. I wish you would make it your goal to do more of the things that bring you joy, because that's the surest path to fulfilling your ultimate purpose and having a career you really love.

We're so engaged in doing things to achieve purposes of
outer value that we forget the inner value, the rapture that is
associated with being alive, is what it is all about.
—JOSEPH CAMPBELL, *The Power of Myth*

Exploring and telling your stories is an access point to untold joy. Reveling in the unique experience of being alive and of being you, warts and all, will enrich your life more than any new job could. Start your day not with 30 grams of protein or a vigorous workout or learning something new. Start by appreciating something about you just the way it is, and then see what else you're inspired to achieve that day.

Though on the surface this book is about interviews, at a deeper level it's about finding and sharing your voice. It's about taking your own narrative by the reins and using it to drive your life where you want it to go. It's about speaking words—true words about yourself and your experiences—that inspire and uplift you and others. It's about sharing your humanity with the rest of us humans and creating deeper, more meaningful, and more beneficial connections. It's about creating the conditions to live your life on your own terms and fulfilling your wildest dreams.

All of that is in your power, and your magic wand to create it is communication. Share vividly, be honest about your humanity, and connect with Confident Humility. You've now got the ability to do that in any circumstance where you're the subject of conversation. If you can leave someone inspired by who you are during even that most stressful of circumstances—the job interview—then you can inspire anyone anywhere. And most importantly, you can inspire yourself.

So my second wish for you is that you will take the tools of this book and any others you pick up on your journey and create the life, the career, and the impact that's worthy of incredible, awesome you. If you do that, then you'll be making the world a more hospitable and welcoming place for all of us. And you'll be fulfilling your potential in this life. The world needs you. The world needs you just as you are. So go out there and give the people what they want: you.

Wonderful, beautiful, flawed, human, feeling, magnificent you. To quote my favorite story guru one last time . . .

The privilege of a lifetime is being who you are.
—JOSEPH CAMPBELL

Recommended Reading

Books You Might Find Useful and Enlightening

The Hero with a Thousand Faces and *The Power of Myth* by Joseph Campbell

Story: Substance, Structure, Style, and the Principles of Screenwriting by Robert McKee

Screenplay: Building Story through Character by Jule Selbo

The Anatomy of Story: 22 Steps to Becoming a Master Storyteller by John Truby

The Seven Basic Plots: Why We Tell Stories by Christopher Booker

Power vs. Force: The Hidden Determinants of Human Behavior by David Hawkins

Descartes' Error: Emotion, Reason, and the Human Brain by Antonio Damasio

Influence: The Psychology of Persuasion by Robert Cialdini

Mirroring People: The Science of Empathy and How We Connect with Others by Marco Iacoboni

Trust Factor: The Science of Creating High-Performance Companies by Paul J. Zak

Books That Might Inspire You to Inspire Yourself

Ask and It Is Given: Learning to Manifest Your Desires by Esther and Jerry Hicks

The Artist's Way: A Spiritual Path to Higher Creativity by Julia Cameron

The Gift: Creativity and the Artist in the Modern World by Lewis Hyde

How to Be Interesting (in 10 Simple Steps): An Instruction Manual by Jessica Hagy

The Alchemist by Paolo Coelho

Tiny Beautiful Things: Advice on Love and Life from Dear Sugar by Cheryl Strayed

Notes

CHAPTER 1

1. Jennifer S. Lerner, Ye Li, Piercarlo Valdesolo, and Karim S. Kassam, "Emotion and Decision Making," *Annual Review of Psychology* 66, no.1 (2015): 799–823. https://www.annualreviews.org/doi/10.1146/annurev-psych-010213-115043.
2. Lerner, Li, Valdesolo, and Kassam, "Emotion," 799–823.
3. Antonio Damasio, *Descartes' Error: Emotion, Reason, and the Human Brain* (New York: Putnam, 2005), Preface.
4. Antonio Damasio, "The Somatic Marker Hypothesis and the Possible Functions of the Pre-Frontal Cortex," *Transactions of the Royal Society*, 351(1996): 1413–1420.
5. Antonio Damasio, Daniel Tranel, and Hanna C. Damasio, "Somatic Markers and the Guidance of Behaviour: Theory and Preliminary Testing," in Harvey Levin, Howard Eisenberg, and Arthur Benton, eds., *Frontal Lobe Function and Dysfunction* (Oxford, Oxford University Press, 1991), Chap. 11, 217–229.
6. Daniel Kahneman and Amos Tversky, "Prospect Theory: An Analysis of Decision under Risk," *Econometrica* 47, no. 2 (March 1979): 263–292.
7. Olivia Goldhill, "Humans Are Born Irrational, and That Has Made Us Better Decision Makers," *Quartz*, accessed March 4, 2017, https://qz.com/922924/humans-werent-designed-to-be-rational-and-we-are-better-thinkers-for-it/.

CHAPTER 2

1. Liz Mineo, "Harvard Study, Almost 80 Years Old, Has Proved That Embracing Community Helps Us Live Longer, and Be Happier." *The Harvard Gazette*, April 2017, https://news.harvard.edu/gazette/story/2017/04/over-nearly-80-years-harvard-study-has-been-showing-how-to-live-a-healthy-and-happy-life/.
2. Jane O'Reilly, Sandra L. Robinson, Jennifer L. Berdahl, and Sara Banki, "Is Negative Attention Better Than No Attention? The Comparative Effects of Ostracism and Harassment at Work," *Inform Pubs Online* (April 2014): 774–793, https://doi.org/10.1287/orsc.2014.0900.
3. Alexandra Sifferlin, "Why Loneliness Is a Public Health Threat," *Fortune*, August 2017, http://fortune.com/2017/08/07/loneliness-public-health/.
4. Emily Jarrett, "The Far-Reaching Effects of Workplace Loneliness," *Good & Co*, accessed March 2018, https://good.co/understanding-workplace-loneliness/.
5. Michael Gibbs, "Reward and Performance Management Challenges: Linking People and Results," Global Narrative Report for Towers Perrin, 2003.

CHAPTER 5

1. Paul J Zak, "Why Your Brain Loves Good Storytelling," *Harvard Business Review* (October 2014), https://hbr.org/2014/10/why-your-brain-loves-good-storytelling.
2. Lea Winerman, "The Mind's Mirror: A New Type of Neuron—Called a Mirror Neuron—Could Help Explain How We Learn through Mimicry and Why We Empathize with Others," *The Monitor*, 36, no. 9 (October 2005), http://www.apa.org/monitor/oct05/mirror.aspx.
3. Salvatore M Aglioti, Paola Cesari, Michela Romani, and Cosimo Urgesi, "Action Anticipation and Motor Resonance in Elite Basketball Players," *Nature Neuroscience* 11 (2008): 1109–1116, https://www.nature.com/articles/nn.2182.
4. *Merriam-Webster Online*, s.v. "story (*n.*)," accessed March 6, 2018, https://www.merriam-webster.com/dictionary/story.

CHAPTER 6

1. *Merriam-Webster Online*, s.v. "hero (*n.*)," accessed March 6, 2018, https://www.merriam-webster.com/dictionary/hero.
2. Diane K. Osbon, *A Joseph Campbell Companion: Reflections on the Art of Living* (New York: Harper Perennial, 1995).

CHAPTER 7

1. Dictionary.com, s.v. "fail (*n.*)," accessed March 6, 2018, http://www.dictionary.com/browse/fail.
2. Dictionary.com, s.v. "mistake (*n.*)," accessed March 6, 2018, http://www.dictionary.com/browse/mistake.

CHAPTER 9

1. Julian Treasure, "How to Speak So That People Want to Listen," filmed 2013, TED video, 9:58, https://www.ted.com/talks/julian_treasure_how_to_speak_so_that_people_want_to_listen.
2. Amy Cuddy, "Your Body Language Shapes Who You Are," filmed 2012, TED video, 20:56, https://www.ted.com/talks/amy_cuddy_your_body_language_shapes_who_you_are.

CHAPTER 13

1. Michael E. Porter, *Competitive Strategy: Techniques for Analyzing Industries and Competitors* (New York, Free Press, 1980).

Index

Behavioral interview preparation, for
   success stories *(cont'd)*
   overview, 153, 156–157
   practicing a little, Step 6, 170–171
   success inventory, Step 1, 157–161
   using details, 155, 161–162, 175
Behavioral questions, 60, 153. *See also*
   Behavioral interview
   timing your story answers to, 172–173
   your past and behavior (interview
       stage), 49, 52
Body language, 173–174, 260–261
Boss, not liking your, 24
Breaking the ice (interview stage), 49–51
Breathing, deep, 278–279

C
Campbell, Joseph, 16, 78, 109, 289
   The Hero with a Thousand Faces, 82–83
   Hero's Journey and, 82–84
   storytelling and, 82–83
Candidate for employment
   Airport Test in assessment of, 23
   when you're not best candidate,
       225–226
CAR framework, 81
Career Bucket List, 229
Career professionals, as leaders, 1–2
Carnegie, Dale, 50, 57
Case interviews, 10
Change, in Epic Failure Story, 132
Change, in Epic Story, 94–95, 110–111
Cher, 153
Chitchat, 266–268
Choice
   interview questions and, 100–101
   Why Line as chronological choices
       and motivations approach,
       200–201, 210
Choice, in Epic Failure Story, 131, 132
Choice, in Epic Story
   choices defining character, 100–101
   in Conflict Sentence, 101–102
   questions about, 110
   in response to conflict, 101–103, 145

as revealing who you truly are, 104
uniqueness of you revealed by, 145
Climax of story, 139
Clothing, for interviews, 262
Coelho, Paulo, 61
Communication, 50
   common ground and good, 264–265
   confidence and, 37
   emotions and, 39
   good communication, 203–204
   information compared to, 9
   as shaping experience of life, 134
Communication mistakes, 125
   made while avoiding arrogance,
       40–42, 44
   overusing "we," 41–42, 44
   preamble disclaimers, 40–41, 44
   sticking to facts, 41, 44
   tearing yourself down, 41, 44
Companies
   employee happiness and performance
       of, 25
   information they have pre-interview,
       21–22
   why they interview, 21–22
Company research, 239
   advanced research, 251
   getting more intimate with firm and
       industry, 251–253
   Interview Hero secrets about, 257
   overview, 241–242
   primary research, informational inter-
       views, 253–257
   speed reading comp and, 242–243
   staying on top of news, 251
   SWOT Analysis, 252
   use target company's stuff, 253
   using information gathered for inter-
       view preparation, 250–251
Company research, targeted information
       gathering
   company's position in market, Step 2,
       244, 245–248, 250
   company's values alignment with
       yours, Step 1, 244–245, 250

About the Author

Angela Guido runs Career Protocol, the web's most refreshing destination for no-nonsense career advice and innovative professional development services. Her pioneering work helps aspiring business leaders cultivate the self-awareness, communication skills, and relationships they need to get into schools, achieve their dream jobs, and have more impact and more fun at work. Her clients land at amazing places like HBS, Stanford GSB, Chicago Booth, Google, BCG, McKinsey, Goldman Sachs, and many others.

She's created and taught programs for over 10,000 aspiring business leaders and MBAs all around the world, and her uplifting talks routinely receive the highest overall speaker ratings at conferences and training events. Angela speaks to companies, schools, and associations throughout the world about storytelling, confidence, networking, and active career management. For availability, please email **questions@careerprotocol.com**.

Learn more at **careerprotocol.com**.

CPSIA information can be obtained
at www.ICGtesting.com
Printed in the USA
LVHW090950160720
660851LV00001B/25